For Rosemary, such
who has, keep
kind eyes to understand —
trying to understand —
Thank you,
Rheta Grimsley Johnson
Oct. 21, 1987

RHETA GRIMSLEY JOHNSON

★★★★★★★★★★★★★★★★★★★★★★★★★★★★★★★★★

AMERICA'S FACES

RHETA GRIMSLEY JOHNSON

****

AMERICA'S FACES

****

ST. LUKE'S PRESS • MEMPHIS

Library of Congress Cataloging-in-Publication Data

Johnson, Rheta Grimsley, 1953-
America's Faces

"The pieces brought together in this book were first printed in
The Commercial Appeal of Memphis"—Acknowledgements.

Includes index.

1. Southern States—Social life and customs—
1865—   I. Title
F216.2.J64   1987   975'.04   87-16336

ISBN 0-918518-58-X

For Michael Grehl

Acknowledgements

The pieces brought together in this book were first printed in *The Commercial Appeal* of Memphis, either in part or in their entirety. They are reprinted here with the permission of *The Commercial Appeal*.

I am indebted to Walter Veazey, assistant managing editor of *The Commercial Appeal*, for his tireless support in collecting and publishing this material first and second time around.

He hired me a couple or three times. He listened to hours of gripes and defeats and doubts. He bought me a new dictionary when the one I'd been using for seven years finally came up missing a spine, the "Ps" and some of the "Qs." Once, he even loaned me $5 for gas money to get home.

I also owe thanks to one Jimmy Johnson for his patience, expert copy-editing and innumerable suggestions, all of which made my writing better. He stayed home alone, without ever complaining, as I chased stories and a half-baked dream across the South.

This book is his, too.

Rheta Grimsley Johnson

Foreword

In a red dress she wore even in the staid environment of the Mississippi Research and Development Center, Rheta Grimsley Johnson burst from oblivion as copywriter to bureaucrats after an editor from the old school saw past her uncommon beauty and found raw talent that had eluded others. He fed her more rein.

And her talent blossomed into elongated rectangles of type that anchored an open page in *The Commercial Appeal* of Memphis several times a week. This is a woman who simply must write.

She writes not out of ego, and not for having sifted and weighed to isolate the straightest career path. She writes not for recognition, and shrinks from the various attentions that inevitably follow newspaper columnists. She writes because she must, impelled by the impatience of unyielding talent. She writes at any given keyboard, once a Royal, now a Radio Shack, with a pencil behind her right ear. She can write without the keyboard, but not without the pencil.

Adjunct to the tire tool in the trunk of her millionmile Mustang is an orange extension cord, her link from the back country of Mississippi where it would stretch from any country store to a pay phone so the computer could transmit her columns to Memphis.

This is a writer so forcefully in the present that only the daily format will serve as her vehicle. Periodicals that dally with longer deadlines cannot contain the immediacy of what she has seen that day.

Why she must write, she cannot say. I have asked. Maybe, she guessed, it's because she is shy. People seem compelled to fill in her silences. She goes back to the keyboard, lays out the orange extension cord, and tells Memphis what they say. With a craft that she honed in silent hours with the keyboard in funny places and assorted newspapers in Georgia and Alabama and Mississippi, this woman writes as we can only feel.

On the printed page, she absents herself. There is the reader, and there is the subject. At the end, the reader knows the subject as God knows each of us, without pretense and despite defense. In such an honest confrontation the two can come to knowledge of one another. Into the spaciousness created by knowledge, comes understanding. Understanding begets compassion, and compassion, love.

Beverly Crawford
January 1987

Contents

1 / People Next Door

103 Years

James Hundley Broyles still likes a close shave. A nurse, promptly each morning, brings him his Remington cordless, and man and machine get down to the nitty-gritty of good grooming.

It is the habits, the good ones, and, yes, even bad ones, that keep us alive. As much as anything, it is simple routine that arrests the fraying of life's fabric. As the world relentlessly evolves, it is the small, even brush strokes applied daily and mindlessly that keep us at all a part of the Big Picture.

Hundley Broyles is a man of habits and few words, erect and proud in his nursing home wheelchair. He wears a plaid flannel housecoat like some men wear a $500 suit.

I missed his actual 103rd birthday by five days, his party by six. Still, the day I finally show, he greets me with a firm handshake and a trace of a smile. His eyes, behind milky, thick glasses, seem tired but kind.

At least he suffers silly questions he can hardly hear gladly.

Hundley Broyles had been retired five years when I was born, after working as a banker more years than I have been alive. When Orville and Wilbur first swooped over the soft, rolling hills of Kitty Hawk, he was at the legal age of 21. When Neil Armstrong made tracks on the moon, he was 87. He has worn well.

"You don't look 103," I say, and it is true.

"I sure feel it," replies Mr. Broyles.

I resort to the litany of uninspired questions reporters reserve for centenarians.

How have things changed?

"Completely."

Who was your favorite President?

"Roosevelt. Franklin. I didn't take much pains with many politicians."

And, of course: How have you managed to live for so long?

"My mother and my wife took good care of me."

That done, we look blankly at one another, Mr. Broyles too nearly deaf to fool with small talk, and myself too ignorant of this man's life to proceed.

I would find out later he was quite an outdoorsman, loved coon hunting and horseshoes and sandlot baseball. He trapped mink and muskrat until he was 100.

He and his wife Eunice eloped to marry, standing in a flood of car lights on Horse Creek Bridge to recite their hurried vows. He preferred the Democratic Party, James Fenimore Cooper and the Methodists.

Yet, here, in the beige of communal geriatrics, it is easy to dismiss 103 years of individuality. It is easy to assume the very old were born that way.

This is—at first, second and third glance—a room of the aged or ailing, where all energies are mustered for physical therapy, the simple tossing of a half-inflated rubber ball into an upside-down drum.

But it is more. It is a room full of interesting, long lives, passing gradually from us, almost unnoticed.

Fannie Sue Paulk, over there, the only female sheriff ever of Hardin County. She is said to have brought in the biggest moonshine still in county history.

Every resident a story. Every day less likely to be told.

Miss too many birthdays, miss the man.

November 1985

"Don't Talk About UFOs"

NEWCOMERSTOWN, OHIO. Some say Bigfoot stalks these lovely hills.

Even if you are prone to believe in shadowy creatures in gray or black or brown or silver or white, creatures that smell bad, that like women and leave crater-sized footprints with either four, five or six toes, this would seem an unlikely place to spot them.

This is farming country, beautiful and basic, a sweeping vista of gentle contour, the Tuscarawas River a silver snake slithering across it. There are the stark Amish estates and the wonderful old farmhouses. You are as likely to meet a black buggy on the roller-coaster roads as you are to meet another car.

There is an unpretentious, friendly spirit about the people here, too. "No shoes. No shirt. Who cares?" says the sign outside one area restaurant.

But, if nothing else, imagination is roaming these dense woods north of Coal Country, coexisting peacefully with the deer and the bears and the beauty.

About once a month, Don Keating of the Eastern Ohio Bigfoot Investigation Center holds a meeting at Bud's Banquet Room. One night he drew 105 people. Some were believers; some merely curious. Some were local; others came from as far away as Arizona and Kansas.

Don Keating is a polite, unemployed 23-year-old who wants to be a meteorologist. The Bigfoot Center is a small house where he lives with his mother.

He has a wedding to attend this very night, but when I phone Keating to say I want to talk about Bigfoot, he does not stall or hesitate. "Come on over."

Outside his front door is one of those ceramic jockeys, the kind that looks best plotted in petunias. The face on his jockey is painted lime green, and I know Don Keating has to be interesting.

All the most recent Bigfoot fuss started about three years ago. One memorable sighting occurred in late November, 1983. A deer hunter got the feeling somebody or something was watching him.

The hunter claims to have seen a creature, about eight feet tall, lurking in high weeds.

There were numerous other close encounters with Bigfoot — or Something. Heights varied. Colors, too. Kids would go into the woods to pick wild berries and come back out with wild stories.

Not just the children believe. Some who have roamed these woods a lifetime have gotten nervous and stopped. A middle-aged man at Tony's Bar in Newcomerstown, who looked as if he never had a frivolous thought in his life, stared straight at me and said he tended to believe Something was out there. He'd heard too much not to believe.

Keating himself had a brush one night with a set of red, glowing eyes.

People found impressions, footprints if you will, in a sandbar. Keating made plaster casts that he keeps at home, pushed up under a bed, as proof.

I examine the molds but admittedly have had scant training in Bigfoot anthropology. However, if you squint, you can make out indentations that might well be big toes. Not necessarily Bigfoot toes, but big toes.

In the last two years, says Keating, there have been 15 confirmed sightings in a five-mile radius of Newcomerstown. He has several scrapbooks full of pictures.

Alas, not pictures of Bigfoot but of people looking for Bigfoot. Also shots of bent twigs, glowing eyes (which, if you want to look at it skeptically, could be cracks in the film emulsion), sites of sundry unexplained occurrences and several empty landscapes where UFOs are said to have once appeared.

Keating has heard his share of bad Bigfoot jokes. "Hey, Bigfoot," some townspeople yell at him. When a couple of ambitious entrepreneurs started selling "Newcomerstown, Home of Bigfoot" T-shirts, Keating was dismayed.

"I ran 'em off from Bud's, because I didn't want people to think this was just some scheme for me to make money."

Keating is as serious about this as a priest is about prayer. He has talked to a Lion's Club and reporters and just about anybody else who would listen. He truly believes there are many heavy-walking, smelly creatures out there, and he wants to capture one on video tape.

"Some people believe that these things, whatever you want to call them, come from outer space," explains Keating.

"Don't talk about UFOs," warns his mother, who has been silent up to now. "People will think you are crazy."

May 1986

The Toast Of The Town

SAVANNAH, TENNESSEE. Bob Seger sings a sad song called "Coming Home."

Left your hometown for the city lights
You were young and you were strong.
Lots of traffic, lots of sleepless nights
Lots of dreams that all went wrong.
You'll just tell them what they want to hear,
How you took the place by storm.
You won't tell them how you lost it all.
You'll just say you're coming home.

That's the way most people come home. Quietly. Either they slink back, defeated, under cover of night, or they rack up a few intraprofessional triumphs that nobody, especially family, understands. Most of us needing a good dose of humility need only come home. Where everybody knows we are really nobody.

That's not the way Savannah's Pat Kerr came home.

She stood in triumph on her old Central High stage last week and held captive the toughest audience there is to impress—the home folks. She came home an unqualified success.

What a difference clear-cut financial proof makes. Even the most determined detractors cannot argue with customers at

Neiman-Marcus and Bergdorf Goodman, not to mention the homes in a swank Memphis penthouse and London's Regent Park.

So they gave her proclamations and red roses and standing ovations and fancy receptions and a key to the city. They praised her unbridled creativity and said how they always knew she'd make it.

She cried.

When the models wearing her elegant lace creations paraded down the makeshift runway, dowagers and drum majorettes and local housewives alike clapped until their hands were raw. Clapped for a sultry line sure to put Maidenform completely out of business.

City policemen directed traffic, and a Dixieland band played its heart out. Women who probably know more about keeping their place than antique lace were at the high school two hours early to get a good seat.

"I don't design anything anybody needs," said an elegant, albeit ponytailed, Pat, whose regular clients are royalty and movie stars and the otherwise very, very rich.

She can tell you about Prince Charles' sense of humor and Christopher Reeve's up-close good looks.

And, indeed, this was not a practical line of dresses she brought home to exhibit. They were gowns, not really dresses at all, done in the colors you dream in—white and gold and pearl pink and lavender. Her show had not one bride, but a dozen, and children who looked like angels flying too close to the ground.

Pat's creations were lace dresses for lounging about the castle or accepting the Academy Award or attending your own coronation. They shimmered.

Pat Kerr, dressed in lace of course, dedicated the show—not unlike one that recently thrilled celebrities such as Charlotte Ford, Dinah Shore and Polly Bergen in New York's Plaza Hotel—to her parents, Margaret and Hubert Kerr. It was a simple and sweet gesture.

Not only that. She established a scholarship at her old high school in this small town and donated the proceeds from the fashion show to the local Cancer Society. And she was, as she should have been, the toast of the town.

I cannot help but wonder about her reception if the business—an esoteric gamble—had failed. Or if a justice of the peace had married Pat and some poor man, instead of Dr. Norman Vincent Peale marrying Pat and a very rich man.

For the line between success and failure sometimes is thin as fine lace. And all of us need, at times, to come home.

April 1986

The Promises Made

GORE SPRINGS, MISSISSIPPI. His father is a Lutheran preacher: hers is a Mississippi farmer.

Cindy and Steve Haffly got married yesterday in a country church her family helped build, during a ceremony his father performed. They are so young, so happy, so poor and so handsome it hurts to watch.

Cindy wore a dress of white bridal satin, with a bodice of lace and handsewn rosebuds of pearl. Her mother made it.

The word to describe the bride has been banned from acceptable, contemporary vocabulary like red dye from food. Sweet. There, it's said. She looked sweet.

Cindy has a wholesome, country-morning appearance that makes today's pouting, preening models look like Old Testament harlots.

Steve, well, he had been free as a father's advice, a tall, carefree musician who could pack every single thing he owned into an ancient red Mustang with 150,000 miles on its odometer and memories lost like pocket change in its torn vinyl seats. Then he met Cindy.

The romance was swift and sure. They both spent part of the summer on her parents' farm, helping with chores and counting the days. They'd sit making eyes and shelling purple-hulled peas into the hot, summer nights of young love.

Steve teaches. He takes indifferent kids who don't know which end of a tuba to blow and molds them into a high school band. And because teaching youngsters to make music doesn't pay as well as, say, plea-bargaining for crooks, he never makes a whole lot of money. Probably never will.

Cindy, who plays saxophone and plans to teach someday herself, still is a student. Determined to get at least one degree.

So they will struggle and sweat and scheme to manage finances through the cookie-jar stage.

They will be together, though, and sometimes that's all that matters. They will stay together if they count the lean times as a blessing and bolster one another when things go wrong.

There are those who believe careers and bank accounts should be built before marriage. Maybe. But show me a struggle and a little unabashed affection, and I'll give you good odds the marriage will take.

There will be fancier weddings this month, with more attendants and longer aisles and grander receptions. Couples will travel to Bermuda and Rio on wedding trips, to sip rum drinks and bask in the tanning rays of a tropical paradise sun. There will be some grand send-offs for the trickiest of life's journeys—marriage.

But the vows spoken in the little red brick church just past the only stoplight in Gore Springs have a charm of their own. China patterns are just a trivia question at some future garage sale. And taffeta fades.

It's the promises made—or more importantly, kept—that matter. It's keeping a sense of humor when the utilities are due and the checkbook's awash in red ink. It's discovering love eliminates more age spots than Porcelana.

It's knowing if the furnace blows up, the car won't start and the cat's pregnant again, you may kiss the bride. Forever.

August 1984

The Blissit Sisters

TISHOMINGO, MISSISSIPPI. There is still plenty of life about the neat, white house on the dead-end street. Winter has not yet stolen all the green.

There are not one, but two, porch swings creaking ever so comfortably in the considerable December draft.

You can stand in the yard and hear the Tishomingo High School band practicing a few streets over, root-a-toot-tooting in rag-tag formation right down the middle of a public road. In Tishomingo, pedestrians rarely are bullied by traffic.

It is a quiet town, one built mostly of stone and that from a single quarry. The Blissit sisters, LuVera and Gertrude, lived in this particular house, its angles neat and white as a business envelope.

They kept the yard clean and the porch swept, because LuVera had asthma and could not tolerate dust, and because that is just the way they were.

Theirs was an old Tishomingo family, well known and respected. Their father, the late J.T. Blissit, used to run a general store, where you could buy almost anything.

"We even bought our school books there, back before they were furnished by the state," says Ava Hill, now principal of Tishomingo Elementary.

It was Mrs. Hill whom the law called upon recently, to identify the mangled bodies of LuVera and Gertrude and a third sister, Mary Blissit Jackson of Hernando. Mrs. Hill had known all three women all her life, but identification did not come easily.

A car carrying the three Mississippi sisters, ages 77, 73 and 71, apparently was run off the road by an unidentified white automobile that did not bother to stop.

The Blissits had been to visit Mrs. Jackson, who had buried her husband only a few weeks before. They all had done some Christmas shopping. They were returning home, at dusk, down the treacherous spit of asphalt called Mississippi 25.

Mississippi 25 is a virtual racetrack for pulpwooders and other drivers in a commercial hurry, piercing quiet Tishomingo's western border at a parallel, like a splinter lodged beneath the skin. The Blissits and Mrs. Jackson were southbound on the two-lane, southbound to Tishomingo.

Now the town is in shock. Ask anybody. He will tell you. The Blissit sisters will be mourned and missed.

LuVera Blissit taught at Tishomingo Elementary for 39 and one-half years. She was principal for about 25 of those years. She was stern. No-nonsense.

"It was like that E.F. Hutton commercial," says Mrs. Hill. "When she talked, people listened."

Students did as she told them. Nobody talked in the cafeteria. They ate.

The school building is a typical, perhaps even stereotypical facility, with its cavernous halls and clanking lockers, cameo-cropped faces of students smiling down from a dozen composites. For 25 years at least, it was kept immaculate at Miss Blissit's direction.

No teacher left faculty meeting wondering what was expected. LuVera Blissit knew her mind and spoke it.

Gertrude Blissit was much the same way in her chosen profession. She was a banker and the picture of competence for 30 years. When she retired in 1976, Miss Blissit was the branch manager of First Citizen Bank of Tishomingo.

Her customers generally insisted on seeing only her. About a loan. About a problem. About routine, daily business. She was trusted.

The third sister, Mrs. Jackson, also was a retired banker, ending her career as vice president of a Hernando bank.

The sisters were garden club and choir members, the predictable pillars of their respective communities. They took care of their mother. They took care of two arthritic brothers. They took care of one another.

There is an awkward, biblical-sounding verb that seems apt here: to cleave. They cleaved one to another. They stuck fast.

The two new graves at little Spring Hill Cemetery off Mississippi 25 are only a few miles from the accident site. The pastel ribbons on dozens of funeral wreaths have yet to fade or wash to white. Death is fresh.

Even the grave markers have not yet arrived, and you must trust the significance of disturbed red clay and the floral tributes to know where the Blissits are buried.

You can look from those graves to the road where too many travel too fast. And you can only wonder what three sisters who made something of their lives were talking or thinking when those lives ended. They probably never traveled this way without thinking of her.

Velma Blissit Mercer. 1903-1964. Another sister, buried at Spring Hill, too. She was killed within five miles of the latest accident, the triple tragedy that took three sisters.

Killed on the same road, in the same lovely North Mississippi hills. In an isolated place where the woods are dense and the creeks still clear and only one major highway disturbs the peace.

December 1985

Painless Pete

FISHERS ISLAND, NEW YORK. No one waits on the pier today. Fishers Island is floating on the cool edge of autumn, and a soft rain is turning this green dollop of land into a misty Eden.

Sometimes, though, they do come and wait. They stand on the sagging wooden dock with their cheeks puffed from pain, looking for the boat that brings relief.

The pennant flying from the shrouds of "Mistress" is a white tooth on a field of dark blue. Dentist Peter Eckerson is her captain. He relies on a favorable wind to make landfall in time for his Saturday appointments.

His office is the boat—an X-ray machine, the ubiquitous chair, a gleaming sink, the whole works. It is dark below deck, except for an intense spotlight trained on a patient's mouth. The warm hues of teak and the doctor's seamanly calm ease the hurt—with the help of Novocain, of course.

They call him Painless Pete.

The patients come in a steady current, making the leap from land to water and climbing down the boat's dark throat for treatment.

"I get lots of elderly and handicapped patients," Pete says. People with limitations must trust a man who acknowledges none.

For the disabled on Fishers, there is an advantage to a nautical dentist. Sometimes a handicapped patient can be lowered down the hatch in a bosun's chair, a sling normally used for hoisting a workman up the mast. For all his patients, it's easier to visit the dock than to catch a boat to the Connecticut mainland.

Pete is 50, divorced, a red-bearded Viking with eyes the color of old denim. He is slow to answer questions about himself, perhaps too used to talking to people who can't talk back. His hands and arms are agile and strong, his legs useless. An irreversible inflammation of his spinal cord gradually sapped them. He doesn't talk much about that, either.

But it is a strain as he pulls himself up the companionway at the end of the day. A wet wind is slapping the canvas canopy around the cockpit and making a pleasant sound. It's not rain on a tin roof, but it's close.

Exhausted, he sits back with the first gin and tonic. Darkness and cigarette ashes fall around him. Painless Pete speaks of dentists and of his past. Weariness ebbs. Enthusiasm flows. He sounds like a man in love.

"I'm a sailor who practices dentistry, not a dentist who sails," he says with a smile, reminiscing that Humphrey Bogart said the same about sailing and acting. And though he likes his work, he needs something more, something to feed the yearnings that growl inside him.

Peter Eckerson is an adventurer, that endangered American species, still plotting his course by the stars and aspiring to them.

His motives are both noble and selfish. Dentistry helps support his sailing; he provides a service by landing at an island with no resident dentist.

"Mostly, I just can't see spending the rest of my life in an office at 46 North Main, you know?"

He has a prosperous, conventional practice at that address on Long Island; he works there five days a week. The Fishers shuttle is once a week during the warm months.

The weekend expeditions cost him. He must hire a crew of at least one and a part-time hygienist. It's a lot of trouble to hoist sail and make a five-hour cruise to pull a few teeth.

This is a means to an end. That end, like welcome shore, may be in sight. Pete wants to practice solely from his boat, perhaps cruising Europe. In a couple of years, he should be able to do that.

Like most men with an idea, Pete has doubts and bad days. When word first got around about the 37-foot, cutter-rigged boat he ordered from Taiwan in 1979, other dentists started calling him day and night to find out exactly how he equipped it.

There were, it seemed, plenty of other people who yearned to cast off from routine.

But Pete, plenty peeved when he thought of all the expense, trials and errors he'd endured, just stopped talking. Let others plan their own escapes.

Only two other dentists he knows of operate from boats, but he doesn't really count them, because they use motorboats.

It hasn't been easy. He says of his former wife: "She thinks I'm crazy." Not really. The two remain friends.

Yet it isn't up to Pete, really. Something within him dictates his travels, a force akin to that which drove earlier adventurers across the Appalachians, over the Plains and through Donner Pass.

His trips include not only the weekenders, but annual ventures to the Caribbean. And they are all but mental shakedown cruises, preparing him to cruise Europe under the power of bicuspids and sail.

"It takes courage to do something like this I guess. But there are a lot of people who would change their lives if they could."

Pete needs a wheelchair to get about on land. On the sea he is agile and free.

October 1984

Cool, Clear Water

BIG IVY, TENNESSEE. Boyd Franks' barn is red, the color God intended a barn to be. The tin roof on his simple frame house is painted bright red, too. All that crimson jumps out at you from the hillside, makes you want to stop the car and have a picnic, quick, before it disappears.

The whole peaceful scene looks to me like a Paul Detlefsen painting. You know the ones.

Detlefsen's barns are always very red and his trees very green. The season always is summer. His most famous painting is of a blacksmith in a very red barn working at an anvil.

Detlefsen prints hang in doctors' offices or furniture stores and get sniffed at by art snobs who think only Cezanne could paint a tree.

Boyd Franks knows he has a picture-pretty place. People traveling from Memphis or Nashville through the Tennessee countryside often have stopped and made snapshots—or sometimes, generous, impetuous offers to buy all or part of his 647 acres.

"It's my home," Franks says. So no deal.

Franks is an ordinary looking but tall man, probably about 6-foot-3 and none of it flab. He is dressed in a cap that shadows a kind face and in overalls labeled "Washington Dee Cee." His hands are the most extraordinary thing about him. They are big—no, huge—and permanently stained from honest work.

He pulls one of those big mitts from his overalls pocket and holds it out for inspection. The hand is about as unsteady as a mountain.

"You wouldn't think I could do delicate work with these," he says. But he does, stripping and braiding leather for mule whips. A few of the intricate leather braids hang between the hardware on his overalls, strung like Third World military decorations across his broad chest. The governor once commissioned some of his leather work for display in Nashville, he says.

The best thing about the Franks place, though, is its running water. It flows from several springs down the hillside and into a long, wooden trough that Franks rigged. He replaces the trough every seven years.

Why every seven years?

"That's how long it takes it to wear out."

Something about clear country air can make a perfectly good question sound silly.

The water is cold and pure and nothing at all like city water, Franks says. The sound of it pouring down the manmade route is a noise he dearly loves to hear. I walk with Mr. Franks across a footlog to his sluice network and aboveground "well."

"Try some," he offers, and I do. By now the constant rush of running water has made me thirsty and started me to thinking of a song from an old book my piano teacher nagged me through one year.

(All day I've faced the barren waste, without a drink of water. Cool. Clear. Water.)

The song was written in the comfortable Key of C, no sharps or flats; therefore I could play it; therefore it was one of my favorites.

Franks' water tastes good, though I'm no connoisseur. I only drink water when the Coca-Cola machine takes all my change. But those who know say it is the best.

A nurse from Cincinnati comes by the Franks farm annually and gets enough spring water for making coffee all year. Any water worth a drive from Ohio must be Grade-A.

This day, Franks is filling water jugs to take into town for his sick wife, Annie Mae. She is hospitalized in nearby Savannah, and the water there is giving her a stomach ache, he believes.

Something about the thought of the farmer loading those jugs into a 1953 pickup to haul into town renews your faith in matrimony. In sickness or in health, like the vows say.

The Franks have one child, a daughter, who lives in New York. "I've told her I'll pay her plane fare any time she wants to come home, but I'm not going there," says Franks.

I take a last look around. The firewood is stacked neatly. The house is held up off the ground with fieldstone and washed a forest green. Corn past its season pops in the wind like a good wood fire. And water sweeter than wine beats a path to the door.

No sane man would sell. No sane man could leave.

November 1985

"The Army Was Good To Me"

WEST POINT, MISSISSIPPI. He will fool you, this Gains Hawkins.

On the one hand, rotund, retired Army Colonel Hawkins, central CBS witness defense against the libel charge brought by Gen. William Westmoreland, seems about as apt to rock the boat as Mister Rogers. Between puffs on his customary Roi-Tan, Hawkins delivers a merry monolog some standup comic, somewhere, would kill for.

He talks about anything and everything—his short-lived, post-retirement job selling recycled pantyhose, or how he survived college days eating mainly Mr. Goodbars.

He wears a bright, red and blue checkerboard shirt—Ole Miss colors, he specifies—and drives about this beautiful old town in a small truck that he stops in the middle of the road at the least provocation.

Friends—he certainly seems to have them—rush right over to the driver's window and pass the time until traffic starts lining up behind him.

Before, during and since the Westmoreland trial he's gotten more ink than singer Michael Jackson. A lot of it was spilled trying to describe him.

David Halberstam called him "the most anonymous of men, balding, a little overweight, hard of hearing."

"I don't know where he got that hard-of-hearing part. I'm not," says jovial Hawkins.

Various others have called him pudgy, cherubic and a dead ringer for Jedi master Yoda of *The Empire Strikes Back*.

"I don't know this Yoda," says Hawkins. "What movie is he from?"

Gains Hawkins looks to me like your favorite uncle, Edgar, the one who comes bringing a surprise and then puts it behind his back and makes you choose which hand.

This is the man who stripped the oil cloth from the tables at Dugan Memorial Nursing Home, which he has run since 1981, and replaced it with elegant linen. He works the sunny halls of Dugan like a politician, using first names and handshakes.

Hawkins lives on 22 green acres just outside of town with his wife Bettye, a Nancy Reagan near-look-alike but with much softer, prettier features.

He helped head the Clay County Republican committee for Ronald Reagan's re-election. He was reared Baptist but turned Presbyterian. He rarely misses a Rotary Club meeting.

There is a flip side to Gains Hawkins, though, a devastating intellect beneath the Southern-fried crust. Uncle Edgar never thought like this.

He is the man who challenged a military superior, in open court yet, laying bare 17-year-old memories about the sculpting of enemy strength.

"It's not easy to point your finger at a four-star general and say, 'This man directed a monstrous fraud, and I carried it out,'" he says, dead serious all of a sudden.

"The pressure was pretty severe. I wasn't getting any hero play. My hands were dirty, too."

But the revelations, he says, "had to happen."

When CBS filmed the documentary on Vietnam that Westmoreland called libelous, Hawkins was less than delighted to be approached. He said to himself, "You've used up your allotment of denials. Are you going to sit there and let that poor damned rooster crow himself to death before you decide to be counted?"

Hawkins was counted. Life goes on. He will talk about it or not talk about it. For Hawkins is at home discussing Vietnam, Aristotle or hound dogs.

He flew to New York not long ago to address a meeting of the National Coalition against Censorship. He came to the attention of the organization after the Mississippi chapter of the American Civil Liberties Union honored him for his fight against an anti-pornography group waging indiscriminate war in Clay County. The anti-porn group had even insisted T-shirts with the Playboy bunny insignia be removed from local department stores.

If Gains Hawkins sounds like a native of Flora, Mississippi, eleventh son of a struggling shopkeeper, he is. If he sounds like a sophisticated, bi-lingual thinker, he is.

A young Hawkins on the GI bill stayed between the University of Mississippi library stacks researching his thesis, "Tragedy In Transition," while outside Charlie Conerly was throwing touchdowns, and Ole Miss was rocking. "I don't think I saw one ballgame."

He became an English teacher for a while. But a military career seemed the thing to pursue, and he never returned to teaching.

"The Army was good to me," he once wrote. "It taught me Japanese, sent me to Asia, then launched me permanently in the area of intelligence by sending me to Stanford University to concentrate on the countries of the Far East."

Instead of "keeping the books on the Communists," Hawkins now writes remarkable fiction that a New York agent recently discovered and plans to start peddling seriously.

While an undergraduate at Delta State University in Cleveland, Mississippi, Hawkins was sweepstakes winner of the Southern Literary Festival.

If this paradoxical package is confusing, it also is inspiring. Gains Hawkins inspires intense love or hate and has the mail to prove it.

He has been called a liar, Uncle Cornpone, Sultan of Smut, Prince of Porn and a disgrace to the uniform. He's also been compared favorably to Joan of Arc and William Faulkner.

CBS' Mike Wallace, whose autographed picture sits beside Hawkins' desk, has this to say to the colonel: "Thanks, comrade."

One of the Westmoreland trial jurors, an art teacher, has written Hawkins and praised him for his testimony. He keeps the letter in a bulging file.

"I don't let any of it get to me," says Hawkins. Then, seconds later, "But you know, you can't help feeling it some."

There it is again, division and contrast in a man stacked like an Oreo cookie. Crusty exterior, smooth interior. Part of him seems to enjoy the notoriety, the challenges—"I'd go anywhere to talk against censorship." Another part spent a quarter of a century saluting and taking orders.

The only order he could not follow, at least not indefinitely, was the one to lie.

July 1985

Never Too Late

JACKSON, MISSISSIPPI. Joe Olczak was disgustingly happpy. For a man with only 18 cents in his pocket, his smile was obscene.

He had been standing on the same spot alongside busy Interstate 55 here for more than two hours, waiting for the rides that would complete piecemeal his trip from New Mexico to Illinois. Cars weren't exactly lining up to oblige.

Beside him were two ancient suitcases, one the blue-green color of a swimming pool bottom and the other a dirty gold. Both were bound loosely with thick ropes. You didn't have to ask if he wanted a ride.

Because he was wearing so much of his clothing on his back, Joe could have been peeled down layer by layer like a Vidalia onion. Underneath the jacket and three shirts showed small patches of the leathery kind of skin Mammy warned Scarlett about. White hair bushed from underneath a black baseball cap, great tufts of it escaping around fleshy ears. He looked every one of his 64 years, plus 20.

Joe had been drinking lots of water at service stations and sleeping under bridges. He had been sampling the cigarette stubs thrown from passing cars, smoking them to keep his mind off the growls echoing in his empty stomach.

"I bet I've smoked over 40 brands. Some I didn't even know existed," he said, settling in for an 80-mile respite. His last job, boarding house caretaker, was the best one he'd ever had. But then the owner sold out and moved to a nursing home, and Joe was odd-jobbing his way around New Mexico with no permanent prospects.

Then he had an idea. He changed a $10 bill into quarters and dimes and fed them into a greedy pay telephone. He placed the call to an Army buddy he'd seen last in 1946. It connected.

The two of them had once vowed that the one of them who made it would help the one who didn't. It was a vow of young men. But Joe's buddy hadn't forgotten.

Now Joe has a job on a demolition crew in LaSalle, Illinois, and a place to stay once he gets there. He's only 600 miles away from a bright future.

"I'm just a late bloomer, that's all. Next time you see me, I'll be a man of means." He stopped talking only long enough to eat his first meal in two days. It wasn't like watching Princess Di mince around a tea table. French fries he sucked up like a new Hoover eats dirt. He ate every green inch of lettuce on his sandwich and saved the toothpick to nibble later. He even ate his ice.

Joe interspersed his lively talk with Polish sayings his mother, an immigrant, had taught him. He had hundreds, delivered in fluent Polish and then translated thoughtfully for the listener.

"It's never too late to be what you might have been." That was his favorite right now.

"Ninety percent of the people don't mean what they say. But my friend, he did. He told me he wouldn't take 'no' for an answer, to get myself to LaSalle." Then Joe broke into Polish: "Even a parrot can be trained to repeat the wisdom of the gods."

Wisdom, Joe said, has nothing to do with education. It has to do with living. So Joe catalogs the bits of wisdom he collects along the highway, storing them to share with the next friend he makes along the way to LaSalle.

"I rode with a salesman who was from Germany. And he gave the best description of America I've ever heard. He said this country was great, because the matches and maps are free at service stations. How about that, heh? The matches and maps here are free."

Joe said goodbye—and thank you—in Polish, pulling his ugly suitcases behind him into a spot he'd staked out in the Crimson Clover. He was still smiling and tugging at the overcoat hiding a busted fly zipper.

"I must be living right!" Joe yelled as the car pulled away. "I'm the luckiest man alive."

He pulled his toothpick from his pocket and chewed on the end without the cellophane twist.

May 1983

Life Without Walter

OCEAN SPRINGS, MISSISSIPPI. Mary Anderson Pickard has that special look of a long-time coast resident. Her hair is windblown, casual. She is pretty in a natural way, with no makeup or jewelry to weigh her down.

Her gauzy blouse and Katherine Hepburn pants are slightly rumpled, suggesting an afternoon nap. She never seems to hurry but strolls almost regally about rooms filled with pottery the blue-green color of sea foam. She is a daughter of artist Walter Anderson, perhaps the child who knew him best.

He was the father who used to give puppet shows for his children or make elaborate Greek ships to illustrate "The Iliad," which he read to them aloud.

But he also was the father who eventually left—for all practical purposes—and disappeared into his own reclusive world.

He did block prints, figures, line drawings, ceramics and pottery design. For money. For the rest of the world.

For himself, for art's sake only, he painted fabulous watercolors, now often compared to the work of Van Gogh.

He was the man who would row a skiff 10 miles across the Mississippi Sound, his painting supplies in a garbage can, to desolate Horn Island. There he would spend weeks, sometimes months, painting or dancing, living his wife has said, "like an animal."

He was a true eccentric, which took some doing on the tolerant Mississippi Coast. But Walter Anderson went the extra mile, strapping himself to a tree to study a hurricane or climbing to the top of a tall pine to observe a fire and then refusing to come down for a week. The accommodating family sent his food up by rope.

He was, Mary Pickard believes, a genius. The rest of the world finally seems ready to agree.

"My mother taught us to have great respect for his privacy, which was essential to him and his art and not just an indulgence," says Mary. Privacy is an understatement.

Walter Anderson lived the last 14 years of his life alone in a cottage almost hidden by brush on the ocean-front grounds of Shearwater Pottery.

This was and is an artists' compound, populated by one family. The Andersons have all been potters and artists going back to Walter's mother.

Walter Anderson's children and his wife, Sissie, lived about 100 yards away from him in a comfortable, converted barn. Most of the time, they might as well have been on another planet. When he was at the cottage, they left his meals on the doorstep.

Sometimes he would leave on his old bicycle, sending postcards from Texas or Virginia. Sometimes he would take off to Egypt to study a certain animal. They never knew, as he pedaled off, if he was going a block or a continent away.

Then he would return, not to them but to his cottage. And to Horn Island, his spiritual home.

"I went through a period of resentment, but it didn't last long," says Mary. "He just reached a point where art had to be everything, where he couldn't work with children looking over his shoulder." When she speaks of him, it is in almost worshipful tones. He died in 1965.

Now people pay thousands of dollars for his watercolors, most of them painted on typewriter paper. The mural he painted on the walls of Ocean Springs Community Center is valued at $1 million; he charged the city $1 for it, using the money to replace the tube that had blown in his bicycle tire.

This year has meant the first major Walter Anderson showings outside his native South, with exhibits in Philadelphia and New York. Critics with no regional bias have raved.

A new edition of *The Horn Island Logs of Walter Inglis Anderson* was released. And Anderson's wife is working on a book about life with—or maybe without—the artist.

Mary Pickard, who has devoted herself since 1978 to studying and promoting the work left by Anderson—including some 8,000 watercolors and voluminous writings—is confident her father is finally appreciated. And she is ready to spend time on her own pursuits, which lately include drawing.

There is a certain symmetry in all of this. Walter Anderson finally providing for his family while they pursue their art.

"He wouldn't like it if he knew I was spending all my time working on his things," says Mary.

She knows him well enough to say that. Now.

June 1985

Every Red Cent

Talmage and Louise know where their money went. Every thin dollar. Every plug nickel. Every red cent.

The Heathcotts live in Tennessee, in the small town of Gates, in a charming brick house, within their means.

Mrs. Heathcott is a compulsive record-keeper. She has a ledger to make an IRS auditor polite. She has kept diligent, hand-written records of every cent spent for her entire married life, the last 50 years and 9 days.

On Jan. 11, 1936, the Heathcotts bought a skillet for 20 cents.

On Feb. 10, 1947, Talmage paid $7 to have a tooth pulled.

On May 18, 1959, daughter Nancy Heathcott paid $2.90 for a high school diploma cover.

On Dec. 4, 1959, Talmage drove to nearby Ripley, dropped 2 cents in a parking meter and weighed himself for one cent. He bought a 30-cent lunch.

On May 28, 1966, the Heathcotts bought a package of Feen-A-Mints for 43 cents.

Every expenditure—down to a single postage stamp—is recorded on lined paper collected in dusty, loose-leaf notebooks. The cost of those notebooks is recorded, too.

"I don't know why I started this," says affable Mrs. Heathcott. "It's a hobby, I guess."

Talmage Heathcott is proud of her. You can tell.

"The IRS would have to believe her. A jury would have to."

The first full year the Heathcotts were married—1936—they spent the following:

Groceries—$131.34
Clothes—$62.08
Church—$21.58
Miscellaneous—$41.63
Gas and Oil—$10.97
Haircuts—$3.85
Help to pick cotton—$56.77
Grand Total—$328.22

What can I say? They were young and foolish. In later years, as times got better, the Heathcotts added a "Recreation" column to their ledger. In 1960, for instance, they spent $2.60 recreating. I don't think they made it to Disneyland.

Mrs. Heathcott does not limit her listing to finances. In 1951, she kept up with the Saturday movies Talmage and the children saw, while she stayed home to wash her hair. On Jan. 21, it was "Fancy Pants" with Bob Hope and Lucille Ball. On Jan. 4, "I'll Climb the Highest Mountain" with Susan Hayward.

You would be surprised at the family arguments she solves. "If they know the approximate date, I can find it."

She also lists Christmas cards sent and Christmas cards received, funeral home visits and food taken to shut-ins. On July 19, 1977, Nellie Baker was the recipient of a lime Jell-O and pineapple salad. You can never tell when you might need that information.

Mrs. Heathcott has two stacks of cards wrapped tightly with rubber bands. One is the stub of every phone bill she has ever paid. The other is all her utility bills. The financial list, though, is her first love.

"Many times I've said, 'I'm not going to do this another day. I'm going to put this away and forget about it once and for all,'" says Mrs. Heathcott, sighing.

But then Talmage would come in and dutifully write down what he had spent for his wife to record. "I'd think to myself: 'Well, I'll just add these two or three items.'

"Then I'd start to reason, 'Well, I've been at it 25—or 29 or 49, however many—years. I can't stop now.'"

It has become like brushing her teeth or saying her prayers. Hard habit. She trained her children to report every cent they spent. Try to teach a kid to do that today, and he might beat you over the head with his Twisted Sister compact disc.

Talmage Heathcott was a farmer. Farmers have to keep good records, even if they are written in red ink.

Dec. 15, 1941: Heathcott killed a spotted sow that rendered 55 pounds of lard. In 1939, the family ate 25 fried and baked chickens and gathered 2,036 eggs.

Mrs. Heathcott has never added all the years' totals together to see what a lifetime of spending comes to. She says the thought is tempting, but too scary.

January 1986

Tater George

NEW SITE, MISSISSIPPI. An eloquent champion of women's suffrage died last week in the Mississippi hills. He was better known for his sweet potatoes than his politics.

He dug so many in his lifetime, they called him "Tater George."

A newspaper obituary last week described George Bryan Denson as a "retired farmer," accurate as far as it went. What it didn't say was Tater George and his family dug an average of 1,368 bushels of sweet potatoes per acre in 1915, setting a record probably not broken to this day.

What the 84-year-old man was proudest of, though, had nothing to do with digging potatoes on the farm called, you guessed it, Tater Hill.

His nephew, Curtis Coghlan, told me the story last winter, before we drove deep into Prentiss County to look for Tater George. It had been a while since Curtis had visited his uncle, and soon all the rambling country roads began to look alike.

We figured we were close, but nowhere could we spot the old house where George Denson was born in the year 1900—and where he died last week.

Finally, we gave in and asked directions, stopping an old farmer on the side of the road to see if he knew George Denson.

"He's lived somewhere near here all his life," said Curtis to the farmer.

"George Denson. George Denson." The old man scratched his head. He thought and thought.

"They call him Tater George," said Curtis.

"Oh! Tater George. Sure." The farmer beamed his recognition and told us the way. We found his home but not Tater George, who was in poor health then and staying with a daughter.

So I never got to meet Tater George or hear his tale firsthand. But this is what happened.

Back in 1919, the thorniest political problem in this country was whether to give women the vote. George Denson was a senior at Tishomingo Agricultural High, a co-educational boarding school in rural North Mississippi. He started classes three months late that year, delayed by the fall potato harvest.

When Tater George finally made it to school, classmates already were planning a debate to argue if the 19th Amendment ought to be or not to be. Nobody wanted to speak for it.

Tater George agreed to defend women's suffrage, asked for 30 days to prepare and then went to work.

The night of the debate, 5,000 spectators came from Mississippi, Alabama and Tennessee, jamming the auditorium, proof the issue was a hot potato.

It took a three-man team only 15 minutes to give the anti-suffrage side. Tater George used the rest of the scheduled four hours, a lone but powerful voice, orating late into the country night.

"Women's apron strings have been tied to the kitchen table post since time began on Earth. I say cut those apron strings and let them go out the kitchen door into the wide-open world and get some fresh air."

That's what he said in a nutshell. He remembered those words 60 years later.

"Being elected president of the United States wouldn't have meant as much to me as making that speech," he told his nephew.

Tater George saw the 19th Amendment ratified on June 4, that same year. And he followed closely the political career of the first congresswoman and determined suffragette, Rep. Jeanette Rankin, a Democrat from Montana. He even wrote and recorded a song about her called "Montana Land."

Tater George died farming.

He was back at home, helping tend strawberries, peach trees and, yes, sweet potatoes, when he fell.

"He died like he wanted to," said his daughter, Jane Moore. "We found him out by the peach trees, sort of sitting on a plow."

The family hasn't decided what to put on the tombstone where he's buried at Little Brown Freewill Baptist Church.

Tater George?

"It'd only be right, since that's how everybody knew him," said Mrs. Moore.

He reared seven children and raised countless crops. And one night he stood up and spoke his mind about what he thought was right.

Tater George might not have made history, but he sowed some seeds for change.

February 1985

Up From Winona

WINONA, MISSISSIPPI. Mabel and Pete Peterson have been married for 53 years, a long enough time to work out the kinks.

He sits quietly minding his stay-for-preaching manners while his wife chats about antiques and astronauts, wallpaper and cut glass. He doesn't like to interrupt.

Pete, at 91, still tools around Winona in a bright yellow Volkswagen bug that once upon a time was new. He has the face and movements of a much younger man, the no-nonsense manner of a practiced bill collector, which he once was.

Mabel, at 86, is an active, brass-polishing Episcopalian who proves that sometimes broad minds come in small packages. For over 50 years the diminutive woman headed her church's welfare committee, bucking a small town's tendency to kick the dog that's down.

If these two cling to the past, it's only in the form of hardwood family pieces that comfortably furnish their home, the second-oldest residence in Winona.

The winter just thawed has been a long one for the Petersons. She has been sick; he has been patient, fielding phone calls and visits from friends.

There have been a lot of both lately. For next week, Pete and Mabel's oldest boy, Donald, will walk in space.

Mission specialist Donald Peterson, 49, paid for his ticket to the stars with years of hard work, his parents say, and neither one of them would want the trip canceled.

Peterson will be accompanied by three other astronauts —Story Musgrave, Paul J. Weitz and Karol J. Bobko—on the five-day maiden flight of the Challenger space shuttle, scheduled to lift off from Cape Canaveral carrying the world's largest communications satellite.

While astronaut Peterson performs the last-minute rites of space flight, his mother and father pack their bags for Houston thinking entirely different thoughts.

Mrs. Peterson likes the ground and would just as soon keep both feet and both sons on it.

"But I'm proud of him, and I know it's what he wants and has worked so hard for. I just have to have enough faith to know God can take care of my son in space the same way he has taken care of him on the ground."

It hasn't been easy, watching the world change so drastically during her lifetime. "I remember when I saw my first automobile," she says, shaking her head in belated wonder. "Someone had told me a man I knew bought one, and that he sometimes drove it by our home."

Mabel Peterson, then about 8, waited patiently for the alien sound of an automobile, which eventually came. "It was some kind of steamer and as red as fire. I flew into the yard and onto the porch. I'd had enough of the automobile."

Pete Peterson is different. "I would like to go up with him," the father says, and there is genuine envy in his voice. "I've always been enthused about flight; I think it's the safest, best way to travel. And I'm excited over this flight."

Though this is his son's first trip into space, Donald has more than 6,000 flight hours, which Peterson brags about like grandchildren. "Donald was afraid he'd get too old and wouldn't get to go in space at all. When the space program first started, you know, men over 30 going into space was out of the question. Now they're sending them as old as 50."

The Petersons see nothing that unusual about having reared an astronaut and a former movie actor in Winona, Mississippi. It is, they insist, on the way to the stars.

Their younger son, Gilbert, who has given up the movies and now sells real estate in Los Angeles, was always the athlete. Donald, the scholar, won an appointment to West Point and then joined the Air Force. Gilbert played football for Mississippi State University and joined a small orchestra that eventually led to Hollywood.

"I've never told anyone about this," Mrs. Peterson says in a conspiratorial whisper. It was Donald's high school homecoming, senior year, and the diminutive Winona lineman was among the players escorting campus beauties onto the field at halftime. Mrs. Peterson, who had been busy selling concessions, made her way out of her booth to watch the traditional procession.

Suddenly, two jets blew by overhead, and the high school band stopped playing. Everyone looked up.

"I looked at Donald's face instead of the planes, and from what I saw then, I knew he would be a flier.

"I tried not to think about it. I went back to selling sandwiches and never said a word. But I knew."

April 1983

The Sounds Of Sunday

He was square as Andy Hardy when it came to cutting class. He just wouldn't.

The rest of the Kappa Alphas might be catching rays on the mansion's rooftop or brewing something noxious and purple on the patio below, but Jack kept his nose in a textbook. That stunt was no gimme in springtime. Auburn students knew how to suck the nectar of the season.

Husky farmboys from Dothan and Wadley and Ramer—the ones who'd be driving tractors and pitching hay for their fathers all summer—now engaged in such idle pursuits as throwing Frisbees across College Street. They wore the uniform of the young—shaggy, faded cutoffs, rubber thongs and shoulder-length hair.

Before them sashayed the light of some daddy's eye, tanned girls decked out in bright, brief finery, bought with a credit card from the Polly-Tek or maybe even Atlanta. School was as incidental as a sneeze. Except for pivotal test weeks, academics were the last thing anyone was studying.

Jack simply couldn't afford the pleasant loitering. Engineering is what he'd settled on. He was forced to study hard.

Originally, he'd been drawn to journalism. He could write, too, this smart Birmingham boy with eyes the color of mahogany and black, black hair cut short for ROTC. He'd rush into the cluttered, basement office of the campus newspaper, loosen his shirt collar and draw pure magic from the worn keys of an old Royal manual.

But Jack wanted career security and a hundred job offers. He wanted desperately to make good. And he cherished a challenge.

Perhaps writing came too easily.

So Jack was plugging through his Sophomore year, skipping the lazy afternoon drives to Opelika or the beer busts held beneath his open window in the Shalimar-scented nights. Jack of the conscience. Jack of the drive. All work threatened, but never succeeded, in making Jack a dull boy.

Everybody liked him anyway. He would only come out and play on Friday and Saturday, and soon his friends accepted that. The desk lamp projected Jack's handsome silhouette against his bedroom wall night after night.

On Sunday's, he always went to church. "The sounds of Sunday with Floyd Cramer" was his favorite album, this in the days of Foghat and Santana and acid rock.

But if Jack heard a different drummer, he still kept pace with his peers. He was a campus leader. "Please don't lose sight of the necessity to do your best always, for if you do your best at all times, success is inevitable," he once wrote a harried friend. "Keep smiling, believing in yourself, dreaming up bold ideas and working hard."

They planned the house party weeks in advance. Cars filled with giggling, gorgeous coeds and their proud escorts left at hour intervals from Fraternity Row. The cow pastures and Mom-and-Pop groceries of east Alabama blew by, bucolic blurs to the carloads making their way to the lusty Florida Panhandle.

It was a weekend of surf and sand, not slide rules. Not even Jack brought his books along.

He had carefully marked these days for diversion. For a few hours, at least, he was just one of the carefree crew.

Three of them died that Sunday in 1974 when a drunk hit their car near Wewahitchka, Florida. John Haim, Kathy Ray and Jack James, all gone too soon in a season so inconsistent with death.

Word filtered back to Auburn slowly. Telephones started ringing through the long dormitory halls, shrill bells signaling the news.

Jack, who invested his youth as carefully as a broker does his own money, was not coming back. For him there would be no more frivolous times.

April 1984

2 / Sweet and Sour Notes

Good Time And Hard Time

LELAND, MISSISSIPPI. Son Thomas has a Trophy Room, just like Elvis. Son's Trophy Room also serves as living room, TV room, dining room, music room and bedroom. For it is one of only two rooms in a tired hovel on Sinclair Street.

Photographs of Son Thomas paper the walls. Son singing the blues in England, in the Delta's Freedom Village, in the White House. Some of the photos are framed, some are not. Some hang straight, some do not.

In the small, sad room is a sagging bed, its blue coverlet so old the chenille bubbles have burst. There is a black and white television set with nothing to offer but reruns of "Benson."

Skulls—primitive sculpture Son fashioned from the Yazoo gumbo—stare mockingly with their empty-sockets. If I lived here, I'd have to cover those grim heads each night, like some bird in a cage.

Son Thomas has a pressing, paying engagement. For $150, he will sing the blues into the night on a barge floating the Mississippi River. The barge party is raising funds for something or other, he's not sure what.

To Son Thomas, $150 is good money. A University of Mississippi blues archivist, Walter Liniger from Switzerland, lately is helping the bluesman manage his appointments and fees.

Son Thomas has been singing the blues all his life, with nothing to show for it but a bottomless well of material—hard times, faithless women, broken dreams. He sells me an $8 album from a cardboard box stored in the back of Liniger's truck. The day has been a big one, financially, for Son Thomas.

Later—two days and many thoughts later—I will visit the home of another singer. Graceland is all I have heard and then some.

I stand on the portico as a chipper guide tells all us eager tourists that Elvis' aunt, Delta Mae Biggs, and her 10-year-old Pomeranian still live here in Presley's hillside house. They live here with the 24-karat grand piano and the life-size portraits and the carpeted ceilings and two Stutz Blackhawks.

They live in this Tupelo-come-to-town mansion, with its pink Jeeps and 14 TVs and countless gold records and rhinestone-studded suits. And each day busloads of tourists come to visit, buying $7 tickets and walking through this 1939 home all done up in 1968 trappings.

Fans sometimes leave a message on the rock wall outside Graceland, something clever or sappy. Some paean to Presley. Or, rarely, something mean-spirited.

"We're glad you did it Your Way."

"Until we meet again in Heaven."

"Enjoyed your house, Elvis. But do something about that Jungle Room."

Elvis had things, lots of things, which he couldn't take with him. They remain. The horses and snowmobiles and chandeliers so big they had to be broken down to fit through Graceland's doors. A pool table and whirlpool and wet bars. The Ferrari, the Cadillac. A glut of goods and gold.

Talent is not unlike a prison sentence. You can do good time or hard time, but do it you must. Success may swamp you or elude you, but that is beside the point. Beside the talent.

Some men simply are born to sing or paint or write. And it seems to me we give them too much or nothing at all.

May 1986

Royalties, Loyalties

MERIDIAN, MISSISSIPPI. If Jimmie Rodgers was the Father of Country Music, Elsie McWilliams is the midwife.

She delivered the music and lyrics when Rodgers needed them, not for royalties or fame but to help her ailing brother-in-law start his brief but sterling recording career.

She is 87 now, bedridden much of the time, yet still the spunky, generous woman who wrote over 30 of the Singing Brakeman's songs and contributed to far more. The proper daughter of a Methodist minister, she refused to sign some of his bawdier, trademark yodeling numbers that she polished.

Her old bungalow sits on a steep incline amidst bushes that need clipping. Time has done a remodeling job. The roofline sags a bit, and screens are rusting. She has only recently returned after a long stay in the hospital. Pipes that burst during the winter aren't replaced yet, and she's using water from buckets.

"I never envied anybody their fancy houses, 'cause maybe they don't have friends all over the world like me," says Miss Elsie. That's what everyone calls her.

"I got some money from the songs, but I guess I've spent it all. That's what they tell me. I don't need any money now; my children buy me everything I could want.

"They say when I have money I just give it all away. And I guess I do."

The story is simple, really. She's told it hundreds of times.

Drifter Jimmie Rodgers married her younger sister Carrie. When the railroad jobs ran out, Rodgers made a recording of an old ballad, "Sleep, Baby, Sleep." It was an instant hit. Rodgers needed more material. And he needed it fast.

"He thought because I wrote poems and songs for the children to sing at church I could do it," says Miss Elsie. She laughs a laugh as rangy as a Jimmie Rodgers' yodel.

"Well, I wrote him a batch, but my notes must not have been right or something, 'cause he couldn't get anybody up in

Washington—that's where he was living—to play 'em." Only one, "The Sailor's Plea," was recorded.

Rodgers kept after her, though, to come to New York and "show him how they should sound." Miss Elsie reluctantly left her three children with her mother and went North to make music with Jimmie. "I'd listen to him talk about his daddy and home and things like that and come up with the inspiration."

During one 1928 session Miss Elsie wrote "My Old Pal," "My Little Old Home Down in New Orleans," "Daddy and Home," "Lullaby Yodel," "I'm Lonely and Blue" and "My Little Lady."

"At one point we had just written the six new ones Victor (recording studio) wanted, and Jimmie and I were so proud we had them ready. Sister Carrie had a good turkey dinner waiting for us. Jimmie grabbed her up and danced her around the table and said, 'Kid, if I can just keep you and my old guitar, I'll go to the stars.'"

Miss Elsie turned right around from the supper table to the piano and wrote "You and My Old Guitar."

Rodgers had to persuade Miss Elsie to sign a contract. "I didn't want a penny for those songs," she says. "If there was any money coming, I wanted him to have it. He was sick and broke, and I loved 'em both so much, too.

"Finally, I agreed to accept ½₅th of one percent.

"I told him if I got 50 cents or $50 it was going on the new church we were trying to build."

When Miss Elsie's first royalty check for $256.56 arrived, "I nearly fainted. I signed it right over to the church."

The music has always been in Miss Elsie. As a child she'd pull her small chair up to a larger one and pretend to be playing the piano. "Before I could nearly touch the pedals I was playing the organ by ear at revivals. Someone else had to work the pedals for me." A sister finally taught her how to read music.

"I still put my own expression in, though, all the runs and things that aren't there on the page."

She looks feeble, under the covers in the four-poster bed. But when she talks about music, Miss Elsie beams. Music has been her ticket to travel and fun. Her house is literally crammed with mementoes from admirers of Rodgers' music.

"I never bought one piece of bric-a-brac and look at this place," she says proudly. There are piano music boxes, ceramic railroad men, portraits and photographs of Jimmie Rodgers everywhere. On the mantel are the bronzed, child-sized gloves Rodgers bought her daughter when he made his first recording money.

Miss Elsie didn't end her music-writing career with in-law Rodgers. She also wrote five songs for a San Antonio disc jockey, one Ernest Tubb.

"I got him started," she says, matter-of-factly. "He had a folio full of my lyrics, though, that he never used. He said he just couldn't get into my music like he wanted to."

On Miss Elsie's front porch sits a crippled man working a jigsaw puzzle. He rents the house next door, and she takes care of him. "I love him like my own grandson, but I'd love him even more if he were a Christian. He just won't talk about God."

She's still the minister's daughter. "Some things they call country music today are trash in my estimation. Some of the words, and the beat of it, are just trash. I've got a song I wrote about that that nobody's ever paid any attention to."

Miss Elsie is trying her best to get ready for Meridian's annual Jimmie Rodgers festival held in May. She is reserving her failing strength.

Carefully she emerges from beneath the covers, walking to an upright piano in the living room. Her gnarled fingers coax an incredible sound from the chipped ivories.

The whole room seems to shake with sound. The artificial flowers Merle Haggard sent her dance about on top of the old piano.

March 1983

Red, White And Blues

JACKSON, MISSISSIPPI. It was a white crowd, mostly, calling out for country classics involving blue eyes and red heads.

Willie Nelson was headliner, and quite naturally he drew a country and western audience. Spectators wore denim uniforms and high-heeled boots and wide leather belts tooled with their names. It was a Red Man crowd come to hear a white man's blues.

And they did. A gargantuan Texas flag unfurled dramatically behind Willie's family, and the Whiskey River flooded the coliseum floor. Everybody took the ribbon from his hair and let it fall, so to speak.

But Willie didn't come alone. Bluesman B.B. King and his saucy, best "girl" Lucille appeared, too, giving a flip side to the concert and the night.

Those in the crowd were lucky. For the price of an ordinary concert ticket, they got one of those unpredictable and unique gems of living called a "rare moment." When the two men sang, the people heard the masters of two southern musics, heavyweights in arenas and sounds both similar and oh-so different.

One man had learned to sing the blues in rural Mississippi, where he explored the rudiments of the guitar by plucking a single strand of broom handle wire strung across the wall of his momma's home. From Indianola, a brief interruption in the long crop row called the Delta, B. B. King made his way north to fame.

The other man teethed on hard times and honky tonks in the Lone Star State and old Nashville, mostly surviving before his middle-age mug finally became more familiar than George Washington's.

Willie Nelson's lyrics and music preceded his fame as a singer, but now if you haven't sung a duet with Willie, you're not off the country music bench.

One was black and one was white, but both sang their own brand of the blues with the kind of feeling you had to believe wasn't inspired exclusively by gate receipts. Both seemed to know what they were singing about.

They smudged the boundaries between their two musical forms that evening, Willie singing "Night Life" with B.B. King and B.B. King joining in on "Uncloudy Day."

The country audience didn't need a course in blues appreciation, either, to warm up to bluesmaster B.B. King.

It's true that the blues still languish in esoteric circles here in Mississippi, their native state, while country music dominates. The speech is the same; just the dialect is different.

If modern Rock is a strange hybrid of international influence, Country ' n' Western and the Blues are pure stock. Purely American.

More importantly, they are both music spawned in the heart, where toil and trouble take their toll. That trouble might be Jim Crow, a landlord or a faithless love, but trouble has no particular color. They may sound different, but they feel the same.

And that's what seemed to matter to the congregation the night B.B. preached and Willie gave the invitational.

July 1984

THE *John Denver?*

SAVANNAH, TENNESSEE. Tipper Gore's traveling rock pornography show comes with a warning: Explicit.

"Rock is a subject that really does offend," says Tipper Gore's warm-up act, a local woman charged with introducing the crusading Tennessee senator's wife.

"These slides are pretty graphic. But when you're dealing with rock, this is what it's about."

Nobody leaves the junior high auditorium. Then Mrs. Gore takes to the microphone. "I can quote or spell out the offending words," she offers. "I ask this as a courtesy. Which shall I do?"

Hearing no opinions and sensing everybody in the audience can spell anyway, Mrs. Gore decides to give it to us straight. The lights are dimmed.

The audience holds at least as many teenagers as adults. They are good kids, you can tell, more likely into Lionel Richie than Heavy Metal. This is the Bible Belt, after all, and teens probably spend more time at Baptist Training Union than at Twisted Sister concerts. We are the world, not the worldly.

A handful of teenagers on the front row has come to defend "their" music—one girl wears a black, Motley Crue jacket—but most are here as church or class groups in complete support of Mrs. Gore's campaign against gore. Just tell us what to do.

Now the kids sit squirming in their seats as they see flashing before them album covers you don't find in the stacks at Wal-Mart. You get the uneasy feeling these kids have never heard so many naughty words in a stream.

It is impossible, of course, to disagree with Tipper Gore about the repulsive nature of much heavy metal music —the blood theatrics, the excesses. No normal kid or adult really relishes seeing the simulated decapitation of a woman, or some uninspired singer drinking blood from a human skull.

And that's probably why Heavy Metal music has a relatively small, determined-to-be-outlandish audience.

I wonder about Tipper Gore's responsibility. To context. By slipping album covers of Olivia Newton-John, the Rolling Stones and Sheena Easton into her slide show between the really hard-core stuff, she manages to trash several octaves of rock.

I wonder if the parents attending will go home and purge the stereo cabinet of the Rolling Stones or perhaps Olivia singing "Grease" when they fail to turn up any Judas Priest.

I wonder if Tipper Gore is giving the normal teenager too little credit and normal rock music far too much blame.

Teen suicide, undeniably a real concern, may sometimes result from a disturbed teen's interpretation of rock music, she says next. Then she flashes grainy mug shots of children who ended their own lives, and whose parents have connected those various tragedies with rock.

It is hard to argue with a grieving parent or for a pro-suicide cut some sicko sings. But Tipper Gore goes beyond condemning songs that glorify suicide. "It is the interpretation we worry about. Even if there's a chance the child could misunderstand the lyrics, you have to look at the effect."

Interpretation. Charles Manson slaughtered to a Beatles' tune about an amusement-park sliding board. Surely Mrs. Gore—lover of wholesome rock that she professes to be—would not take the Fab Four from us. Warped minds could find warped meaning in "Mary Had a Little Lamb."

When the lights come back up, and Tipper Gore winds down, the audience gets its chance.

John Denver is a priest in the Church of Satan, one man flatly states. I suppose he means the John Denver of Muppet fame.

Labeling albums with explicit content—Mrs. Gore's solution— is not enough, says another man.

"That's sort of like helping an alcoholic become a social drinker, isn't it?" he asks. "Why not go ahead and go all the way and ban it?"

It is the excesses that worry me—in censorship as well as rock.

"I feel more akin to the rebels than the reverends," John Fogerty, formerly of Creedence Clearwater Revival and one of music's more intelligent lyricists, told *Time* magazine last fall. He was speaking of Mrs. Gore's labeling plan.

"This whole thing sounds kind of dangerous to me."

I second that emotion.

April 1986

"Be Cool, Chicken"

SOMERVILLE, TENNESSEE. When you are asked to judge the Fayette County Egg Festival's World Chicken Beauty Contest, you know you have arrived as a serious journalist.

Actually, I was in good company. The local funeral home director, a Somerville grocer, the sheriff and Mr. Funky Chicken himself, Memphis bluesman Rufus Thomas, also helped judge.

In fact, there were more of us judges than there were chickens.

The first year Somerville held the chicken beauty contest, there were about 40 fine-feathered entries. Last year there were 12. This year four.

They didn't really need the CPA who tallied the scores. Little Miss Egg Festival could have figured it out on her fingers. I don't know why the poor showing. Maybe some contestants scratched at the last minute.

A chicken named Granny Clampett won the gleaming, four-foot-high trophy, a bigger loving cup than Sparky Anderson and his Tigers got last year for winning the World Series.

I hate to get technical, but the inaccuracy of the winner's stage name offended me. I couldn't vote for her. Granny, of "The Beverly Hillbillies" fame, was a Moses. Daisy Moses. She was Jed Clampett's mother-in-law, not his mother. Certainly not a Clampett.

There probably hasn't been such blatant beauty pageant fraud attempted since Miss New York iced her cupcakes in a last-ditch attempt to win Miss USA.

I preferred Miss Fayette County, anyhow, a classic red hen dressed in red taffeta skirt and red shoes. She looked like a winged version of Scarlett O'Hara, all decked out in crimson—that naughtiest band of the rainbow—to go to Ashley's birthday party.

The chicken beauty contest was late starting. Mostly, the judges all sat around waiting and listening to Rufus Thomas talk about being famous.

"It ain't always so great, being Rufus Thomas," he said.

Just about then, a beauty operator who is also an aspiring singer interrupted him, asking for an autograph.

"We're cutting hair at a booth on the corner," she said. "Come on out, and I'll cut yours."

"You'd have to find it first," said the 68-year-old singer. Then he laughed heartily at his own joke.

"I went to this place out in the county a long, long time ago," said Thomas, picking up his story. "You went through a gate, and they locked it behind you.

"There was whiskey drinking and gambling inside . . . . And I walked into the room and folks over there in a corner right away started hollering 'Hey, there, Rufus.' I ducked out of there fast."

There are some places, Rufus Thomas decided that night, where you had just as soon not be seen.

The bluesman's fans kept filing by. A couple of people asked him to sing. I don't know that he ever did.

One woman pulled him over to her refreshment booth and gave him a couple of homemade brownies. He carefully put them with a bunch of foil-wrapped rib bones he planned to take home for his dog. Finally, we did our judging.

And Miss Egg Festival crowned the World Chicken Beauty. Then, as a surprise, they presented Rufus Thomas with one of the four contestants, a big, white rooster dressed as Jesse James.

"Be cool, chicken, now be cool," Rufus Thomas admonished the rooster, which probably didn't understand why it was being held up to a throbbing microphone as a strange man boomed his thanks.

As I was leaving, I looked back. The gregarious old singer was standing in the middle of all his admirers, holding a white rooster under one arm. The rooster was wearing six-shooters and a cowboy hat and, no longer cool, was flapping about wildly.

Fame, I decided, is a strange bird.

October 1985

An Outlet, An Outrage

I have never been married to Jerry Lee Lewis, which possibly puts me among a minority of southern women. Jerry Lee Lewis has spent more money on marriage licenses than most folks spend on white bread.

Last year in Ferriday, Lousiana, he buried one bride. Last month in Memphis he took another. The grass was not growing on the Ferriday grave before the Killer was courting and wedding and bedding. He's enlisted more young girls than the Brownies.

Just as it did when Lewis married his teenage cousin decades ago, the world now clucks like a schoolmarm at his latest action. Ol' Jerry Lee Lewis has done it again.

The decent folk who adore his music condemn his lifestyle. When will they learn they're one and the same?

There probably is some complicated, fancy, psychological explanation for what makes George Jones drink and Jerry Lee marry and Willie smoke dope. There is a financial one as well.

The world doesn't pay to hear these men sing about the life of a 9-to-5 accountant. We pay to hear of their mischief, their sorrow and shame. They wallow in the excesses most of us will only know vicariously. They reinvest their money in what made them famous— the fast life.

Rural towns used to tabulate the divorces after touring Jimmie Rodgers passed through. Hank Williams left an Alabama trail of heartbreak and havoc. The world expects a little depravation from these men, and most of them don't disappoint.

Only, every now and then reality intrudes and the honky-tonk lights are replaced with unflattering daylight and the legend becomes a louse. The IRS or death arrives and unceremoniously dumps these country kings from their throne. And we recoil in sanctimonious horror that someone with everything would risk it all for a few cheap thrills.

Only tragedy makes these people real to us. Usually they and their bodacious lifestyles are an outlet, an outrage. We want to see

Jerry Lee in his white suit and red, ruffled shirt, leaping from wife to wife the same way he leaps an octave. We chuckle or stare wonderingly as he does all the tacky, wicked little things that normal folks just don't do.

If he sells the story rights to his sixth wedding to *National Enquirer*, Jerry Lee Lewis is a card or a cad, depending on how you look at it. But what matters is you're looking.

"I may forget a line or two, a few words now and then. It takes a drink to make me think, and live it all again.

"This gray you see don't bother Jerry Lee, and neither do these lines. I may have seen some better days, but God knows I ain't reached my prime. I got some scars from a woman's war . . . but Lord only knows, if I had the time, I'd do it all again."

That's what he sings. That's what he means.

That aging bluesman Son Thomas, residing in a hovel in Leland, Mississippi, had his utilities turned off last year while he was away at a singing engagement. His wife shot at him in a barroom for paying too much attention to some young thing in the corner. He's still singing the blues, because he's still got them.

And if anyone ever sang from the heart, it's Jerry Lee.

That's the way it works. It's not always comforting, but it's the price we pay for hearing what we want to hear. We can feign surprise, but if you insist on a Mormon lifestyle, you get Donnie and Marie.

As for the Killer, there's always been a whole lotta shockin' going on.

May 1984

"Sing That Bird Song"

PHILADELPHIA, MISSISSIPPI. You may not know Bob Ferguson, but you've heard his song.

Ferlin Husky recorded it first, leaving out the verse that called Jesus by name so the song could play on honky-tonk jukeboxes. George Beverly Shea sang it, Jesus and all, at those open-air, three-hanky Billy Graham crusades. And Kitty White gave it the rhythm and blues treatment.

Or maybe you live in a cave and first heard Bob Ferguson's song from actor Robert Duvall, who portrayed a country music singer in the movie "Tender Mercies."

Ferguson scribbled the lyrics to "The Wings of a Dove" on a brown paper bag as he drove between work and his Nashville home one day in 1958.

"It's hard to believe they can wring all those different sounds out of one little song," says Ferguson. He is a lean, modest man with a deep, Hughes Rudd voice.

"That song doesn't belong to me anymore, anyhow. It has a theme that's echoed a million times to a million different people."

He was a Tennessee state employee then, filming 15-minute television shows called "The World Outdoors" for the Game and Fish Commission. "I was so elated, because I had met a tough schedule, and there were going to be a certain number of films ready at a certain time. I had this burst of elation, this prayer."

The result was a song, a simple classic, that sold more than 10 million copies and stayed on the top of both the pop and country charts in 1959 for 36 weeks. Even then it fell only to Patsy Cline's "I Fall To Pieces," and nothing mortal could compete with that.

It was translated into Swedish and German and distributed worldwide. It was heralded by the Catholic church, but banned in England—why, Ferguson still doesn't know. "Wings" was a cross-over (country to pop) hit before the term was invented.

Bob Ferguson lives with the Choctaw Indians near Philadelphia now. But for a long time his heart and home were in Nashville. "I'm not a songwriter. I'm just someone who every now and then writes a song. There's a difference."

Maybe so. But after the phenomenal success of "Wings," Ferguson scored again with "Carroll County Accident," also written on the road, this time between Carroll County, Tennessee, and Carroll County, Mississippi. That song was the Country Music Association Song of the Year in 1969.

"I write better driving, about 100 miles from where I've been or 100 miles from where I'm going. I just sort of loosen up."

For 15 years Ferguson worked with Chet Atkins, producing records for big stars like Charley Pride, Dolly Parton, Lester Flatt and Porter Wagoner. He even worked about 12 hours once for Elvis and Colonel Tom Parker, but the business details and the advance road work expected of him just weren't appealing.

"The bottom fell out of country music in 1955, what with Elvis and all. You could book Ernest Tubb for $50, anywhere."

But before he settled in with Atkins, Ferguson made ecology films for the state and—every now or then—wrote a song.

His old friend Ferlin Husky happened to invite him over for Easter dinner in 1958. "We sat around singing and talking, and I sang him the song I had written."

Before they wound down, Ferlin asked, "Sing that bird song again." Ferguson did.

"Bob, that's a hit," the singer said. "Not a country hit. A Top 10, pop, country, smash hit."

Ferguson smiles and looks down, afraid of bragging even after all these years.

"I thought he'd gone off the deep end. He asked if he could record it, and I didn't say 'no.'"

Since then, people everywhere have relayed stories to Ferguson about how "Wings" comforted them in bad times. Ferguson is not particularly religious—"I have spurts"—but he's pleased the song means something to somebody.

Ferguson eventually went back to school in Nashville for a master's degree in anthropology. It took him six years to finish, but since then he has published two books on the subject. One of his various film-making projects led him to the Mississippi Choctaws, and he fell in love with the Choctaws. He was smitten with Indian culture and one particular Indian woman named Martha. They are married and have four children.

Ferguson now produces videos for the Choctaws, films used for attracting industry to the reservation. Lately he's thought about recording some of his own songs. Maybe even singing "Wings." It would put him in pretty good company.

April 1985

3 / Beaten Paths

Room 711

ATLANTIC CITY. Miss Lewis, of all people, came to mind when I first stepped into the glitzy Claridge Casino to watch suckers shovel their money into the slot machines.

She has gone to her reward now, but once Miss Lewis was a formidable Vacation Bible School teacher, a former missionary to China who made all of us youngsters sign pledges never to smoke, drink, gamble or dance, so long as we lived, so help us Lottie Moon.

What would Miss Lewis, with her white hair and sequin broaches, have said about Atlantic City? Jesus and the moneychangers would have been a peace conference next to the late Miss Lewis turned loose in this half-acre of legalized lunacy. One thing about growing up Baptist. You always lug your guilt around with your Samsonite.

I don't know what I had expected. A younger, more glamorous gaming crowd, for one thing. Women in glittering gowns and men in dinner jackets. A Robert Wagner and a Cybill Shepherd playing blackjack.

The people spilling off the junket buses and into the gambling emporiums were all ages, including old. Lots and lots of them were old. Grandmother types were pushing quarters into slots as fast as their arthritic arms could operate, a look of fierce determination on their faces. Women who should have been home preserving strawberries or bouncing grandbabies on their knees were wearing Celluloid visors and pulling the silver levers in a regular rhythm that looked about as exciting as work on a factory production line.

There were the tourists, too, of course. They were dropping a pre-determined $100 or $200 at the tables, laughing and then ambling on to hear Perry Como or the McGuire Sisters dust off some songs from the past. They were staying in the fancy hotels and buying salt water taffy on the Boardwalk and then going home for a decade or two.

But the regular, repeat patrons—the ones wearing work clothes and an eerie, purposeful look on pinched faces, the ones jostled in from Philadelphia, New York and Newark on the free buses, who didn't have rooms in the gaudy hotels, who didn't hear Rita Moreno or Don Rickles or Nipsey Russell, who spent all their time and money at the slots—were the ones who were depressing. They were the ones who made me think Miss Lewis may have been right, if for the wrong reasons. They would be back. Just as soon and as often as they had more money.

Atlantic City Mayor James Usry, a former Harlem Globetrotter and a personable Athens, Georgia, native, said double-digit unemployment still plagues the "new" Atlantic City, which plays host to 30 million visitors annually. There are unaddressed housing needs for the poor and elderly. The police budget is $97 million—yes, $97 million—and crime is still a problem.

The poor here seldom collect $200 and often go directly to jail. The glittering casino world and the rest of Atlantic City have yet to merge.

And, according to Usry, there is real division. "A black mayor in this city of 40,000 would be acceptable," said Usry, who is black, "if it were not for all the money involved. What it boils down to is this: Some just don't want a black man handling all that money."

I sat in my Room 711 (really), resting a moment from the deafening noise of money being lost, won and lost again. It as a nice room, all in blue, with a color television and a complimentary fruit basket.

From seven floors up I had a grand view of the famous Boardwalk and gray beach, both of which look better from a distance. It is funny how height lends a charm to many things, including milling crowds. From on high you see the sea gulls and the sailboats and the colorful, throbbing blend of humanity, ants walking purposely toward some neon sugar cube. Three floors below me, inside, men and women were standing in line, impatiently waiting their turn to fatten the casino coffers. They might as well cross the street and throw those cups of quarters into the ocean.

I ate a free banana and thought about it all.

April 1986

John And Abe

WASHINGTON. During the day allotted for museums, I saw everything from a special exhibition on the evolution of women's gym shorts to Mister Rogers' red sweater.

I caught a splinter of culture running past Renoir. Somewhere between the French Impressionists and Lichtenstein's spatters, I quit caring. Washington was eluding me. Mostly it was hot, and my feet hurt.

Night falls on the seat of government, too, though it does not mean much. People keep moving. They pile into an amazingly clean subway called the Metro, reading paperback copies of *Iacocca* or discussing Gramm-Rudman the way you and I would talk Baskin-Robbins. And they ride willfully into the night, into the suburbia of reclaimed swamps like Foggy Bottom.

Only the tourists stare wide-eyed at the monuments and tombs and buildings that all look vaguely familiar from some textbook. But there are enough tourists so that gawking does not matter.

The moon was almost full and the night revived me. So I went to stare at the Lincoln Memorial. That's where I met John Elliott. He had been staring at Mr. Lincoln for five years, and five years will make you a little proprietary.

John is a guard with the National Park Service and Lincoln his charge.

"There is very little reverence, very little respect," he said, motioning toward the hundreds milling about. He had a point.

It was late, past 10 o'clock, but throngs of people still were circling Mr. Lincoln. Four teenaged girls were standing at Lincoln's Georgia marble feet, waiting to have their picture made. Arms were linked, mouths twisted in idiotic smiles. All of them wore Minnie Mouse T-shirts. Yes, John Elliott had a point.

"I grew up in Washington," said Elliott. "Used to, when I was young, you could come in and hear a coin drop. Not anymore.

"Now you get groups of kids who are dropped here off some bus. Their chaperones stay down at the concession stand and drink a beer. I've thrown whole busloads out of here when they got too loud.

"I like to watch the people after midnight. Sometimes you'll get someone who gets to the very top of the steps, and he'll stop and wipe away a tear."

Elliott wiped away an imaginary tear for emphasis. He approved of the visitors who felt something.

Elliott knew his monument. From top to bottom, inside-out. He pointed out the Alabama marble in the ceiling, treated, he said, in vats of beeswax to promote translucence.

He had once lived in Alabama, Elliott explained by way of footnote, down in Enterprise, where the only monument is to the boll weevil. Studied police science at a junior college there. Now his wife lives in Arkansas, and he is here, assigned to Lincoln. "Haven't seen her since April."

Not even beautiful Abe Lincoln makes that seem right. Elliott said he wanted a transfer.

"They are afraid if I get down on that Buffalo River with a fly rod, they'll never see me again."

He cast a make-believe fly toward the reflecting pool. The moon and the pure lines of classic architecture were ganging up to make a fool of upstarts like Lichtenstein.

I stared some more. Elliott gave me a park service brochure on the Lincoln Memorial, but not before making two corrections in the printed text. There are 20, not 28 blocks of marble in the statue. The Piccirill brothers spent one year, not four, carving it.

"I've been trying to get that corrected for four years," he said. Then he walked outside with me, to the top of the stairs, a proper host showing his guest the door.

Yes, he said, sometimes he does come here on his day off.

I finally left the two of them, feeling like I at last had a fix on this mind-boggling place.

Sad John Elliott, angling the white waters of the Buffalo.

Sad Abe Lincoln, presiding over the simple dreams of us all.

June 1986

One Town, Two Worlds

NOGALES, ARIZONA. This would be considered one town if the tall chain link fence didn't split it in two.

You don't notice the fence at first. Standing on a hillside in Nogales, Arizona, the landscape directly across the way in Nogales, Mexico, looks similar, part of the whole. But in the ravine between the two towns runs the fence that is the international border.

On either side are the bustling shops and the dark eyes in brown faces. You might call the fence an artificial boundary, but that wouldn't be accurate. It doesn't just separate the land that belongs to the United States from the land that belongs to Mexico. It separates worlds.

On the Arizona side, Nogales looks a little shabby—crowded, old, yet full of a border town's imported color and charm. You can eat a hamburger at McDonald's and walk 50 paces to the border inspection station, which looks about as intimidating as a post office. An American can walk into Mexico as casually as he mails a letter.

Nogales, Mexico, is different. It's on the wrong side of the vertical tracks.

There the shop owners are imploring, desperate to please the gringo tourists on whom they depend. The homes clinging to the steep hillside are ragged by northern standards. And there is the smell of sewage, of poverty.

If Nogales, Arizona, looked a little shopworn before, from the Mexican side of the fence it looks like paradise.

It's not hard to understand why Mexicans are clambering into the United States in greater numbers each year. They can get lowly jobs here, paying more in a few weeks than they'd make in six months back home.

All that's standing between them and paradise is men like Tom Fredrick of the U.S. Border Patrol. He wades in the river of illegal immigrants, trying with a teaspoon to catch as much of the flow as possible.

Tom's head is shaved slick as Formica, and he has a kind of Jack Nicholson sneer. He might have been sent over from central casting to play a border patrolman. As a captain, he wears two silver bars on his shirt collar.

"Just call me Tom. We used not to have military ranking, but some guy in an office somewhere decided it would be neat, I guess." His manner is less intimidating than his looks.

Tom was riding to his job in a Sears toy department years ago when he heard a radio ad recruiting for the border patrol. It sounded exciting—"Of course, anything would when you're working in a toy department"—and Tom Fredrick passed the tough written and physical tests to join the patrol.

It doesn't tax his Princeton economics degree for Tom to understand he's fighting a no-win war. As long as the economic differential keeps getting larger between the two countries, poor people are going to climb through the fence. The work, like the stream of illegal aliens, is steady.

Mexicans keep scampering through the holes, which have been patched up and ripped open more times than Joe Namath's knees. If they don't make it the first time, they try again. And if they don't make it the tenth time, they try again.

"And if they keep trying, they eventually make it."

Most of them are so poor they have absolutely nothing to lose; the border patrol simply processes the ones it catches, then hustles them back across the border. It's a routine that takes only a couple of hours.

There are no apparent hard feelings. For the captured aliens, it's like losing a hand of gin rummy. They'll be back. As long as American employers are happy to give jobs to Mexicans willing to work for little or nothing. And politicians are reluctant to address the sensitive issue.

Tom will keep scouring the landscape, knowing he's earning a paycheck, not stemming the tide. Border patrol work is a lot like housework; the sheer repetitiousness of it can be depressing. Nothing ever seems accomplished.

So burnout is a real problem. "Some guys can't sleep if they think there's one illegal alien in all of Los Angeles. That type burns out pretty quick.

"Then you have to guard against the other extreme. And that's the feeling it's all so futile you might as well sit in a coffee shop and drink coffee all day 'til it's time to go home."

Tom has a simple approach. It's his job and a job worth doing. ("The law is the law.") But at quitting time he quits, riding into the sunset on one of his beloved motorcycles or crossing the border himself for a steak dinner.

He seems to have mastered the ability to depersonalize the Mexican immigrants, not in a cruel way but more in a posture of emotional self-defense. He talks like he's catching statistics creeping across the border, not people.

And, too, he's maintained his sense of fun, finding it as best he can in the grim pockets of hillside where humans hide and wait for dark.

On a dirt road directly paralleling the border, a black and white dog suddenly stalks the patrol car, snapping and barking and raising Cain right in the driver's window. Tom stops. He takes his radio microphone from its cradle, holds it out the window and transmits the angry dog's howls to headquarters.

"Ten-four," comes the matter-of-fact reply. Border patrol humor is dry as the desert.

Along with the increased alien traffic have come increased numbers of smugglers and traders ready to make a buck off America's new pilgrims. Shame is compounded.

"Ten years ago, I used to pick up these good old boys with leather feet who had walked up here from Guadalajara or someplace. They would just come through a hole, and then you'd pick them up on the road or on a railroad track heading north.

"It's much more organized now. Smugglers are more active. They'll pick up a large group and, for a fee, move them by automobile or truck."

He knows the favorite pickup points, some of them in the most innocuous places. He pulls into one behind a convenience store. It seems so absurd. This slab of uneven pavement, behind a milk-and-bread store and next to a garbage dumpster, is an O'Hare of illegal alien traffic.

You ask and he answers. "Yeah, I think I'm good at my work." And he does seem to read a face or a movement the way most of us read a newspaper. He knows his business.

And to him, that's just what it is. Business. Nothing personal.

October 1984

Chaos In The Round

ATLANTA. The Martin brothers of Tennessee are right where I left them 22 years ago. One is lying prostrate on the hard ground, his gray uniform covered with blood. The other brother, dressed in blue, is bending down to offer comfort.

And Old Abe, the Wisconsin war eagle, a veteran of 42 battles, still circles in the smoky sky. Not much changes in a war that is over.

I thought I had outgrown Grant Park's Cyclorama, which sits snug to a zoo and depicts the Civil War Battle of Atlanta. It's not exactly among the Atlanta "in spots" you think about visiting nowadays.

There's too much else to do in Hot 'Lanta. Six Flags Over Georgia keeps adding to its rides and Ted Turner to his roster. There are so many stylish clubs and restaurants the city's Yellow Pages are thicker than a Russian novel.

This very night, I'm scheduled to cover a regional aerobics competition in a trendy, lively joint called "Sneakers." Maybe that's why I'm here, at the good old Cyclorama.

It keeps a slightly unfashionable appeal. It's not unlike nearby Stone Mountain; you figure it will always be here. Besides, I'm more than willing to spend a couple of dollars and 20 minutes to find out if the world's largest painting still gives me chill bumps.

It does.

Oil on Belgian linen, a football-field-and-a-half long, the Cyclorama is, of course, a painting in the round. Its themes of duty and death are perversely fascinating, like war itself. But the Cyclorama also is an amazing art work, the Sistine Chapel of the South. There are only 14 other pictures like it remaining anywhere.

This cyclorama was commissioned exactly 100 years ago, before movies, television and other entertainment spectaculars upstaged such pictorial, wrap-around history and made it obsolete.

A Wisconsin man struck the original deal with German artists, back when Civil War veterans were still plentiful for technical assistance. Gettysburg and Shiloh were practically current events then, recent and painful memories, not picnic spots.

An Atlantan eventually bought the enormous painting at auction for $1,000. It's insured now for $5 million.

Only a few things seem different this day at the venerable attraction. They've done away with the red Georgia clay that used to be part of the diorama. It caused mildew and attracted rats.

The canvas now rotates—or is it the floor?—as Sherman warms up for his march through Georgia.

The painting was refurbished 10 years ago, and the colors are all vibrant and new. At least that's what the guide says; it looked just as good to me, or better, when I was 10. Even the audience is basically the same as it was in the summer of 1965. A bunch of Boy Scouts with tall imaginations and short attention spans giggles when the lights are doused. A father wearing vacation bermudas and Hushpuppies pushes his brood along a dark aisle to good seats.

And then we all fall silent as a spotlight sweeps past the tragedies of Kennesaw Mountain and Leggett's Hill. Past dying soldiers and broken rail lines, gutted homes and fallen pines. Past the Martin brothers of Tennessee.

The cannons thunder and bullets fly. History unfolds in four tons worth of paint and canvas.

They fight the Battle of Atlanta the umpteenth time for those of us who happen by. Brother still fights brother. And nobody wins.

April 1985

City Women

Two brassy women with a long ladder signaled our approach to New York. At a stop in Connecticut they tried to board the train with a noncollapsible, eight-foot ladder, an antique treasure held between them like a relative's coffin.

"You can't bring that on board," the conductor said, quite firmly. He cited safety regulations to support his objection.

The women began to argue. Not a wheedling, pleading argument. Something else entirely.

They had taken larger items aboard an airplane, for gosh sakes, one said. They had paid for these train tickets and had full intention of using them, said the other.

Their outrageous straw hats wagging saucily in the night, those women did everything but cuff the white-haired attendant. They cussed him plenty, along with his mother. Finally, he slunk meekly away, as the triumphant New Yorkers boarded with their ladder.

Rudeness is a well-honed survival tool in the city, and it usually doesn't shrink in the face of authority or advanced age.

That was the first thing a couple of rubes hailing from Down South learned about New York. Meekness will get you and your ladder nowhere. And never cross two big-city women wearing over-sized hats.

We spent only three days in the city, our mouths hanging down all the while like pelicans. The city takes lots of money and moxie, and we were short of both.

Our hostess was a sophisticated Associated Press reporter, a woman who had grown up on Long Island. She knew well the ways of the wicked city.

She was patient. Her apartment floor was covered with subway maps, which she repeatedly explained. She knew all the good parts of Central Park and where to find New York Yankees T-shirts. She understood when we preferred gawking at the Statue of Liberty to an Indian restaurant heavy on sitar music.

Margie knew when the flower vendors went to the docks and where Rodney Dangerfield's new club was. She knew to leave us alone and let us watch people. She didn't know why some, like herself, belong to the city, while others never will.

For two years Margie had worked for the AP in Mississippi, renting a home by the lake and away from town. She sailed and swam and had a golden tan. There were never long lines and seldom any muggings. She hated every minute of it.

As soon as she could, Margie headed back to New York, where the creaking subways and jammed busses pump people between their jobs and apartment homes. She is paying more for two rooms than she did for the lakeside home, swimming on a rooftop and parking wherever she can.

She admits it seems strange. If you think about it too much, she says—all these people living on such a small land mass—you go crazy. You can't dwell on all the bad things that could happen to you every time you duck into a subway station. You can't become immobilized by the prospect of lurking evil. Instead, you remember the rules and get into the routine.

Margie automatically tucks her necklaces inside her blouse before leaving home. She rarely carries a purse. She has made her small apartment her private, special island, a retreat in the midst of an unrelenting crush of people. And if her door looks like all the others on the hall, it opens into something distinctive and personal.

That's what most New Yorkers do, I suppose. They create a four-walled garden spot to run to when it all becomes too much. Past row after row of walk-up flats, where residents lean over window ledges for a breath of fresh air, there is a refuge. Past parked cars with busted window glass, no hubcaps and dent over dent. Home sweet home.

Margie pays more attention to one vase of cut flowers than Mobile, Alabama, does to its azalea beds. She gets nature—and beauty—in concentrate.

We stood on the rooftop, marveling at the lights and the unseen people behind each one. The night and such a lofty perch had cleaned up the city and its flaws.

Margie sees first-run movies, Broadway plays and the hottest concerts. Her clothes come from Macy's and Gimbel's. There is a sense of know-how about her, a sense of self-confidence they don't seem to hand out in Colquitt, Georgia, or Bogue Chitto, Mississippi. At 28 floors up, she was on top of her world.

People are different. Some know how to finagle a ladder aboard a train. Others just know how to take that train home.

January 1984

Weaving Dreams

HOLLYWOOD. "Glitter" is probably the word most used to describe the entertainment capital of the world; "grime" would be more accurate.

No, the tour books don't stress the brown film on the world-famous sidewalk in front of Mann's Chinese Theater. But tawdry reality versus stellar reputation is as Hollywood as klieg lights.

Yes, it's actually pretty dirty here at the old Grauman's Theater. It's hard to keep a sidewalk in Los Angeles, even a star-studded one, otherwise.

The theater has an elaborate facade of pagodas and spires painted Halloween colors. It's a shabby kind of showy that is entertaining for a while but then makes you yearn for a long look at the Grand Canyon—and a bath.

It doesn't matter. People still flock to this shrine of American celebrity to worship at the feet, literally, of those who have really made it in make-believe. Foreigners as well as Americans search for the slab of a Bogie or Monroe, lovingly tracing the indentations and calling out to one another to "Come see."

This is a Made-in-America showplace. We might not compete with other countries in manufacturing televisions or automobiles, but Americans dominate the market of imagination.

If movie stars are an industry, Los Angeles is the production line. And Grauman's is the factory outlet.

In Hollywood, visibility is everything, and the stars and starlets would come sit in the wet cement if asked. They want, mightily, to make an impression.

There's not much dignity in bending down to stick your mitts into Redi-Mix, but here in Hollywood there has never been a premium on dignity. What there is is an urgency to be more than a flickering image on a screen, or even more than an accomplished performer.

The thrust is to be somebody, a celebrity, A Name. And you're not A Name until you can write it in the sidewalk at Grauman's.

It is to wonder, watching as a group of Japanese tourists snap each other's likeness at Elvis Presley's star on the Walk of Fame, blushing and grinning and acting as if they are ransacking his underwear drawer instead of merely standing on a bronze star bearing his name.

Why are we so successful at it, this image-building business that permeates our culture? Why are we better at weaving dreams than cloth? Why is it better to be on the cover of *Us* magazine than to win the Nobel Prize for chemistry?

The Japanese export Hondas and Sonys, and we, in turn, send them Dolly Parton jokes. The whole world waits for our inventions of fiction and frivolity, our Michael Jacksons and Hula Hoops. They may not want a Ford, but they'll take two discos, thank you very much.

A good time is America's most durable product. The shelf life is longer on some of our celebrities and fads than you might think. James Dean still sells blue jeans in France.

Some stars fade for a time, but then there will be a revival of interest. Marilyn Monroe one day is only your father's cornball fantasy, then suddenly the hottest club in town is holding a Marilyn look-alike contest.

So pilgrims understandably want to come to the source and light a candle to celebrity. Grauman's is almost the only place left to do it.

The rest of Hollywood Boulevard is about like every other city street in the world, as crowded and nondescript and forgettable. This one is perhaps seedier than most, a magnet for runaways, drug dealers and assorted weirdos for whom the line between what's real and what isn't is vague or unimportant.

Except for the Chinese Theater and a few Hollywood bookstores, there's no way to touch the fanciful business of show. It's long since gone from the corner drug store to behind board room doors.

But at the stomping ground of fame, you can still ponder the anatomical coincidence that most he-man actors have dainty feet. You can match soles with Olivia de Havilland and Richard Widmark.

You can examine the nuts and dolts of the American dream industry.

October 1984

Purplehulls And Hospitality

She was, she said, distant kin to the Faulkners of Oxford, who win Nobel Prizes or write scholarly reminiscences about the Faulkners who win Nobel Prizes.

And sure enough, there in her old high school yearbook was a picture from a time when "flips" were all the hairstyle rage, with a caption beside it that said "Pixie Faulkner."

That is not her name now. She is married and past the age to be comfortable with the nickname "Pixie."

Still, she must have been feeling a little like the old Pixie Faulkner again, riding through the lush Mississippi countryside where she had come of age, returning to the Neshoba County Fair, hallowed be its name.

The Neshoba County Fair is the most revered Mississippi tradition, at least among the white folks. People own cabins on the campgrounds and spend entire weeks just porch-sitting and all-night singing and generally carrying on the way they remember or figure their fair-going ancestors did.

There is a fierce pride about it all. If a little green Martian parked his spaceship on the red dirt fairgrounds, before he walked 20 paces a dozen Neshoba Countians would have stopped him to explain how this unique fair has even been written up in *National Geographic* and all.

The day Pixie played guide, the beef cattle checked out of the fair barns and the dairy cattle checked in. The Suzy Q. Cloggers danced beneath the Pavilion in Founder's Square. The Pavilion is a sagging but sentimentally sound structure where they hold evening dances and politicians hold forth.

It was at a Pavilion dance Pixie fielded her first improper advance. She has forgotten the boy's name but not the moment.

Also that day, a couple of local-lads-turned-politician spoke about federal dams and damn federals and a former Mississippi governor said why he thought Tennessee, not Mississippi, got the new Saturn automobile plant. Something about the winning state being willing to let the governor wear out the state jet between Nashville and Detroit.

We did not tarry long with the Pavilion politicians. You have to be in the mood.

Instead, we went to the cabin of Pixie's old friend, a cabin within a clod's throw of the harness racing and just a short walk from the bustling midway.

The fair cabins are situated cheek-to-jowl and are rather shantytown in appearance. Except these shanties cost $20,000 and better, when and if you find one for sale. You mostly inherit a Neshoba County Fair cabin, like fine silverware or a receding hairline.

Pixie's friend welcomed a stranger with open arms, because it is against unwritten Fair law to do otherwise. She had worked for a week on the food to bring and now was offering it to someone she had never seen before and most likely would never see again. Anyone who has ever shelled a dishpan full of purplehulls knows that is true hospitality.

A bunch of nephews and nieces were underfoot, eating those dried fruit bars that look like a puppy's chew toy. They begged for midway money.

And for a moment there, on the cabin porch, with the children splashing in mudpuddles and purposely spilling their bubble-making solution in front of the window fan, with old folks rocking and comparing horror stories from gall bladder surgery as the politicians whined on in the distance, I thought I knew what Pixie Faulkner meant.

"I hate it, and I love it," she had said.

Ninety-eight degrees worth of sunshine was pouring down, but the ground was still mud from yesterday's rain. There was the smell of close quarters.

Pixie Faulkner probably will be back next year. I may come with her.

April 1986

Romancing The Rails

CHATTANOOGA. Cathy McLeroy was to honeymoon at the Chattanooga Choo-Choo, and we were convinced she had the market cornered on romance.

She revealed her plans at a lingerie shower, back in 1974, when all of us still believed a short nightie and a long night in an anchored Pullman were pretty much the living end.

Cathy was a majorette, and golden, about to marry a man who apparently had the money and moxie to start wedded bliss on the right track. So we sat wide-eyed and envious, watching Cathy unwrap yet another gauzy gown, a Phi Mu princess surrounded by pastel peignoirs and adoring ladies in waiting.

I hadn't thought about the Choo-Choo for a long while. But when you drive through Chattanooga—as I did not long ago —the invitations to the place are not subliminal. They are orange neon. I stopped.

"Pardon me, boys," I said to the Hilton desk clerks; Hilton runs the place now.

"How much does a sleeping car cost? And just how far ahead do you have to make reservations to get one?"

"There are plenty available on a week night," the clerk said. It was a week night. "Yours for only $85."

I stood there, resplendent in my flannel shirt and blue jeans, thinking of that day in 1974 when I had turned green as my cream cheese-and-cucumber finger sandwich, jealous of Cathy in Chattanooga.

I simply was not dressed to do the Choo-Choo. One of my socks was being swallowed gradually by a hungry tennis shoe, and I could feel my hair beginning its day's-end rebellion against bobby pins. But sometimes ladies in waiting can only wait so long. "I'll take it."

There were 48 sleeping "cars," each of them actually half of an authentic, albeit remodeled, Pullman. I had half of the car that was named for Phil Whitaker, whoever he was. The decor was fake opulence. Belle Watling on a budget.

The "brass" bed was only wood painted gold. The black "marble" bathtub was black all right, but not marble. There was a gold velour sofa with fringe. And red curtains with tassels. The wallpaper was black and white and flocked all over.

There is something about gold tassels, even on a train going nowhere, that puts you in a deliciously naughty mood. This would be a fine place to honeymoon, especially if you married right out of high school.

The best thing about the room, actually, was a personal vending machine. You could phone the motel desk, the instructions said, and get things rolling.

"Shall I activate your bell captain?" inquired the desk clerk.

"Do you mean turn on the automatic vending machine?" I asked, always the rube. With the semantics settled, my machine worked fine.

The room lacked the rhythmic motion and the click-clacking of the track joints that made sleeping on a train desirable to begin with. The only huffing and puffing was from the amorous and indefatigable couple in the other half of the car and the only rhythmic click-clack from their gold-painted wooden bed. There was even a little sign in the room, describing to patrons how difficult it is to sound-proof a train car. Forewarned is forearmed.

But, I must admit, the gardens and fountains and torches outside were beautiful, and honeymooners would have no problem getting into the spirit of a richer era.

You could sit in the 1909 depot—now a swank restaurant—and imagine how it once must have been. But the real trains stopped coming through here altogether in 1978.

You can sit all day and all night and all the next day, and no train will roll in or depart. Americans liked the romance of traveling the rails far better than they did the actuality.

And this train yard, for all the gild and glitter and celebration of a catchy Glenn Miller song, is really just one more defunct train yard. Humans have a strange, stubborn habit of romanticizing things, even things we do not really want.

November 1986

"Bill Your Roosters"

OFF AN ALABAMA BACKROAD. Cockfighters have been coming to this same, secluded, tin-topped stadium every other Saturday since right after The War. They come for many reasons. To fight their cocks, to shoot their bull, to place their bets.

The spot is not hidden, exactly, but you have to know where you are going to find it. And once you leave here, you still might not know exactly where you have been. The woods are the apple-green of spring, lush as they ever get, and the wild dogwood looks like random snow.

But inside—in the dusty, dimly-lit barn where roosters equipped with steel talons are tangling—a sport older than the surrounding wood is flourishing. And it sounds for all the world like one continuous corn flakes commercial.

Men pay five dollars. Women get in free. Cockfighters pay a $40 entry fee for the five-cock derby.

There is a permanence about the whole setup you don't expect of something illegal in 46 states, including this one. The place is not some forgotten barn or temporary lean-to; it seats a couple of hundred and was built for fighting cocks, nothing else.

The main pit is ground-level, surrounded with low, wooden sides. There are spectator bleachers, rough and wood-hewn. You wouldn't want to walk under them slowly; the men here spit more than the National League West.

There is a 50-gallon drum equipped with a flue for winter cockfights. There is even a ladies' restroom. The men go outside.

The floors are dirt, packed hard from use. A concession booth sells soft drinks and hamburgers. Two women sitting on stadium seats munch popcorn contentedly, as ever so often a dead rooster is carted from the ring.

A sign inside used to read "No Gambling, No Cussing, No Drinking," but the rules crumbled away with age. Now they are unwritten.

Don't say anything bad about another man's rooster. That is the Cardinal Rule. Insult his wife or maybe his coon dog, but don't say anything bad about his rooster.

The cockfighter has not taught his bird to kill. Gamecocks are born knowing how. But he has specially bred his bird and fed him high protein feed and "worked" him in various ways to strengthen leg muscles. He has invested time; he has bought expensive gaffs to replace the natural spurs, which are cut off.

So bet against him if you will, but don't say anything demeaning about his chicken.

House rules are necessary so the owner of the arena can throw out bad drunks or trouble-makers and nip man-fights in the bud. Keep the trouble down and keep the gates open.

Gambling goes on openly. Men wave $10 or $20 bills and shout out their preference in birds. "Twenty on the gray. I'll take twenty on the gray."

Somebody answers. The bet is sealed with only a nod or meaningful look across the arena. The honor system. Don't welsh on a bet here or you might lose more than your honor. The loser carries his money to the winner after the fight; that's courtesy.

Drinking goes on, but not so openly. There is a constant, human trickle from the barn to a parking lot littered with beer cans and dead roosters. Men fill soft-drink cans with liquor, conversing in the sly, self-satisfied way of those who manage to drink in a region that frowns on it.

The crowd is mostly men; a few bring their women. But these days you also can see a teenage boy with an earring in one ear or a smartly-dressed woman in running shoes and pressed bluejeans.

The actual cockfight has more technicalities than women's basketball. Terms like "Bill your roosters," "Handle," "Pit your roosters" and "drag pit" mean something to the cocking fraternity. But to the uninitiated, a cockfight looks something like two men shaking feather dusters at each other.

Fresh poultry in the ring. The birds take an instant dislike to one another, their long, straight hackles rising Tina Turner style.

Sometimes a high-breaking bird jumps off the dirt floor and puts on a show; more often the birds shuffle close to the ground until the gaffs tangle or puncture some vital organ or other. The winner, basically, is the rooster left alive or the one pecking last.

It is not particularly bloody sport, believe it or not. The sharp gaffs make tiny puncture wounds, not slashing cuts. A better word to describe it would be tedious.

Some would say appalling. And it is not exactly pleasant to watch blood bubbles foaming from a rooster's beak. You can rationalize by remembering the chicken eaten every Sunday, the one shackled to a conveyor belt and stunned with an electrode before his head was cut off, guillotine-style.

At least gamecocks die a natural death.

The fights go on, however you happen to feel, as they have for hours, for centuries. Dust and feathers hang in the slender streams of sunlight that stripe the dark barn. The florescent lights, crusted with dust, will be more important soon.

Outside, two children play in a pile of discarded fowl, using a stick to finish off the roosters that are not quite dead. Mercy killings, I suppose.

April 1986

A Few Great Yowanis

ALONG THE NATCHEZ TRACE. Ride this federally-groomed parkway often enough, and soon you know the signposts by heart.

Instead of the usual highway fare, the billboards for smokes and eats and places to sleep, the government has posted places of historic or natural interest. The bottoms, the sloughs, the swamps and the hollows—all of them identified and explained for the tourists curious enough to stop. Many have musical Indian names.

Some of the signs seem a little silly, a tad superfluous—the one in a bald-cypress swamp, for instance, labeled "Mosquito." I take that one as a courtesy to the Yankees.

But most are informative and a pleasure to read, just as the Trace is a pleasure to drive.

You can see a glade of wildflowers or a pasture full of Indian mounds, a deer or a cotton crop. A narrow screen of protected woods separates the Natchez Trace traveler from the typical junkyards and tin tumors of modern commerce that normally flank any road.

I saw a new sign not long ago, gracing a shaded rest stop area. It said:

"Yowani. Named in honor of a small group of Choctaw Indians who, at one time, lived southeast of here. Little is known of their history. No great battles were fought which would leave the Yowani name to posterity. No great men came from their group. No outstanding events, in which they had a part, seem to have taken place. In short, we here honor these Indians so that they will not have gone 'unhonour'd and unsung.'—(their name is corrupted from Hiowanne, the Choctaw name for cutworm or caterpillar. U.S. Department of the Interior, National Park Service.)"

The sign said something to me about how we evaluate history. Our "great men" are mostly men and mostly warriors, when you stop and think about it. Our outstanding "tribes" or "nations" are the ones that win battles and eventually wars.

After all, a peaceful existence or coexistence is nothing to write home about. Stoking the campfire does not constitute a great happening.

Our most famous and revered presidents preside in war times, and the Indian chiefs we like to remember fought White Men, not the elements.

"How do we know that no great men came from the Yowani camp?" I asked the man in charge of signs on the Natchez Trace.

His predecessor erected that particular sign, he said, "and I assume he did sufficient research to come to that conclusion." That sign might eventually be replaced, he added, "since it doesn't really tell you anything."

I hope they leave it. The Yowani stop is my favorite on the Trace. I get lost in the mystery of the "unsung" people and what we may have missed.

I like to think some Yowani woman made the ultimate piece of pottery or concocted an herbal cure for poison oak. Maybe some

Yowani man was the region's best at following or blazing trails or, perhaps, storytelling and dancing. Maybe they were called "cutworms" because they were a nocturnal people, avoiding the sticky heat of Mississippi days and using, instead, the nights.

I realize I'm nit-picking here, waging my own, semantical war. The sign means to say no Geronimo, Sequoyah, Osceola or Pontiac lived here. Nobody we have heard of or seen portrayed on the Silver Screen.

The sign had to say something. An outfit that didn't miss the lowly mosquito surely couldn't overlook entirely the Yowani.

The government came looking for a few great Yowani men. Nobody obvious stepped forward.

July 1985

Admire The Whitewash

SAND CREEK, COLORADO. The dirt road ends, and there is nothing. Sand Creek is a dry gully, not a town.

Here on the high plains of Colorado, the old notion the world is flat doesn't seem so absurd. You can turn slowly in one spot and take in a cyclorama of unbroken horizon underneath an enormous sky. Painted small on this brownish-green backdrop are occasional trees, windmills and cattle— tons of beef rolling around this grassy prairie like BB's in a boxcar.

It is the emptiness that haunts you, for this is the place where Colorado soldiers massacred a friendly Indian camp because there wasn't room in the territory for the red men.

There is no evidence of its history at the actual site of the calculated slaughter of women, children and old men. But eight miles south on Colorado 96 is a lone marker that refers travelers to "the Sand Creek 'massacre' or 'battle.'" The historians who erected the marker in 1950 still could not bring themselves to call it a shame.

The marker reads: "Many Indians were killed; no prisoners were taken. The white losses were 10 killed and 38 wounded. One of the regrettable tragedies in the conquest of the West. Nov. 29, 1864."

Regrettable.

Commanders from nearby Fort Lyons sent a column of more than 700 soldiers, with cannon, to wipe out a village of Cheyenne and Arapaho. The Indians were camped at Sand Creek in compliance with the white soldiers' orders, and they had been guaranteed safety in return.

There were few braves in camp the day of the attack. This the white commanders knew; they had given the Indian men permission to go hunting for badly needed food.

Many of the Indians killed were gathered at the teepee of old Chief Black Kettle, who flew an American flag. White officers had given it to him and assured him as long as Old Glory flew above him no harm would come to his people.

The winners write the history, it has been said. White Americans "won" the West and gave themselves the benefit of the doubt in incidents such as Sand Creek. Children learn early to appreciate how their shrewd forefathers purchased Manhattan Island for $24 worth of junk.

Briefly, during the past two decades, "revisionist" historians invited Americans to do some soul-searching, but nobody liked what was found.

Now Americans are increasingly rejecting the contrite atmosphere of the '60's and '70's. Oh, most Americans would stand up today and agree that murdering Indian women and children was wrong. Or that Jim Crow and slavery were unfortunate.

However, what really seems to bother most is the immediate past, the era in which Americans openly agreed that, at best, the history books were incomplete.

The shame, it seems, is not so much in the facts but in their admission. We're obsessed with a flattering history of ourselves. We grudgingly paint over the "Whites Only" signs, then proudly stand back to admire the whitewash.

The mistakes of the past are not the trouble—they are inevitable. Anywhere. Still, the old psychiatric admonition comes to mind, that a patient must recognize his problem before anything can be solved.

Then it was buffalo hides and gold; now it's jobs and borders that are jealously guarded, with passage permitted only with reluctance.

It strikes you in a ride across America, all the room and resources that still remain. Simplistic, maybe, but surely there are vacancies for more.

One group makes gains, builds a bridge and then blows it lest another use it.

Black thugs in Philadelphia currently are making life miserable for a community of Asian refugess who are trying to start a new life. The fight is over jobs and federal grants. Not enough, they say, to go around.

What should we do about illegal immigrants? Their children? Their language? What about desperate Cubans and Haitians dumped upon our shore? Have we fulfilled our obligation to the descendants of the white man's slaves? And what about the Indians? Will today's problems be tomorrow's shame?

Today, at Sand Creek, there is nothing—just a vast, empty landscape where people once lived and now don't.

October 1984

Hemming Hemingway

KETCHUM, IDAHO. It's not hard to find the monument to the American writer who believed adventures were for living and adjectives for sissies.

It is as unadorned as Ernest Hemingway's writing style, just a small bust atop a simple marker at the end of a dirt path and next to Trail Creek.

Best of all he loved the fall
the leaves yellow on the cottonwoods
leaves floating on the trout streams and above the hills

the high blue windless skies . . .
now he will be a part of them forever.

Simply follow the stream of tourists to Ketchum, once a normal little town until geography and circumstance forged to make it a resort. Now it is crammed with health food restaurants and overpriced souvenir shops and bars requesting you leave backpacks outside.

There are countless bicycles pumped by tanned thighs, men in sleeveless denim with perfect partners and sporty cars weighted down by the trappings of health and wealth. It's the toxic touch of Aspen and Vail in otherwise wide-open and workaday Idaho, where tourists come but seldom settle and blue skies still hold more windmills than ski lifts.

Past Sun Valley Lodge, made of concrete painted to look like wood, a sign points the way and leads to the Hemingway memorial. Once it must have been an idyllic spot.

Today the sound of bulldozers gorging themselves on expensive Sun Valley real estate overpowers the rush of the running creek. Through the cottonwoods that do, still, drop leaves on trout streams, you can see the many, rising structures that will handle the load of guests who flock here to play in tune to the season.

The backdrop is one of change, of construction and concrete, and admirers seeking a few quiet minutes with Ernest Hemingway might as well take a copy of "For Whom The Bell Tolls" to the nearest video arcade.

You have to wonder about some of the visitors from their plodding and common tracks. On the smooth, white bark of a graceful bough some junior high Juliet has memorialized her pimpled suitor with the pointed end of a fingernail file. "Amy loves Jerome, '83." People have polluted the precious solitude.

There is a political battle raging in Idaho about how much additional land should be designated as protected wilderness. Hemingway's granddaughter Mariel has cried before Congress and aligned herself with the environmentalists who favor protecting more acreage than do, for instance, the Idaho cattlemen.

It is the same old, stormy courtship of beauty and the beast of progress. Idaho is a state of splendor, ripe for spoiling. Who is to say how much protection is too much or too little? Who should be the last entrepreneur, the last developer over the bridge? Should an Idaho native who runs cattle be forced to bend to the whims of a faraway Sierra Club?

"Don't Californicate Idaho," the bumper stickers say. Everybody knows what that means. And though the existing Idaho wilderness and its skirts of prosaic farmland make such visions remote, you have to remember how fast people and their basic accommodations change a landscape.

There is no right approach, at least not a good one, for unclogging our cities and spreading a runaway population evenly over the hills and dales still virgin and vast.

As long as there is beauty, people will clamor and climb and drive to see it, leaving it changed, if not destroyed. Federal fences slow the onslaught and keep our land protected from us. Some will resent it. Some will say it's necessary.

The condos and the hotels make small dents in the sides of the Sawtooth Mountains. There is the whine of the future through wide open blue skies.

June 1984

The Pump

TUSCUMBIA, ALABAMA. What do we expect to find at the birthplaces of our heroes? Clues to greatness? Hallowed ground?

Why do we make pilgrimages to long-vacant cradles and dry-rotted hobbyhorses, Kentucky log cabins and Bethlehem mangers?

There is an unsettling quiet about the grounds of Ivy Green, first home of Helen Keller. Even in winter it is green, this lovely place, with mature, full magnolia, English boxwood and—as advertised—ivy.

Only one dead tree trunk represents winter, rising like a mizzen-mast behind the white house where Helen first met Teacher.

The Ivy Green guides—sealed inside that big house against the January cold—are prepared to talk, by rote, of mohair sofas and antique sugar chests for any tourists who happen by. The two dollar tour tells you more about quaint home furnishings than Helen Keller.

Outside, the clumsier, bulkier gifts sent to Miss Keller in appreciation from around the world form an immobile, unnarrated parade across the lawn. A wrought iron grill from Germany. A wind vane from England. Too bad the possessions always outlast the person they honor.

I have come here mainly to see The Pump. They told us about The Pump in Alabama history, fourth grade.

They gave it to us pretty straight, concerning Helen Keller. There was no gobbledy-gook about states' rights or shades of race to skew the story of her extraordinary courage.

The war we Alabama fourth graders heard about never happened. Turns out, the Civil War did have something to do with slavery. And Jefferson Davis was not the Father of Our Country.

The Battle of Horseshoe Bend—presented as a hard-fought victory over the last, fierce Indian resistance—really was a one-sided massacre of the state's hapless natives trapped at a bend in the river.

Helen Keller as heroine, however, held up well. She lived up to provincial billing as a blind lady of vision.

Anyway, it was a child actress named Patty Duke—not some textbook—who made us really see The Pump. Who made us feel the same cold rush of water and knowledge that Helen must have felt.

That explains why it is not irreverence—only another irksome joke born of mixing history with Hollywood—causing me to hum an inane tune as I stare at the black, workaday fixture.

Our Patty'd rather rock and roll, a hot dog makes her lose control. What a wild duet . . . .

That irrelevant ditty, of course, is from a Patty Duke show far less dignified than *The Miracle Worker*. Actresses, even good ones, have to eat.

But here the famous pump alone is worth the price of admission. For Ivy Green is Alabama's toehold on a legitimate heroine, even if she did leave for college and only return for short, infrequent visits. A birth is occasion enough to claim association. It is reason enough to remember her greatness and goodness.

What we gain from touching Helen Keller's Braille typewriter or walking across her white pine floors is something short of insight. It is reassurance.

Reassurance that some of what we grew up believing is true.

January 1986

"Me Want It Now"

LANETT, ALABAMA. It is the finest playhouse anybody ever built. Made of two-tone brick, with aqua and white awnings and plate glass windows, it stands smack-dab in the middle of the town cemetery.

I used to stop by to see the dollhouse in the graveyard quite often when I lived near here. It has been part of the town cemetery so long the locals don't think a thing about the strange monument. But it remains, to outsiders, both a tender and ghoulish sight.

Little Nadine Earles is buried inside the brick playhouse. You can glimpse her granite tombstone beneath the dolls and stuffed animals and china tea set. She died December 18, 1933. Her Christmas wish that year—her last wish—was for a playhouse.

"Me want it now," she supposedly said.

But time ran out. So Alma and J.C. Earles, grief-stricken and helpless, built their dead daughter a playhouse. Right over her grave.

Our darling little girl
Sweetest in the World
Little Nadine Earles
'Me Want It Now.'

That's what the strange grave says.

The parents have not neglected Little Nadine and her playhouse over the years. You can count four layers of roofing material on its shingled top. The blue carpet and cafe curtains inside are faded, but only a few years' worth.

A small, artificial Christmas tree stands on one end of the granite slab. A tinted photograph of a smiling Nadine— blue dress, blue socks iced with lace, blue hair ribbon—sits on the miniature mantel.

There is also a group photograph of dozens of children, gathered at the unique gravesite for a birthday party in Nadine's honor. What a strange sight that must have been— children squealing with delight over a dead playmate's good fortune.

And then, there are the dolls. You peer inside through the little windows and you see the waxy centurions. One rides a child's tricycle. One doll pushes another in a tiny baby buggy. You can see the years progress through the dolls, from limp, rag bodies to movable, plastic limbs.

One older doll with an organdy dress and long black hair stands in the corner of the playhouse, almost child-size, her face paled by years of graveside duty. When you look through the windows of the house and see those eerie glass eyes staring back, something inside of you jumps involuntarily.

I'll admit it. Reporters tend to haunt graveyards. I guess it is because the way people die is sometimes more important to us than the way they lived. But I have never seen anything that competes with the grave of Little Nadine.

Something new has been added, too, in the decade I've been away. Two more graves are in the Earles' family plot.

"Father," reads one marker. "Julian Comer Earles. May 20, 1909 - Feb. 25, 1976. Daddy of Little Nadine."

The other says, simply: "Mother. Alma. April 1, 1912 - Jan. 28, 1981. Mama of Little Nadine."

They were parents so dedicated they defined their lives, even to their deaths, totally in terms of a relationship with a daughter.

Nadine Earles has been dead 53 years. Had she lived she would be a gray-haired, middle-aged woman. Instead, she is locked forever in a child's playhouse, known to dear parents and curious passersby as Little Nadine.

June 1986

A Coon Dog Indeed

COON DOG CEMETERY, ALABAMA. An era has ended. No trumpets. No hoopla. Just an old man paying a final visit to a quiet spot in the woods.

Key Underwood—founder, keeper, fixture of Key Underwood Coon Dog Memorial Graveyard—is leaving these Alabama hills.

"All good things must come to an end," says Underwood, who today is feeling more than a little sad and introspective. This may be his very last trip to a place dearer to him than just about any other. He stares intently through the car window at every hill and dale and dip in the road, as if the familiar suddenly looks new and strange.

Underwood is 83, his wife has a bad heart, and very soon the two of them are going to live with a son in Texas. Offhand, he cannot recall what town.

For 48 years this man has been a dog's best friend. Since he buried his beloved dog, Troop, in 1937 and inadvertently started a tradition, Key Underwood has felt responsible for the graveyard here in Alabama's Freedom Hills near Cherokee.

Almost every weekend since '37 he has come from his Tuscumbia home to put plastic flowers on the graves or to cut the immaculate grounds. He loves to hear people say the hound cemetery looks better than many cemeteries with people in them. And it does.

Underwood runs a dignified graveyard, and he looks askance at three-wheelers and dirt-bikers whose noisy machines stir up the dust and who don't care they are barreling through what the sign calls "The only graveyard of its kind in the world."

He once read the Riot Act to a bunch of Mississippi revelers who took the whole thing as a joke and unpacked their whiskey right under his nose. "We don't put up with that kind of foolishness here," he told them. They packed up their whiskey crates and were gone.

Hundreds of times he has climbed atop the tin-roofed picnic pavilion and swept away the leaves. And he has held the line on cemetery exclusivity. Only coon dogs, true and tried, are buried here.

"I had a lady out in California write, wanting to know why I didn't allow other kinds of dogs.

" 'You must not know much about coon hunters and their dogs if you think we would contaminate this burial place with poodles and lap dogs,' I told her."

Now he worries that the 10 acres of land leased from a paper mill will not be kept satisfactorily, that coon hunting club members will forget Key Underwood is no longer around to mind the graves.

Ross Sizemore of Leighton, Alabama, has two dogs buried here under store-bought, engraved markers. When Underwood announced at the coonhunters' annual Labor Day picnic he was moving to Texas, Sizemore got worried. "I just wonder if anybody else will take the time to do what he did," Sizemore says.

There is an organization of coon hunters that should pick up the standard; burial is free, but club members pay dues that go for cemetery upkeep and improvements. Not many of them have the time or devotion of a Key Underwood, however.

"A lot of people would say we're all silly, anyway, but they are the ones who don't know the value of a good dog," says Sizemore. His Old Red was killed by a train coming home from a hunt.

"That's about the most hurt I've ever known," he says.

Some of the 150 burial sites are crude. Some are elaborate. Most of the dogs are from Alabama and Mississippi. There are a lot of dogs named Blue buried here. One Old True Blue.

Blue Kate certainly belongs. "Struck by a car while running a racoon," the marker explains.

Also buried are Old Walter, Old Roy, Old Lou and another Old Red. There's Bragg, "The best east of the Mississippi River," and Rusty, "A Coon Dog Indeed."

Some owners elect to use a simple epitaph, stretching a bit of the dog's old collar across the tombstone. Others try to do it with words: "Raleigh Was His Name. Treeing Coons Was His Game."

Underwood walks among the graves, picking up a piece of litter here, plucking an unauthorized mimosa sprig there. He has with him today a scrapbook and a wooden box. He holds them out from himself, carefully, like a kid carrying a birthday present. In the box is a coon skull with a bullet hole dead center. Proof of the best shot he ever made.

A snake's rattler is taped to the front of the scrapbook. Inside are pictures of hunting buddies, many of them now dead and gone. There are snapshots, too, of good dogs, the kind that could strike a cold track and trail it to hell and back.

There are lots of faded pictures of old Troop, who cost Underwood $75 and lived 15 years. Troop first belonged to a moonshiner, who got caught and sent away and whose wife sold the dog to feed her younguns.

A hot, persistent breeze is helping Key Underwood turn the pages of his book, here in this graveyards where poodles and lap dogs are kept at bay. Autumn has arrived. But green and heat are clinging desperately to these gentle hillsides, as if ruing a change of season.

September 1985

Running The River

STANLEY, IDAHO. It's not easy to get lost in Stanley, population 99.

I wanted to. There was a man determined to put me and a bailing bucket in the front end of a rubber raft and float us down the white-capped cataract Lewis and Clark called the River of No Return.

And I was to pay him.

Doug Tims insisted it was the only way to get his story. He had pulled up personal and financial roots, buried generations deep in the Mississippi Delta, to come to this place and operate a raft concession on the Middle Fork of the Salmon River.

Doug was a long way from Cleveland, Mississippi. He was light years from the sluggish river they call the Old Man, far from the humid, thick nights of the Delta.

He knew it. Doug was a kid on Christmas Eve, afraid to go to bed and afraid not to, worried he'd wake up somewhere else besides Idaho.

"Just another crummy day in Paradise," he'd sometimes yell, and the river guides who now worked for him would grin and echo the call off the river canyon walls. Then they'd make another oar stroke toward heaven.

It was late June and hot in the rest of the world. In Idaho, in the mountains, the days were averaging 75 to 80 and the nights about 35. There was still snow icing the peaks of the Sawtooth Mountains, which cut ragged swaths from a Windex-blue sky. You were more likely to see an eagle or elk than a mosquito.

They say you have to learn to spell "pristine" before traveling to Idaho, but "clean" will do as well. Everything was clean. There were no pop tops or gum wrappers on the river, one of only eight stamped as "Wild and Scenic" by federal act in 1968. This was Mother Nature's fancy front parlor, and you could come visit—but nothing better be spoiled when you left.

You caught fish on barbless hooks and threw them right back; even the campfire ashes were carried away on a firepan, becoming part of the baggage.

It all sounded fanatical, excessive, until you saw it and realized what undisturbed nature actually looks like. Until you dipped a tin cup into the rushing river and with utter confidence bottomed-up.

We put in at Dagger Falls, the launch point of a 100-mile trip downriver. There were 16 of us, besides Doug and the guides, half or more novices and at least one scared to death. All of us survived.

The water was cold, not long reincarnated from Sawtooth snow. It was 47 degrees to be exact. Not only well diggers have cold asses in Idaho.

This was an early trip, and the water was high and fast, taking us from camp to camp in record time. Then there was nothing to do but wait while the guides cooked gourmet meals —Cajun pork chops, flown in from Louisiana, one night—drink wine that came in boxes and anticipate the stars. Idaho stars are not related to any I'd ever known.

It also gave me time to hear the story of one man who'd beat the system, who'd bucked a family business and figured a way to make good in this unreal land of geothermally heated waterfalls and cobalt pools.

Understand, you don't just hang a shingle and start running the rapids. The 30 Middle Fork concessions are government-licensed, and getting a permit is like getting University of Nebraska football tickets. You must inherit.

The permits are not for sale and only transferable if the would-be buyer qualifies. When Doug got Northwest River Company, it was the first such Middle Fork business to change hands in more than a decade.

"I'm one of the few folks licensed to bring the American public down the river and allowed to charge for it." He gets that funny, lottery-winner look on his face, and you think he's about to erupt with another river cheer: "It's a good life if a man don't weaken," or some such.

Doug's entrepreneurial gamble would have been more than most stout-hearted Wall Street types could stand. He had turned his late father's $130,000 insurance business into a $3.5 million one, working with three brothers mostly in Mississippi.

He was (is) an unreformed go-getter, who can multiply by a thousand on his fingers and toes. But, and it was a big "but," he loved to run the rivers.

His very first river trip was in a canoe and with his then-pregnant wife Loretta. "I was hooked. Quit hunting. Wore out six vans on rafting trips. Spent all my spare time planning river trips for myself and my friends."

It was at the planning Doug excelled. Now he serves 3,000 meals a season in the wilderness, carrying the food and equipment the same way he transports the paying guests—over black holes and ragged rocks. It just might be the ultimate logistical challenge, which thrills him as much as a No. 6 rapid.

You have to think of things. Women on a trip, for example, mean an increase in the amount of toilet paper that must be carried. Little things like that can make or break your repeat customer business.

On top of floating inventory, he has the constantly nagging river guide's worry—that someone will come to harm. Nobody has yet. He counts heads when there's a spill. Sometimes he counts heads in his sleep.

The danger gets his blood pumping, though. "It's different every time you go. I push myself to the edge of being scared every time."

All the danger talk makes him sound macho. He's not really. Neither are the guides; in fact, mine was a woman. But rafting is still the best way to get to what's left of unspoiled America. And a lot of it is in Idaho.

Doug has to fight his own hustler instincts to keep the two-year-old river company as much a pleasure as it is business. He's already expanded, securing dates on the Selway River in northern Idaho next summer. The Selway is the ultra-fast lane of river rafting, the thrill-seekers' ticket. The Middle Fork is more a combination platter of incredible scenery and reasonably thrilling rapids.

Here, where the telephones don't reach and the river's un-dammed, he's putting down new roots. Friends and family are following him to Idaho, coming for a visit and then, some of them, back to stay.

The state should come with a warning: "Visit to Idaho wilderness could puncture big holes in your current sense of happiness and well-being." There's something in the water.

October 1984

Best Porch In America

FISHERS ISLAND, NEW YORK. I'm sitting on the best front porch in America, and if you can show me one better I'll come sit on it, too.

The spectacular view of the Atlantic is not all that makes this porch special; there are dozens of houses on this island alone with grander, more dramatic views of the sea. Most of them are in purposely isolated spots, though, with no view of island activity.

Between the ocean and this particular porch is Fishers main street, where every car coming over on the ferry called the Munnatawket must pass right by, as if in review. They sound a horn when the ferry gets in, and for just a few minutes there's a flurry of activity with a parade of cars. A troop of Boy Scouts sometimes marches by, single file, on the way to an island camporee.

Then, suddenly, there's just the quiet street and the distant ocean once again. From this porch you can monitor main street action in good measure. It's nice to see everything going on, when there's not much going on.

I suppose you'd call this house Colonial but then that's what I call every house with high ceilings and big windows. It was built by taxpayers for a Navy commander, back when huge gun placements on Fishers were poised to protect Long Island Sound.

I can be more exact about the porch, having investigated it in-depth. There are six wooden steps leading up to a wooden floor, which feels good to bare feet and is plenty wide enough for pacing. There is a white, latticework railing convenient for propping feet or potted geraniums.

This porch has plenty of big, stuffed chairs, indented in the shapes of curled bodies. None of the chairs are those matching, cane-backed rockers, which seem to be the latest in porch fashion. This porch is not fashionable, just used.

You can sit here and see the sun rise before almost anyone else in America, and breathe the ocean air before it's been through Trenton or Detroit.

Every one of us, I believe, will some day have to account for the porches in our past. Did we use them or waste them? Did we shamefully neglect or paint them? Did we share them with others? For those who have ever enclosed a porch, that Judgment Day will be a horrible, horrible time indeed.

Most of the porches I've known have been surrounded by nandina and hydrangea bushes, plants that thrive on dishwater. They were Southern porches, where you had to sit until the house cooled off enough for sleeping. You could crawl right up under most of them, dig in against a cinderblock and listen to the grownups talk.

My grandfather's porch had brick steps he built himself, with an iron rod banister for balance, not show. The fancy wooden scrollwork that once decorated the railing had broken off, piece by piece, until the porch looked like a birthday cake after the party, with most of the icing swirls gone.

That porch gave my great-grandmother Allie something worthwhile to do. She'd come out every evening at sunset and count cars. She was accurate and fast. Every day the numbers grew. Sometimes she'd puff up in a priggish way and say, "They go too fast, Clifford," as if her son, my grandfather, could do something about it.

That porch was "home safe" for a thousand games of tag. It was where you arrived when you graduated "rock school," a game played on the brick steps with one rock and a lot of cousins.

I have stood on that porch and watched as my grandfather killed a rattlesnake, finally draping it over his hoe and waving it like a flag of man's superiority. I have fallen asleep on the unpainted board floor. You could get splinters and a wonderful sense of security from the porch.

Porches have personalities, all right, and this one on Fishers Island is shamefully seductive. You could forget all about what you're supposed to be doing and just sit here like Grandma Allie, counting sailing ships instead of cars.

Ann Denson Morell and Stephen Morell are the people who belong to this porch.

October 1984

Culture In Formaldehyde

FORT WORTH, TEXAS. It's not even twilight and Scott Powers is having his third beer, checking out the women and tapping one boot in time to music the band's yet to play.

"She's gonna come in tonight, Buddy Boy," he says to a close friend of two weeks.

His friend seems awfully young, kind of jumpy, like he'd just as soon "she" wouldn't. He starts to take his cowboy hat off, but then puts it right back on. Off, then on.

Scott moved to Dallas from Des Moines two weeks ago. "Heard there was plenty of work and women."

He found work at a shopping mall; job starts tomorrow. The women? Well, he's feeling good about tonight.

He landed at Billy Bob's his first night in town. Most strangers do. They look around Dallas at the Neiman Marcused men and women and wonder what happened to Texas. Some kid with a slingshot could level the whole city, for chrissakes, there are so many glass walls and mirrors. Everything's so new and boring you'd be better off in Des Moines.

Billy Bob's is where they send you if you ain't got the word that the fleeting chic of cowboy's done come and gone. It calls itself the world's largest honky-tonk and sits at the edge of the old Fort Worth Stockyards. It probably is the world's largest something. A honky-tonk, however, it is not.

This is the big time. Kris Kristofferson's here this week and Willie's due next month. It's clean. A waitress wipes the processed cheese that dripped from the ballpark-style nachos off the table before you can say "jalapeno."

Whole families—mothers and fathers and little girls wearing "Six Flags Over Texas" T-shirts—stroll through the place, stopping ever so often to play a video game or examine a fancy, bronze cowboy sculpture. This place is part amusement park, part saloon, and it accepts all major credit cards.

They run tourists and newcomers like Scott through these stockyards like so many heifers. Then they can go home happy and say they saw Texas and drank Lone Star at a honky-tonk Willie sometimes plays.

Oh, sure, there are locals and regulars, and the nights when the big names sing you get whole vanloads from Waco or Sherman. But you get a lot of tourists, too, who come to Dallas-Fort Worth to see cowboys, first, and maybe that book depository.

The whole place is just culture in formaldehyde for the tourists.

At Mystic Seaport in Connecticut, they've re-created a whole shipbuilding village from stem to stern. They've got men carving spectacular figureheads that will never be near salt water and a sailmaker cutting and stitching as if it really mattered. At the village newspaper office they are hand-setting the type, and in a blacksmith's shop they keep the fires burning.

So if you've driven through New England and been dismayed by all the traffic and wondered where they hide the seaside villages, you can just pay a small admission fee and sop up the past at Mystic.

The regions still have their differences, but New England fishermen and Texas cattlemen now all go home to similar four-bedroom homes with running water and a Sony television. So if it's quaint you want, you get quaint-by-number.

Olvera Street in Los Angeles, for instance, re-creates a Mexican marketplace. Olvera is the oldest street in the modern city, with the oldest house in all L.A. (Casa Adobe). If you want the joy of shopping Mexico without hassling with customs, it's the ticket. There are minor reminders that you're cheating reality—items cost more here than their twins in Mexico—but it's a pleasant enough diversion.

Some places do a better job than others at concentrating and parading their past. Some are so busy living it it they don't have time to display it.

But as sure as Holiday Inn will cash a traveler's check, tourists want to see a cowboy in Texas, an Indian in Oklahoma, a beach in Florida and a lighthouse in Maine. It's just natural.

They don't want to see the Potawatomi golf course in Shawnee, Oklahoma; they want to see drugstore Indians weaving blankets. And they'd be bored stiff touring the shipyard in Groton, Connecticut, where they build submarines—just four miles from mystical Mystic.

Which is not to say shipbuilders and Indians—and, yes, even cowboys—aren't alive and well and in their respective regions. They are.

It's just that we want the *real* thing. You know.

October 1984

4 / Whence I Came

Jilted For Jesus

The year Brad McClain found Jesus and dumped his girlfriend, Belinda, we were only 17.

That is, all of us but Jesus, who had been around considerably longer. You wouldn't have known that to hear Brad talk. He went around acting like an ecumenical DeSoto, charting new and mysterious courses and insisting everyone follow.

Normally, it wouldn't have mattered much to anyone but lovely Belinda, who took being jilted for Jesus pretty hard. Except Brad wasn't just any high school junior but one with the charisma to knock the knee socks off a cheerleader. He had a way of multiplying his women like loaves and fishes, and religion simply added to his romantic sheen.

Most of the devoted were his fellow students at Robert E. Lee High School in Montgomery. There were others, too, from Prattville and Pike Road and Wedowee, the tiny Baptist churches lining Alabama's backroads, where the members took turns cutting the grass and where Brad began an endless series of youth revivals.

His was a conversion that changed, for a time, the whole city. At any Pizza Hut in town you got a youthful interpretation of Saint Paul with your pepperoni. You could turn down the anchovies, but not the Four Spiritual Laws, one campus organization's salvation plan.

Suddenly it was a town of teenagers with dusty knees. Students carried their Bibles with their chemistry books and spoke in tongues, not slang. It became more of an honor to lead the daily intercom prayer than to serve as homecoming queen. Bathroom walls were defaced with "Praise the Lord" and Bible verses.

At the center of all this was Brad, who'd lift his chiseled features skyward and raise his arms and leave his mostly female audience flailing helplessly after taking that high-dive plunge into the deep, dark abyss of his eyes.

He took to wearing white suits and white shoes and shirts of deep pink or tangerine.

The adults were alarmed. It was one thing to swallow goldfish, race hot rods or sneak a cigarette. They were not prepared for a city-wide youth strike against sin, an evangelical earnestness that took to heart the routine Sunday School lessons of childhood. It was one thing to go to church, quite another to take it all so seriously.

Correctly, they put much of the blame for the overnight revival on Brad, viewing him as a combination Rev. Moon and Elvis Presley. Undaunted, pumped full of righteous zeal, Brad kept preaching, his voice a buoyant mimic of every television evangelist who ever passed the collection plate. Salvation with a swagger.

Soon there was a whole network of pubescents behind the pulpits, kids in white shoes skipping classes to witness or preach. When Brad decided Belinda—with her long, sun-streaked hair and shapely body—was more of a temptation from below than a blessing from on high, dozens of other high school romances, too, bit the dust. There was a run on gold crosses at jewelry counters.

Brad almost wasn't able to graduate. He had missed more days than the law allowed, out preaching the gospel. He turned on the 90-watt charm and convinced an administrator he indeed had cornered the market on wisdom.

So all of us graduated, Brad raising one arm from the floppy white gown in a familiar "One Way" salute. Then we scattered.

For a while, I kept half expecting to see him on television. Or I'd tune in some late-night AM radio prophet speaking in earnest cadence through the static. It was always somehow disappointing not to discover Brad's version of doom on my dial.

He sells cattle feed now, not salvation, in Waco, Texas. "I'm not very religious now," he says, half apologetically, as if some movement somewhere is foundering because of him. "I had all the enthusiasm and good intentions you could have. But I didn't have the maturity and wisdom to know I couldn't save the world."

His children by a first, failed marriage live 80 miles away, and he concentrates on them and his new wife now. "The basics, I guess you'd say."

People who knew him before he started selling cow pellets and stopped selling tickets to heaven seemed disappointed, he said, when they would see him in a Montgomery bar or an R-rated movie. That's one of the reasons he went West.

Things were much simpler for all of us when life was neatly divided into six, hour-long periods. Some worked on the school yearbook or directed the lousy senior class play. Brad wrote a prophecy too tough for the class of '71 to fulfill.

But for a while there, a brief while, we knew exactly where we were going.

October 1983

Thy Fearful Cinnamon Tree

He was an earnest little man, with ruddy skin and tufts of hair hanging like worn rug fringe from beneath his baseball cap.

"You got any white dresses for sale?" was the first thing he said.

I was, at the time, conducting the strangest and most damnable of all suburban exercises—a garage sale.

So when he wandered up beneath the carport that day asking for a white dress, I didn't blink an eye. Transvestism would not rank in the Top Ten of weird things exhibited during your typical garage sale.

"What size?" I asked. And, "Long or short?"

"Oh, I don't know, she's nearly a grown woman," he said. "Near 'bout as big as Thelma."

This was not the best time for riddles. I had a carport full of customers and no idea about the size of Thelma.

One man was nibbling at a trolling motor—definitely my Big Ticket item—and a woman was trying to pay me for a pagoda-shaped ashtray. And here I was wasting time with some absurd scavenger hunt.

"It's for her sixth-grade graduation," he offered, weakly.

That got to me. I ran inside the house to look, thinking a few darts and some desperation might tailor a woman's dress to fit a little girl. As I flung garments about my messy bedroom, searching for a dress I knew I probably didn't have, my own sixth-grade graduation came to mind.

I wore pink. My grandmother took a couple of yards of polished cotton and a rope of white velvet and made me the prettiest dress worn that day. Or at least Mother assured me it was.

My graduating class sang "Somewhere Over The Rainbow" and recited a William Blake poem:

Tiger! Tiger! burning bright
In the forests of the night,
What immortal hand or eye
Could frame thy fearful cinnamon tree?

I found out years later "cinnamon tree" was "symmetry," and the poem thereafter made a lot more sense.

That graduation probably was more important than subsequent ones from junior high, high school, even college. For we weren't leaving just dear Dalraida Elementary, with its wonderfully shady playground and teachers eternally searching beneath their voile dresses for the ever-elusive bra strap. We were leaving childhood.

As we trudged across that old wooden stage—plunk, plunk, plunk—we were headed straight into the looming jaws of puberty and pimples, heartbreak and driver's licenses. And on some stage, at some graduation beyond this, we would become adults. It was sadly inevitable.

At one point that day—perhaps between the solemn recognition of our most diligent patrol boys and those fearless students who cleaned their lunchroom plates an entire year—the enormity of what was happening hit me.

I didn't know about the rest of the fools singing full-volume about lemon drops and chimney tops, but I wasn't ready to leave. Childhood was home.

I had heard about Junior High. You were expected to dash from classroom to classroom within mere minutes and to remember always your locker combination. There were tough, MALE teachers who notched their paddles for each discipline problem conquered.

A beast named "Algebra" was said to lurk inside certain rooms, devouring even the most conscientious pupils and then spitting them out into a rubbish heap burned at the next pep rally bonfire.

The popular junior high elite scorned the hoods who terrorized the nerds who hunkered in dark hallways until high school made them only a little more acceptable.

Junior High was Hell.

So I lingered in Dalraida's empty sanctuary that graduation day, lovingly etching my name in chalk dust and whirling about in my wonderful pink dress for effect. This was a world I could understand, with its papier-mache hallway murals and linoleum-defined reading circles.

Each classroom had one designated "Bad Boy" and one "Star Pupil." The rest of us were equals, the way we'd never, ever be again. Cheerleading squads and organized sports and high school sororities would soon take care of that. Forever.

I went back to the garage sale in progress empty-handed.

This time the girl, tall and redheaded, stood by her father. A woman, presumably Thelma, stood there, too.

"I just ain't gonna pay no store prices for a dress for a sixth grade graduation," said the father.

The girl said nothing, but looked hopefully at me as if I might pull a white Oscar de la Renta from my sleeve.

You can't ever tell about fathers. Maybe he relented. Maybe he changed his mind and bought her one.

If he did, and if he paid dearly, that white dress won't cost him half as much as not buying one will.

Maybe Thelma remembers.

May 1985

The Easter Egg Tree

There was no particular ritual associated with the raising of my family's artificial Christmas tree. We simply took the long, green pipe cleaners from a box and stuck them in the Made-in-Taiwan plastic trunk.

Chances are we were decorating under protest, anyway, after having demanded—in various years, in vain—a live tree, a live flocked tree or the snazzy tinfoil type with a rotating colored accent light.

This tree is good for another year, my parents always said. At least we won't get needles in the rug.

Oh, but the Easter egg tree. That was an altogether different matter. It took months of careful, exacting preparation.

From early fall until early March, we ate scrambled eggs. Blown, scrambled eggs.

The four of us children sat patiently each morning at the Formica counter, stair-step style in order of our ages, while Mother bowed low over the kitchen sink blowing through a pinhole in one end of an egg as our breakfast oozed out the pinhole in the other end.

It was a tedious process that did nothing for my queasy, early-morning stomach.

Gradually the bowl of hollow eggshells would build, a fragile monument to our consumptive power and Mother's good wind. Then began the fun part.

If there is a way to decorate a dyed egg she did not know, I will eat a purple eggshell. Whole.

Mother would dip a shell smeared with glue into dyed rice. She sometimes used bits of lace and ribbon or even the white, circular reinforcements made to repair the torn punches on our lined notebook paper. She used sequins and old jewelry and whatever other flotsam there was to be found in the bottom of dresser drawers.

You cannot be clumsy or thumb-heavy and stick a sequin on an empty eggshell. You must have hands like a Labrador retriever's mouth.

Mother had them. Each year she became more daring. I think I left home about the time she began eyeing the grits box.

Ornaments ready, we now had to help find the perfect tree. Unlike the plastic bough for Christmas, not just any tree would do.

Mother wanted a symmetrical branch, with plenty of thorns for hanging eggs. When she found it, all of nature's "flaws" soon disappeared beneath several coats of gold spray paint, the color often used to paint model Stingrays.

You cannot imagine the playground power of having a mother with an Easter egg tree. For each spring she would loan my classroom the tree.

There in the middle of the reading circle would sit glorious proof that no mother laden with pink cupcakes and no PTA officer adept at appointing committees had anything on my mother at all.

The only other mother who came close was Terrell Finney's, who once a year wore the Indian garb she bought on a trip to the West and did an exotic-looking shuffle around the reading circle.

The teacher was always especially nice to me while the colorful egg tree remained. I was not above staring meaningfully at the hanging yolk carcasses when it came time for her to pick some lucky soul to dust erasers.

March 1986

Don't Cry, Young Lovers

I thought about Ellyn Dudley the other day.

I was drinking banana punch with a group of English teachers at a fancy reception and Ellyn Dudley, of all people, came to mind.

Miss Dudley taught music, not English, at Robert E. Lee High. Or at least she tried.

"You sound just like a Baptist congregation on Easter morning," she would sometimes say, shaking her head sadly when we were over-zealous and off-key.

"I can say that, because I'm Baptist," she always added.

We figured volume made up for anything. She figured it did not.

Ellyn Dudley was my favorite teacher at Lee. Ellyn Dudley was almost everyone's favorite teacher at Lee.

Each day she wore a uniform, of sorts, to a school that required none. It was a long, straight skirt, brown or navy, with a short-sleeved blouse to match. Her shoes were sturdy, not stylish. Her glasses had solid black rims. She was overweight and underpaid.

We were young, romantic and conceited. We felt dreadfully sorry for her.

Once we thought we saw tears behind her glasses when we sang "Don't cry young lovers whatever you do. Don't cry because I'm alone. I've had a love of my own . . . ."

We imagined she had been jilted; we wondered by whom.

Each day we waited on the rickety risers for Miss Dudley's arrival. We sat and waited and talked about important things:

Did you know that Brad saw Belinda talking to Tommy behind the school, back where the biology club let the frogs out that year while they were taking Beauty pictures for the annual and the girls all were running around crazy in their formals, and, anyway, Brad asked for his friendship ring back, that little gold one with the real diamond chip that is set in a rose except Belinda chipped the petal a little at a swimming pool at her aunt's house in Prattville?

When Miss Dudley entered the room, we swallowed our gum and our gossip and followed the firm direction of her hand as she led us through "Anthem for Spring" or "The Snow." We became, for an hour, disciplined and marginally musical.

We saw her out of uniform only twice each year, at the Christmas and spring glee club concerts. She looked strange in an evening dress; it was a lot like seeing a man who always wears a hat without his hat.

Then, with her back to the audience, Miss Dudley would make a funny, cross-eyed face to keep us loose. We would drain our voice boxes for her.

We would leave those concerts in our new formals, their hems dirtied by black shoe polish from some clumsy tenor behind us, eager to feel over-dressed in a pizza parlor, our boyfriends in tow. Miss Dudley always went home with her mother and the roses we gave her.

When I was a senior lots of teachers signed my yearbook. They said, "Best wishes" or "I have enjoyed teaching you."

Miss Dudley wrote this: "You have always meant so much to me. Thanks for everything you have done to make these past three years the best of my life. Have a happy life, but especially try to make others happy. I love you. E. Dudley. Phil. 1:3."

We all promised we would come back to Lee and visit her. I never did.

While I was away at college, Miss Dudley, still young and still teaching, died. My mother mailed me her obituary.

I remember trying then to think of the words to "The Snow," but time already had them.

October 1986

Tough Cookie

I hold what I believe to be the singular distinction of having eaten every Girl Scout cookie I ever sold. Both boxes.

When no stranger would buy my wares, I paid for a couple of boxes so as not to insult my gung-ho Girl Scout leader. I hid them in the bottom of the closet behind my Sunday School shoes and ever so often rewarded myself with a stale peanut butter sandwich.

An article in *Smithsonian Magazine* got me to brooding once again about my total failure as a cookie salesman. Girls Scouts sold 130 million boxes of cookies in 1984, the article said. That is $225,000,000 worth of cookies. A quarter of a billion dollars. That is Big Time.

One scout alone, Elizabeth Brinton, sold 11,200 boxes in 1985, bless her little merit badges.

I wanted to sell cookies, I really did. Top troop saleman in my neighborhood got to change the flannel board pieces the leader used when telling us Bible stories. We didn't learn to tie fancy knots or build campfires in my particular troop; we were too busy hearing about the Pharisees and Sadducees.

But I truly wanted to be the one to raise flannel Lazarus from the dead and rip down the cloth walls of Jericho.

I always began the annual Cookie Wars with an ambitious 25 boxes or so, figuring those few surely would be gone after only a couple of houses.

Mother pressed my uniform, heard me rehearse an impressive sales spiel and then sent me out, an irresistible little angel with delectable and relatively cheap cookies held before me in a cardboard box. Nobody wanted them. Nobody. My courage faltered.

I trekked those weary vales of curbs and gutters until holes appeared in my Mary Janes. At each stop my will grew weaker.

"I don't suppose you want any of these half-melted chocolate mints, do you?" I found myself asking.

Nobody did. Nobody knew anybody who did.

Sometimes through a screened door I would see, sneering in the background, some smart scout already home from The Wars, her cookies snapped up, no doubt, by hungry customers who had not eaten since the last Mean Season.

Sometimes I would see, three houses ahead of me, a quicker scout unloading dozens of boxes on a soft-touch husband who was unaware his wife bought three boxes yesterday. Men, as you probably know, melt.

But by the time I made it to his door, he had steeled himself to the pitiful pleas of a desperate 10-year-old. The best the kind man could do was to offer to pour me a glass of lemonade.

I would start home, finally, rumpled and sad, dragging the official gold kerchief of the Girl Scouts in the dust behind me like a limp, crushed tail.

"How many did you sell?" my parents always inquired.

"Oh, a couple of boxes."

I still couldn't sell missiles to Reagan. But it hurt more then, pitted against my peers, vying for the spectacular honor of helping a felt Zacchaeus climb a felt sycamore tree.

May 1986

A Minimum-Wage Romance

We made housecoats, mostly, the summer I worked at U.S. Lingerie.

They weren't the gauzy, pastel numbers the firm's name implied, but rather furry, bulky robes of purple or lime to be worn with matching mules and varicose veins. They all seemed to be Size 18 or larger, and it made you hot just to look at them.

The garment plant was the pride of Donalsonville, Georgia, a land where corn fields are plowed next to steamy cypress swamps. The locals called it "The Sewing Room." It was a steady source of minimum-wage money for mostly middle-aged women who would have kept Gulliver in trousers to get out of the infernally fruitful South Georgia gardens.

They bought the defective garments at reduced prices and dreamed of wearing them other places.

Behind industrial-sized sewing machines, the women buttonholed and quality-inspected their way to weekly paydays. A tough old broad they called "Miss Beulah" paced the floor all day, refereeing frequent spats that broke out between the bolts.

But it was mostly the purring sound of their own precision that lulled the employees of U.S. Lingerie into productive submission, that kept their seams straight and their zippers tight.

I got a job there because I knew someone, a tough old broad who loved me, Aunt Beulah. She put me to work bundling pattern pieces, the least skilled of all the chores in the finery factory.

Using the methodical motions it took only a day or so to learn, I'd pick up two sleeves, a collar, a right bodice, a left bodice and the rest of the puzzle parts to deliver to the appointed seamstress.

The work, while monotonous, had its moments, sweet sensations that had something to do with knowing there was nothing for you to take home, except maybe a couple of aching arms and the piece of pink fuzz stuck up one nostril.

When the whistle blew, the day was done. There were no Happy Hours afterwards where you could compare notes on career advancements and office romances. The women clocked out, went home and cooked supper.

Because mine was a temporary visa to this never-ending sewing bee, it was a summer of contentment. It was a time of bare, calloused feet that left dust on the bedsheets. It was long, long afternoons on wide front porches and fireflies that beat the darkness into the sky.

And the mornings never came too soon. They were as pleasant, in their own way, as the nights, with the slight shock from the time clock marking each new day at the sewing room.

By noon, the plant's floors would be strewn with scraps and buttons and busted zippers, but in the early hours things were as orderly as a fussy widow's sewing basket. The smell of machine oil had yet to be conquered by the stench of middle-aged sweat, and the radio would carry a gospel music program.

It was among the pattern bundlers that I made my summer's best friend. She was a pretty girl, much younger than the rest, who wore lightweight nylon shells and bermuda shorts to work. She had an even temper and tan.

My friend showed me the ropes and how to measure carefully your steps and effort till 4 o'clock. Her employment there, like mine, was temporary, she was quick to say. She was saving money to move to Florida.

She'd sing and flirt her way down the crowded sewing room aisles, where bobbins spun like colorful buoys marking a cloth-lined channel. She used her dreams like a thimble, keeping herself beyond pricking distance of reality.

Together we'd rejoice over minor things, a change to material with lighter weight and a smoother texture. Sometimes she'd hold up half a dress front and prance around the cutting room floor in an exaggerated model's walk. For that place, it was rich humor.

We'd settle into our day's routine, choosing a topic to talk about to make the time and the cloth before us go faster. She believed in a Hell, where she was sure she was bound. Church of God tent meetings had convinced her. But still she liked good times, country music and beer. She had a certain sewing room savvy.

The summer ended, leaving me with enough money for a full quarter's college tuition, and with a permanent aversion to bathrobes. My friend took me for a farewell hamburger at the local drive-in, where she leaned over a scarred jukebox and sang "I"m an All-Day Sucker When It Comes to Loving You" in a clear, young soprano. But the outing wasn't our finest. The conversation already was winding down, as if the final four o'clock whistle had blown.

I saw her once more, less than a year later, when a bunch from the sewing room gave her a baby shower. She looked plump and tired.

Aunt Beulah says I wouldn't know the plant; they've expanded. They make pantsuits and dresses now, not just lingerie and play clothes.

My friend left the sewing room and the town with a pattern cutter, a shy, smiling-eyed man I barely remembered. The edge to my aunt's voice when I asked about my friend hinted at scandal. There, where air hoses blow away lint and where buttons are stored in bins, she had found a little romance.

I hope they made it to Florida.

March 1983

Something About Donnie

I'll never forget the day I found out Donnie Nobles was a boy. It came as a shock, though I first met him months earlier.

I knew in the literal, physiological sense that he was the opposite sex. My father even called him "That Little Fat Boy," an oxymoron that fit.

But as a playmate and friend, he was an absolute neuter. A red-haired, slightly pudgy neuter. I figured we both were.

The first time I saw him he was staring at me through the spokes of my new Schwinn. I was sitting curbside, checking the air pressure in a tire. There was ample air and I knew it, but sometimes it felt good to sit down and spin those marvelously balanced black rubber doughnuts against the flat of your hand.

I remember I had on one of the Lumberjack Meat T-shirts my father brought back in assorted sizes from a sales meeting in Atlanta. They had a picture of a lumberjack hefting an ax and were supposed to sell bacon.

"Is that a 22 or a 24?" this strange kid asked, referring to my bicycle tire size. Schwinn spokes subdivided his acres of freckles.

"Oh, it's just a 22."

But a fine, sleek, fast 22, the pinnacle of racing machines, I wanted to say. Instead, I gave the tire one more purposeful spin, the ten-year-old's answer to gunning a motor.

Thus did our relationship begin, in the safe and circumferential realm of childhood. And for a while it was a beautiful thing.

We lived three houses apart if you counted houses on the left side of Ware Hill, and only two apart if you counted those on the right. Every summer morning I gave his parents time to leave for work before pedaling down to Donnie's.

Donnie's grandmother lived with the family and took good care of him. She was a mewling, fragile sort of woman, always dusty with an orange, loose powder that came in cardboard canisters.

She was nothing at all like my ample-lapped, sturdy, country grandmothers, who in the mist of distance always seemed more like pink, aproned angels than real people.

Sometimes Donnie talked back to his grandmother. Once he completely lost it and cruelly stomped his foot. She never told; she would just shrink into the ranch house, retreating to her naps and soap operas, probably wondering why at her advanced age she was once again rearing children. And we would go about our business, doing whatever it was she didn't want us to do.

I am ashamed now for my tacit part in terrorizing the old lady. But at the time it seemed the only thing to do; children love an easy target. That's because children are little adults.

Donnie and I spent most of our time collecting old pop bottles. The implicit danger in balancing glass in cartons dangling from handlebars appealed to us.

So did the refund money from the grocery store. We spent most of it on candy or other sweets. We knew nothing of delayed gratification. One day we ate a whole jar of marshmallow cream, taking turns jabbing our index fingers into the white sap, refusing to admit how fast a good thing got old.

We also built a chemical laboratory in my playhouse. There were shelves of hideous, brownish concoctions labeled "Secret" and "Poison."

There were certainly the former—we never bothered to record or remember recipes—and probably the latter.

When the smell became unbearable in the lab we tired of that and soon became private detectives, chasing neighborhood "mysteries" the bored but persistent way dogs chase cars. It took just two days to pinpoint a spy, a neighbor with such odd hours he couldn't be anything else.

We decided to spend the night together and stake out his house. Surely at midnight, when the televisions along Ware Hill were darkened and normal people slept, his devious commerce had only just begun.

Donnie's grandmother said I could stay over. Donnie didn't even have to raise his voice.

But my mother looked alarmed and sent me to Daddy, who began with much embarrassed hemming and hawing and ended by saying "no." I had to figure out for myself what was wrong, and I somehow, instinctively, did. Little girls didn't plan spent-the-night parties with little boys.

I told Donnie a lie that involved my cousins arriving from Georgia that very night. Our plans were off. Maybe it was my imagination, but we never seemed to have as much fun together again.

I liked him much better before I knew.

April 1985

5 / Black and White

Good and Peaceful Reputation

It seemed like a family reunion, like a ritual gathering deep in the country where there are no secrets or pretenses and where the black sheep break bread and belch loudly with the rest of the clan. The children run barefoot and unchecked, and old men spit wherever they please, as acceptance prevails.

That's sort of the way it was. Relatives huddled around a prodigal son who grudgingly put in an appearance.

The women wore tentative smiles with their Dacron summer finery and carried patent leather bags on arms mottled by the Mississippi sun.

The men held back to avoid the endless hugging and to clear their throats. Then, those not desperate for a smoke moved in with handshakes and conspiratorial winks and whispered reassurances for their white friend and neighbor who had shot and killed a black deputy sheriff.

It was a somber, special occasion. A funeral where everyone got to speak to the corpse.

At each brief recess, the crowded courtroom seemed to shift forward as a high tide of women lapped around defendant Jimmy Lancaster of Van Vleet. He smiled a weak smile summoned from somewhere in his uncomplicated past and allowed himself to be pressed and pitied. He knew his role.

Lancaster periodically fingered his wide, polyester lapels to find and fasten the missing galluses. The suit was a strange new uniform for the jail-paled, lanky welder who liked to hunt and keep to himself. He held his head stiffly erect, as if his shirt collar was a razor. He had the self-conscious look of someone posing for a Polaroid.

His supporters might not have comprehended the seriousness of the offense; the months in jail awaiting trial had almost convinced Lancaster. Still, here with a forgiving family and well-wishers cooing over him, even Lancaster must have found new hope.

If the district attorney wanted to avoid the case and the considerable controversy it generated, he didn't let on, leading the prosecution with the barely-bridled ferocity of a Baptist preacher. He made the most of bloody clothing and color photographs of the victim; there was nothing half-hearted or cavalier in his manner.

The dead black man's law enforcement status made it more respectable to aggressively prosecute a white man for the murder, but it still wasn't politic.

And the state's confidence was mostly superficial. They had a dead deputy and the man who said he shot him eight times in self-defense. But they had only one black on a Chickasaw County jury that came from, and would return to, a largely segregated society.

Lancaster told his own story. Robert Kirby had come to the front door of his home early one morning, ringing the doorbell and then waiting. When he answered the door and asked what the deputy wanted, Kirby for no apparent reason shot up from his hip, through the bottom of his holster and the glass storm door.

Only grazed, Lancaster told how he grabbed a rifle and started firing at the fleeing deputy. For better aim, he dropped one gun and went for his powerful 7mm hunting rifle with scope.

At least eight rounds later—after watching Kirby's body bounce from the impact of the last bullets—Lancaster said he felt a little sick and went back inside.

The district attorney pulled an undamaged holster from Kirby's stained clothing to refute the Lancaster story. The defendant was slightly injured by flying glass from his own shots through the storm door, not one of Kirby's bullets, he said.

Kirby was trying to do his job. He was trying to deliver an assault warrant filed against Lancaster by his wife, who the day before had provoked a beating.

A parade of character witnesses attested to Lancaster's good and peaceful reputation. A Methodist minister, a farmer, a shop foreman and an elderly, former justice court judge all took Lancaster's part. One such witness was the employer of a white juror. In the audience, reporters could hear other testaments to Lancaster's worth. "He deserves a medal," one man sniffed to no one in particular.

Robert Kirby couldn't demand justice. That was in the hands of a white district attorney who must worry about re-election. It was in the purview of a white judge. It was up to a mostly white jury whose friends sat on the white side of a distinctly black and white courtroom.

Dick Gregory wasn't there. There were no banners or rallies or network television cameras. There was a crowd, but it was composed of local folks who waited for a verdict.

The widow of the slain deputy waited, too, across a narrow aisle from Lancaster's supporters. Her husband had been brash enough to interrupt a white family's feud, and he'd gotten himself killed for it.

After the trial, Robert Kirby's widow went home alone. The friends of Jimmy Lancaster disbanded.

The jurors, who had looked down the barrel of Lancaster's rifle and seen the moment of one man's death and another man's madness, went to their homes in towns where not much changes, where progress must be diluted and served up in small doses. They had been drafted to serve justice and were going home from a war with their own consciences. They had been color-blinded by the truth.

In Mississippi, there are two white men serving life sentences for killing black men. One of them is Jimmy Lancaster.

November 1982

"Is Anybody Out There?"

FLORENCE, ALABAMA. Virginia Foster Durr's white hair is swept up regally with red combs. She looks the part of an 83-year-old grandmother of 11, which she is.

Today, this grandmother is speaking to students at the University of North Alabama who are young enough to be her grandchildren. Most of them are too young even to remember the 1960's.

Bright lights sweep the stage but leave the audience a faceless void. A young man in black sweat pants rushes in late and parks his backpack in the seat beside him. He immediately slumps in his auditorium chair, as if to nap. Two girls three rows in front of him are busy scribbling something into a notebook. The program begins.

"Can't somebody turn up the lights?" demands Mrs. Durr. "I want to see if anybody is going to throw something at me."

Don't be fooled by her aristocratic looks and soft edges. Mrs. Durr is no typical Montgomery, Alabama, matron. Somebody has called her a southern radical in white gloves.

"You young people just drive me absolutely nuts," she begins with characteristic candor. "You are happy, healthy, beautiful. But you don't do anything."

The audience is quiet. The boy in sweat pants remains low, motionless in his seat. Other students fidget.

"Is anybody out there?" asks Mrs. Durr. More silence.

Mrs. Durr, a native southerner and daughter of a prominent, white minister, was a Montgomery civil rights activist when that role was reserved for what George Wallace called "outside agitators." She housed leaders of the movement in her Montgomery home. She cooked bacon and scrambled eggs for northern volunteers like the three young men eventually buried beneath an earthen dam in Philadelphia, Mississippi.

"If you're from the South, you cannot help but be born into original sin," she says, matter-of-factly. "Our families had slaves, servants, who waited on us hand and foot. All these modern conveniences don't amount to a pin if you've been waited on by slaves.

"I was 33 years old before I realized I was still living in sin. I paid a cook $10 a week, a nurse $10 a week. I had a yard man and a woman to do the laundry.

"And I was free to go out and pursue the rights of black people. We equated sin with things like kissing boys. That's real minor compared to keeping people in servitude.

"One day I went into the Montgomery library, and a black girl came in after me. They wouldn't give her a book. I never had anything strike me as hard."

A panel discusses Mrs. Durr's book, *Outside the Magic Circle*. Each panel member praises her in turn. After hearing Mrs. Durr talk, the panel discussion seems sterile and a little pompous. One scholar from another university credits Mrs. Durr with helping to lead the South to a new and brighter day. She interrupts.

"You are such a sweet, nice man, but if you think blacks and whites now love each other you are living a myth.

"I would love to think I led the South to a world of joyful brotherhood. But it just ain't so. There's very little integration today in Montgomery. Blacks don't trust whites. You can't treat people so bad for 300 years and expect them to love you."

In Montgomery, Mrs. Durr says, 50 percent of the black men in their prime, their most healthy and productive years, can't get jobs.

"Alabama's answer to that is to build new penitentiaries. In Alabama prisons, 85 percent of the population is black. I don't believe it's because blacks are naturally bad. I believe it's because they can't get jobs.

"Doesn't that make you mad? Isn't anybody here willing to go on a march? I'm 83, and I'll go on my one good leg."

The grandmother is now begging the students for a response. Silence.

There is polite applause following her speech. A few people gather around her to ask questions. This has been a part of what the university calls a "values colloquium."

The student in black sweatpants is stirring, strapping on his backpack and preparing to leave.

What did he think of Virginia Durr?

"I didn't like it when she called Ronald Reagan an idiot," he says. He hoists the canvas bag onto wide shoulders and makes his way down the dimly-lit aisle.

October 1986

Shoeshine Man

GREENVILLE, MISSISSIPPI. They wouldn't dig John Odis' grave until the cash was in hand.

So the weary old black man was buried just yesterday, only after a group of white lawyers spent a week raising $165 for a country cemetery plot. Through a small burial policy, John Odis already had paid for his cheap wooden box.

It had begun as a bad year for the gnarled town fixture, a shoeshine man. He had been mugged once by the hoodlums who lurk like cats in Greenville's riverfront alleys and had his Social Security check stolen a couple of times.

His pride and joy, an outboard motor he affixed to rented boats routinely, had been stolen. Even his tackle box, filled with the second-hand lures that hauled in respectable showings of Lake Washington crappie, was taken from him.

"They took advantage," says Mike Cordell, a lawyer and John Odis' friend.

The sundry ailments that swarmed John Odis—stomach ulcers, weak kidneys, palsy and a deadly collection of fluid around his heart—kept his shoeshine stand closed some days. But Greenville's well-shod would wait on a John Odis shine, the one that came with lively conversation.

He endured, his crippled legs fluttering around a walking cane like lifeless ribbons. He'd maneuver down Washington Street in time to his own incessant, tuneless whistle.

Outside Robert May's downtown office building he set up shop. May helped him build the stand and charged him no rent for the sidewalk spot.

"I first met him in Hollandale, Mississippi, in 1940," May recalls. "He had a kind of sleeping sickness and would fall asleep while washing a window. There he'd be, eyes closed and rubbing in one little spot."

Then about 1970, John Odis showed up in Greenville, asking to erect his shoeshine business. May let him, though a messy tobacco habit and the sizable crowds John Odis could draw created what May terms "a nuisance."

John Odis would hobble from office to office in the May Building, collecting, usually, for the Friendship Baptist Church choir with which he sang. He'd bring along an authorization letter from the pastor, presumably to lend credibility to his collection efforts. In last Sunday's services at Friendship, they announced John Odis had died but took up no collection for burial.

Sometimes John Odis would ride the May Building elevator with a mess of fish beaded on a stringer. He would stop on each floor and proudly hold high the pungent trophies.

Cordell co-signed the bank note that allowed John Odis to buy an old, metallic blue station wagon. John Odis rented space in the car for fishing parties, hauling his friends—for a small fee—to nearby lakes. He never missed a car payment, Cordell says.

"There was an elderly widow near Hollandale who had a little dog that was continually getting out and running away," May recalls. "She'd pay John Odis 50 cents every time he'd track that dog down and bring him home.

"John Odis would feed the dog bologna every chance he got. And the dog kept getting away every chance he got, costing the widow 50 cents a rescue."

About six months ago, no longer able to care for himself, John Odis went to live with friends, the Emmett Rileys. He came to the May Building with a big smile on his wrinkled face, its color the flat brown of unbuffed shoe leather.

"He said Mrs. Riley had put him in a bathtub and bathed him all over, the first time that had happened since he was a boy," Cordell recalls. "He kept wanting to unbutton his shirt and show me how clean he was."

It was a bright spot in a lackluster year. John Odis was convinced he lived in a mansion, where floors were clean enough to eat off. The Rileys carried him back and forth to the South Washington County Hospital in Hollandale, where he died last Friday.

Cordell thinks John Odis was 75. May says John Odis didn't even know his own age. His one living relative, an 80-year-old aunt from McComb, Mississippi, couldn't travel all the way to Greenville for the funeral.

John Odis, who had been a doctor's chauffeur and finally popped a rag for a living, sometimes was ridiculed by other blacks for his subservient lifestyle. And he was a master of shuck and jive.

Yet John Odis was more. He was the personification of what's right and wrong between the races.

In his scrappy, self-styled way, he made his own living. His white friends were genuine, and in the end they were the ones who buried him. But then, he was satisfied with a borrowed piece of the white man's sidewalk.

July 1983

Jesse and The Furor

They pulled the canvas off the statue about sunset. At least a couple hundred of us stood beside an Alabama cow pasture, watching.

It was a sleek, summetrical affair, so simple and small and clean of line you had to marvel at all the fuss it had caused. They planted it in a briar patch at a crossroads called Oakville. A group of black Masons, most of them elderly, cleared the half-acre of stubble and built a flower bed around the statue's base. They poured sidewalks and directed them across the stark landscape to nowhere in particular. The homemade walks looked like gray, grosgrain ribbon, tying up Oakville's humble gift to its most famous native son, track star Jesse Owens.

Nobody else wanted the little obelisk. White county officials in Moulton would not allow it on the courthouse lawn. They feared, they said, "a flood of similar requests."

The statue finally saw light in Oakville on a bittersweet November day. A crowd came. There were joyous songs and long speeches but only allusions to why all of us were standing in the middle of nowhere, unveiling Jesse.

You might leave Alabama, win gold medals and single-handedly one-up Hitler, but come home to Lawrence County and it's back to the quarters, boy.

The first time I saw Oakville, the debate had been raging and the unwanted memorial collecting dust in storage. I wasn't sure it was the right place. There were no signposts or storefronts. There was a cinder-block building that looked like it might be a church, though no cross nor stained glass proved it.

A small man in work clothes and baseball cap greeted me.

"Is this Oakville?" I asked him.

"Everything you see," said Marvin Fitzgerald.

I told him what I was after.

"Jesse Owens was my first cousin," he allowed.

Small place, Lawrence County.

Now, two more years have passed since the unveiling.

Only children are here today.

The Masons have added a playground-style basketball court to their modest park. A dozen or so young men are using the court, following with rapt exertion the familiar thud-thud-thud of rubber against concrete.

Somehow, it is fitting.

The white movers-and-shakers in Lawrence County might have—inadvertently and stupidly—done something right. For often, the best memorials rise up unexpectedly, surprising you in some unassuming little place like Oakville.

Statues in a park tend to run together. Competitive granite. On a courthouse lawn they are unappetizing, required reading. But here, standing alone, this compelling hunk of stone commands full attention. It does not share space with obligatory monuments to anonymous veterans or the ubiquitous Confederate dead. It is in a remote spot, but worth hunting, amid surroundings not too different from what would have been in 1914, when Owens was born.

The last of this year's cotton crop is strewn, giving the roads a snow-melt look. The two-year-old memorial is shining in the sun, looking like a fresh grave in an ancient cemetery.

Behind it, black children with limited advantage are playing and running with ferocious concentration. And in unconscious tribute.

October 1985

"We Might Win This Time"

OXFORD, MISSISSIPPI. It would be easier to confiscate all Izod alligators than to dislodge symbols of the Old South on the campus on the Unviersity of Mississippi.

People here spike their toddies with liquor from the Rebel Package Store. High School students backseat romance at the Rebel Drive-In. Coeds get their hair punked and permed at Rebel Hair Styling.

The symbols abound, official or not.

The week itself is annual Dixie Week, an innocent celebration of food and fun that is distinctively Southern. *Gone With The Wind* is showing at the Grove. "We might win this time," promotion posters say.

Black cooks are barbecuing chicken to sell as the Reggae Rhythms of the Raft play for a patio full of students, their faces flush from beer or early spring trips to the beach. Championship wrestling is on inside Tad Smith Coliseum.

In this isolated and fragrant Eden, the sky is Bonnie Blue and the median age is twenty. Life is a full ice chest. Students are smirking their way through college, waiting for Friday when the original Drifters will mix soul with the sunshine permeating nearby Sardis Lake.

But there's a fly in the ointment, sand in the suntan oil. On a campus with 8,000 whites and 700 blacks, a minority is making demands. And from the looks of things, they might as well try to take the cross from the Christians.

Judi Griffin is a fresh-faced Ole Miss senior in a flannel shirt and blue jeans. She is snub-nosed and bright eyed, with a rebel flag stuck in her textbook: "The blacks who are making an issue of this thing are the racists. They're the ones making race the issue."

Confederate flags and Rebel colonels and "Dixie" mean Ole Miss to Judi, not slavery. You have to believe someone with a snub nose and bright eyes. For all she knew, the Confederates borrowed . their flag from the Ole Miss football team.

Her male companion says the flag furor is just the beginning, that, by gosh, a few people are going to make life miserable for the contented majority. He says reporters have only been interviewing the blacks, ignoring the whites.

Actually, the "white" side is hard to miss. It looks like a football weekend on campus, with Rebel flags flying from automobiles and dormatories and fraternity windows. Portable signs outside of restaurants use thier plastic letters to spell "Save the Flag," and plump sophomores scream the Rebel yell to nobody in particular down University Avenue. There is the other side.

Alvin Calmes, who is black, actually wouldn't like being positioned on either side of the controversy: "I've been here five years now, and I just want to graduate."

But the articulate history major with books under his arms and purposeful stride sees the minority's point.

"The first year I was here, you know, when I got my first yearbook, I thought it was the most beautiful thing I'd ever seen. On the cover it looked like a million Confederate flags all together, and that, to me, just meant Ole Miss and school spirit."

The first time it occurred to Calmes that just maybe he should be offended by all the Confederate hoopla was last year when the Klan was in town.

"There are the pictures of klansmen holding Rebel flags, and all of a sudden it all means something new to me."

Should a few blacks dictate symbolic dressing for a mostly white university? Should a minority be able to tamper with a revered tradition? Calmes has thought about it. He believes demands, even sometimes excessive demands, might help the University image.

"Friends in my neighborhood back in Tupelo said I was crazy to come to Ole Miss."

There are block parties this week, when neat, khaki-clad guys with Army-inductees haircuts and clinging dates go from fraternity house to fraternity house, comparing bands and brew.

One fraternity house on this campus sits apart from the rest, a small shingle and brick house that would be dwarfed by the antebellum-style mansions on The Row. It is the campus' only black fraternity, across the street from a Danver's Restaurant and light years away from the real heart of this campus.

It is empty, quiet, at mid-afternoon, with members in class or listening to the Dixie Week band. No rebel flags hang from its screenless windows.

April 1983

A Solemn Occasion

PHILADELPHIA, MISSISSIPPI. Their names sound like a law firm—Schwerner, Goodman and Chaney. So, by fate, are they linked forever.

They are partners in tragedy, bound not by law but by the lawless. Black-and-white pictures of the three young men are embedded in the granite of a tombstone-like memorial outside tiny Mt. Nebo Missionary Baptist Church. The pictures look like a page from a high school yearbook— unlined faces, open collars, eager expressions.

Beyond the monument, inside the red brick church, old men who remember sit by the open windows, waving cardboard fans with metronome regularity. A crowd has gathered on this, the first day of summer, exactly 21 years after two New York Jews and a Mississippi black were murdered and buried in an earthen dam.

Michael Schwerner, Andrew Goodman and James Earl Chaney, victims of the Ku Klux Klan and unreasonable hate, summoned up once again from Mississippi's darkest day for commemorative bluster. This should be a solemn occasion.

Jesse Jackson has come to place the wreath and say the words that mark the day. But like all made-for-television memorial events, this one has lost its dignity somewhere between intention and execution. Microphones are propped on the pictures of the dead men, and the prayers offered up seem orchestrated, empty.

A truck with a television station's call letters painted on its side roars out of the church yard before the ceremony is complete. There is pushing and shoving where there need not be.

Maybe all history is doomed to be trivialized, debased. Presidents' birthdays are remembered with white sales and martyrs' graves strewn with plastic roses. But the episode for which this particular remembrance was planned seems too recent, too raw, for cavalier treatment. It deserves more than a blurb on the 10 o'clock report.

"Today, men and women, black and white, stand together, and none are afraid," Jesse Jackson prays as the minicams hum.

True, nobody is afraid. But the crowd is 99.9 percent black, unless you count reporters. Jackson's rainbow has a few missing hues.

The white mayor of Philadelphia is here, and that his presence is politic is at least a sign of grudging progress. But where in the audience are the white townspeople, the ones sickened by past violence and eager to show the world two decades make a difference?

The crowd is slow to scatter. Football star Marcus Dupree is giving out autographs, and Jackson's entourage is weaving slowly through the churchyard, working the crowd the way Jackson does so well. A lot of the children have come to see Marcus, who came to see Jesse, who came to be seen.

Theresa Judon, 14, manages to shake Jackson's hand and get Marcus' autograph. She says she knows nothing about the three dead men. Which is not her fault, of course, considering she was seven years the other side of the womb when Schwerner, Goodman and Chaney were shot to death.

Her companion, Brenda Graham, draws a blank, too. Maybe despite all the confusion, maybe even because of it, they will be moved to learn more about the fresh faces in the old monument. Maybe they will ask the old men, the ones trying to stay cool inside Mt. Nebo Church, why three names from the past draw us here in the present.

When the cameras and crowd have rushed to the next stage, maybe Theresa and Brenda will stand here and study the simple shrine. Maybe they will see from the dates that Goodman and Chaney would now be only 42, Schwerner 46, if they had lived.

Maybe they will learn something when the news conference is over.

June 1985

Frozen In Time

BOSTON. Theodore Landsmark was running a little late for a City Hall meeting the day six white kids and a motor-driven camera stopped him dead in his tracks.

"It was the day I discovered that even in a three-piece suit, as a lawyer, you can't necessarily walk the streets of this relatively civilized city safely as a black."

It was the weapon that made photographer Stanley Forman's picture — shot in the Bicentennial year — a Pulitzer Prize winner. An anti-busing demonstrator was using a flagpole with Old Glory flying from it as a lance, poised as if to run Landsmark through, while other white youths attacked him from all directions. His attackers were all high school students from South Boston, one of them the president of his junior class.

Landsmark remembers: "I was late, walking quickly. I hadn't even had time to read the newspaper that morning, and I wasn't aware of anything in particular going on outside City Hall. The first thing I saw was a couple of kids carrying a sign that said, 'Resist,' and I didn't even know at the time what it meant."

They showed him. Landsmark walked into a crowd of about 200 people, people ready to vent anger at anything black and moving.

"I got ready to do a classic Ichabod Crane; I figured I could take three or four steps and slip right by them. But one kid jumped me from behind, then another blind-sided me with a fist.

"The whole thing didn't last long. There were about a half-dozen kids involved at some level or another.

"The one with the flag never actually hit me. It would have taken my head off."

The resulting picture is nauseatingly ironic; the story behind it the same.

Landsmark grew up in Harlem, frequenting the New York art museums, partly because they were free. Eventually, he made it to Yale and the fringe of Boston establishment. Sipping white wine in the courtyard of Boston's elegant Gardner Art Museum, he has become the personification of all that's gone right for American blacks in the past two decades. Yet he's famous for all that's still wrong.

He stopped practicing law not long ago to become, at age 38, the graduate dean of America's only public art school, the Massachusetts Institute of Art. Landsmark is an unpretentious, cheerful scholar, a veteran of early civil rights campaigns who once worked for liberal Republican Nelson Rockefeller's gubernatorial campaign "to see what it felt like to be on the well-financed side."

The ugly incident, captured for contemporary history on silver emulsion, broke his nose but not his spirit.

"I first felt incredulity and a little bitterness. I mean, I was just on my way to work. Nothing that bad had happened in my activist days in Selma."

Landsmark remembers the dark, unlighted streets of Selma's black neighborhoods, where just the sight of approaching headlights could scare you: "I remember finding a very comfortable spot in the bushes."

But he didn't get his head knocked once by Southern nightriders. His date with violence would come much later, after enough laws and time had passed to lull him into complacency.

While one of few black students at progressive Yale, Landsmark used to dream of becoming internationally famous for his skillful handling of some landmark civil rights case.

"In a perverse way, I achieved my goal. The subject was correct—civil rights. It happened at about the right time in my career. It was just the wrong procedure, that's all."

He has achieved the kind of "international fame" of the American Express commercials. "Do you know me?" For a while, people knew his name but not his face. Then the name and the incident faded. Now, only once in a blue moon does someone want to talk about the beating. He's glad.

"Sometimes being associated with the photograph is like being inside a pair of bronze baby shoes."

Landsmark himself is an enthusiastic amateur photographer and readily appreciates the impact of the famous picture. It "turned a lot of heads," he says. Its shocking statement helped quell the ugly mood of Boston at the time.

Boston blacks used it to force new lines of communication. Landsmark himself became the first black member of the city's transportation board.

Times are better, superficially. Landsmark leads an impromptu tour of the gallery, pointing out a Rembrandt self-portrait as his favorite work in this museum. Surely strolling through these opulent halls of refinement beats the days of nose-diving into roadside ditches on the Alabama front.

Yet, when asked, Landsmark says he's glad he came of age when he did. For college-age black youths, he believes, it will be rougher now then it was in the '60's or '70's. The support organizations so visible in the activist days are all but gone; government is reflecting the conservative mood of a white-dominated society.

Some people gave lip service to black advancement, while others made token stabs at it; now all feel they have done their part. Blacks, equal on paper only, are on their own.

The number of blacks being admitted to college is down, he says. "And motivation is not what it was." Blacks are going to have to help one another more in the future, Theodore Landsmark believes, to keep gains from unraveling.

In the us-against-them mentality of modern America, blacks are still "them."

October 1984

Maycomb, Alabama

They cut down Boo Radley's oak tree in 1976, when its diseased limbs started falling around the heads of Monroeville school children.

That tree was one of the last authentic props in the town where Nelle Harper Lee learned from her father it was a sin to kill a mockingbird. She won a Pulitzer Prize for trying to teach the world the same lesson.

By then, most of the houses along Alabama Avenue, including the old Lee home, already were razed and replaced by fast-food palaces, car dealerships and the mill offices of Vanity Fair, the world-famous clothier that transforms cheap Alabama labor into a harvest of pastel undergaments with New York Fifth Avenue labels.

More Alabamians know about the Vanity Fair outlet store there than about the south Alabama author who gently—and with much humor—poked at prejudice. The town's only physical acknowledgement of Miss Lee's literary genius is a limited, autographed supply of *To Kill a Mockingbird* in the downtown religious book store. There the books are stacked alongside Anita Bryant's life story and Debby Boone sheet music.

There are no libraries or roads named in her honor. No one wonders aloud any longer about what she'll write next. It even took a stubborn stand by history buffs to keep the old courthouse intact when county business outgrew it.

It persists in the square, with a new courthouse right beside it. Old men, just as persistent as the structure shadowing them, play a continuing game of dominoes on the lawn. A narrow walkway between the two courthouses splits the square where Harper Lee once romped with her growing imagination.

For years, Mary Ida Carter was caretaker at the Old Courthouse Museum. She was one of those people who make fictional characters seem dull. A Yankee writer from Harper's ran into Miss Carter one day, discounting her in print as "a languid old woman who claimed to be Truman Capote's aunt." She was Capote's aunt, one of several who kept him on a seasonal basis during most of his childhood.

It was during those hot, south Alabama summers together that Capote and Harper Lee became friends bound by a love of words and a recognition, yet forgiveness, of Southern idiosyncrasies. The character Dill in her semi-autobiographical book was based on Capote. Several of his short stories, including "A Christmas Memory," have Monroeville backdrops.

There are literary experts everywhere in Monroeville. Just ask them. Some say Nelle—the town calls her Nelle— exhausted her childhood memories in *To Kill A Mockingbird* and that's why she's never finished anything else. Others say Capote wrote—or heavily edited—her one, lauded novel. Others say she had a heavy hand in his stories. A few say they've never read the nonsense.

Harper Lee comes home now periodically to visit her sister, lawyer Alice Lee, who is as civic-minded and outgoing as Harper is reclusive. One doesn't hear that Nelle's in town, only that she just left.

The town's still smarting a little at her portrayal. The Lady's Society and missionary tea mentality that marked Maycomb, her fictionalized Monroeville, still is alive and well and pouring punch. Polite society is quick to claim Harper Lee, but they stress the dwindling landmarks and soft-pedal the poignant attacks on hypocrisy that made the book a classic.

Worldwide attention helped the town get over its first anger. The Hollywood set-makers came to town to copy the courtroom, adding a rail or two to the outside but making an exact interior reproduction. They studied angles and arches; Gregory Peck studied ambience.

Peck spent a few days there to prepare for his Atticus Finch role, and that visit's something the town considers real scrapbook material. A local bank teller looked up from counting bills one day to stare into Peck's celebrated face. He presented a check for several hundred dollars and asked to cash it. "I don't think I'll cash it, Mr. Peck," said the star-struck teller. "I think I'll just keep it."

"That," Peck is supposed to have replied, "will be just dandy."

Then the movie was released, its courageous Atticus Finch hopelessly defending a black man accused of raping a white woman right there on the giant screen, and the quiet resentment came again.

It's a town that still has more stop lights than Catholics and where newcomers are held at arm's-length until they prove themselves. An all-black section conveniently located just out of the city limits is referred to as "Clausell Quarters." The Atticus Finches still are grossly outnumbered. They still are objects of curiosity, if no longer hate.

But to deny a celebrity—even one like Harper Lee, whose spotlight faded years ago—is not easy in a town the size of Monroeville. There is a grudging respect for the woman who is one of them, yet apart. They have forgiven her for making good and for telling the truth in a prize-winning way.

November 1982

And Then It Was Gone

It's where blacks in Jackson, Mississippi, dressed up and went on Saturday night. Farish Street was down around the tracks, where life showed a little leg and and bosom, and the earth trembled from passing freights and heavyweight jazz.

It was Mississippi's Beale and Bourbon. Nighttime was Duke Ellington or Louis Armstrong at the Crystal Palace, the darkness and their music a welcome salve for the days. For there was a day side to Farish Street, too, a bustling if burdened society that stayed and grew inside the lines Jim Crow drew.

Mississippi's first black millionaire lived in the Farish Street area, and the state's first black physician hung his shingle there. Jackson's seven oldest black churches and Smith Robertson, the city's first black public school, were there, too. Farish was the main, pulsating artery to the heart of an all-black world. The road led to commerce and good times and religion.

And then it was gone.

Times change, and so do cities. White-owned department stores and restaurants and theaters now depend on the black trade that once shopped Farish. Whites adopted black music. Assimilation and migration drained Farish Street, leaving it littered, used up and haunted by crime. Where they could, when they could, successful blacks left the reservation, because they could.

For 364 days a year now, Farish Street is like any other street where business and boom have been and gone. There are a few businesses and corner groceries, mostly struggling. Prostitutes in tube tops patrol the street. The Alamo Theater stands empty. Like hundreds of similar streets across the South, Farish now connects a deflated ghetto to the rest of the world.

The Louis Armstrongs of today play in fancy clubs and coliseums, not at the Crystal Palace. Bluesmen like Son Thomas sing at Republican fund-raisers, not the Birdland Lounge on Farish.

On Farish Street now the beat is the hard, lifeless one of jukeboxes and the unemployed racking pool balls.

But for one day a year—for the past five years—Farish Street remembers. A dedicated group of Farish Street activists hope the memory will finance improvements.

This year the celebration was small but determined. A band heavy with African rhythm thumped out its history lesson, while vendors hawked barbecue and beer. Muslims touted their "fruit of life," a variety of prescribed foods and pamphlets. A black artist offered a painting of Martin Luther King and copies of Frederick Remington.

Booths sold "I Love Mississippi" T-shirts along with Malcolm-X biographies. A woman demonstrated the cosmetic benefits of the juice of the aloe vera plant. All this in an effort to revitalize the street shell-shocked by progress. For all its worthy intentions, the movement to pump life into decay along Farish Street has made little visible progress.

What has happened to the Farish Streets and Harlems is a crime without a villain. The sweet butterfat has been sacrificed to homogenization. When nobody else wanted the black business, the black talent, the black heritage, the black man built his own schools and streets and stores, and with them his pride. In Tuskegee, students made their own bricks and raised their own classrooms and chapels and dormitories. The sons of slaves learned trades or poetry and then applied their knowledge in a white man's world. They lived and worked and played on the Farish Streets.

In reality, their dollar is the only thing truly welcome in mainstream America, yet blacks today know the future, ill-defined as it may be, is with the whole. The time has passed for completely self-contained black centers of politics and religion, culture and carousing.

There is an understandable reluctance to fold the tents that for so long provided the only shelter. Black colleges vehemently resist the suggestion that, if all goes well, they will not be needed. And this festival is held to keep fresh the memory of the spiritual and commercial sustenance Farish Street provided.

But what used to be the poor side of town has become the bad side of town. In the pursuit of a new, rightful order, the good of yesterday has been thrown out with the evil, or at least diluted in a much larger world. The high-heel and silk-stocking nights on Farish Street have been reduced to slices of darkness between the burglar bars.

Most of those who stay on Farish Street do so because the economy, not the law, now posts the limits. The residents still are all black. They sit on cramped, sloping porches, wearing poverty's bright colors and watching the festival crowd pay hefty sums for slim portions of barbecued ribs. But they must be wondering how to leave, not celebrate, Farish Street.

October 1983

Pale As A Peeled Apple

TUSKEGEE, ALABAMA. She didn't know, growing up in Tuskegee, that blacks weren't meant to ballerinas.

"It wasn't until I left here that I realized all dancers were supposed to be blond and pink like the Sugar Plum Fairy."

Dyann Robinson is not blond and pink. She is the warm brown of polished teak, with black, liquid eyes and a cap of close, dark curls. Her angular features and fist-hard body are, indisputably, a dancer's.

Growing up black and proud in Tuskegee is about the only way it's done. So when young Dyann saw Margaret O'Brien pirouetting across the movie screen, she decided to become a dancer. And nobody told her she couldn't.

Dyann's first dance teacher was a white woman, who used the spare room of a black funeral parlor to hold her one black class. The studio was reserved for whites only (even Tuskegee was in the Old South), but that slight didn't faze Dyann.

She left this rural, east Alabama oasis for blacks and danced her way from Broadway to Brussels.

Now she is home once again, an accomplished teacher and dancer, the city's director of cultural affairs and founder of the Tuskegee City Dance Theatre. Black children aren't curtsying among the corpses anymore.

Her studio is in a rustic, brick building with good light and two stunning fireplaces. It once was the town's white country club, back in the days of segregation and minority rule. Dyann never even saw the secluded, hilltop place until she returned home in 1980.

"I wanted my office here for all kinds of reasons," she says, smiling rather wickedly.

Soft sunlight splatters across the empty studio floor, where an hour from now black children will prance. Dyann props herself gracefully against a ballet bar and talks of color barriers in a most unlikely place—the world of fine arts.

"In dancing, the artistic license is a license to discriminate. You can turn a dancer down for the shape of her nose. So not choosing a black is very, very easy.

"There are still only token roles for blacks in the major dance companies. Just take a look at them."

If she sounds bitter, she's not. There's more spirit than stridency in the lithe, 42-year-old woman who credits her hometown with giving her boldness. In Tuskegee, blacks are not the minority. The town offers more in role models and statuary than the obligatory Confederate soldier.

"All of my high school classmates did well, just about," Dyann says. Johnny Ford, one of those classmates, became Alabama's first black mayor and still holds office in Tuskegee.

Dyann hopes her dance company will significantly expand the roles for blacks in American ballet. She has always stood her ground when the issue is color.

"As a kid I never would use the crayon called 'Flesh' to color the skin in my Bible pictures. It wasn't the color of my flesh. Yet I knew white people believed in Jesus, too, so I didn't want to use brown. I compromised with burnt sienna."

There was no compromising when it came to ballet tights and slippers. She insisted, as the only black member of Maurice Bejart's Ballet of the Twentieth Century in Brussels, that pink tights and shoes only made white dancers appear natural. She wanted dark stockings and brown shoes.

"If I did nothing else for the world of dance, at least now black dancers wear tights and shoes the color of their own flesh."

Prejudices are harder to conquer than balletic pose. After a performance of Broadway's "Bubbling Brown Sugar," a white interviewer asked, "Do you people train?"

Dyann raises her eyebrows and puts her hands on slim hips as she did that day. I told her, "Oh, no, absolutely not. We black people jump out of bed every morning doing that."

Once Dyann Robinson chanced to read a famous ballet master's description of the ideal ballerina. He wrote of long legs and interesting features. He described perfect torsos and arms. She matched all those requirements.

"And the dancer should be," the master concluded, "pale as a peeled apple."

The woman of sienna burned.

March 1985

6 / Back Rooms And Boudoirs

What A Doll

She had a waist about the size of my ring finger and flaxen hair that cascaded down her porcelain-smooth back.

Barbie was about three-quarters skinny legs and one-quarter torso. With narrow hips and no rear end and awesome plastic breasts that forever defied gravity, she managed to to fill out quite impressively her strapless swimsuit.

We all wanted to look just like her.

That's why it comes as no surprise to read about a recent survey indicating nine out of ten American women are dissatisfied with their own bodies. It figures.

For exactly 25 years this year, little girls have been dressing their Barbies, examining those lean limbs and assuming on some magic date they, too, would have Barbie Doll proportions.

Blame the current "fat" panic on the male fashion designer, if you will; he does seem to have a "creative" preference for a young boy's body. I, for one, however, put the blame squarely on Barbie.

Since that siren's debut in 1959, she has shaped much more than just our bodies. We got our ideas about love and life, what they held in store, from those long hours we spent on childhood's bedroom floors, playing with Barbie.

Remember her clothes? Each outfit was purchased separately, complete with the appropriate accessories. There were "Prom Night" and "Wedding Day" and "Country Picnic." Barbie never had to rummage through the closet to find a clean white shirt for "Another Monday Morning." She reached for black sequins and "Evening on the Town."

She had a "Dream Car" and "Dream House." A Western Barbie had a perfectly groomed horse and a satin riding outfit. Malibu Barbie kept an even tan.

Barbie adapted to each new fashion or trend quicker than the state of California. She didn't cling to her ponytail when the "bubble" was the rage. She whacked off the long hair without so much as a second thought, and the new style, of course, worked beautifully.

Redheaded, freckle-faced Midge was her best friend, a cute girl but certainly no threat to the glamorous Barbie. She was the perfect complement, as trusting and loyal as an old hound dog.

Midge "dated" Poindexter, an obvious egghead with less brawn and sex appeal than Barbie's clean-cut Ken. Ken never looked at Midge. Barbie never flirted with Poindexter. Midge never winked at Ken. It made for the perfect foursome.

The Christmas I first got Barbie she wore a black and white stretch swimsuit and toeless black heels. Mine was the blonde, regulation, official-issue Barbie. I couldn't wait to show her to my country cousin Donna, who had been dreaming of a Barbie, too.

Even at the insensitive age of eight, I felt badly for Donna. Her "Barbie" obviously wasn't. It was some cheap, imitation doll with a ragged ponytail. Donna's attempts to smooth and wash the doll's hair had turned it the green color of an old penny. It lacked the pert, upturned nose and perfectly shaped brows of my model.

You could tell. It wasn't Mattell.

Donna handled her disappointment that day in a child's brave way. She refused to acknowledge a difference. We played. That night, under the covers, she bawled.

It seems funny, now, 23 years later, to realize Donna got the far better gift.

Her Barbie with green hair and lumpy features and cotton clothes let Donna deal with the truth early. We weren't ever going to dress, or look or live like Barbie.

Our "Dream House" came with utility bills. "Prom Night" sometimes would be spent at home. Ken might take the "Dream Car" and run off with Midge. A "Country Picnic" had rain and ants.

Those of us who had regulation Barbies, on the other hand, spent adolescence buying her latest wardrobes and clinging to the myth. As adults we jog and lift weights and skip dessert and assume that, some day, our bodies will be like Barbie's. For she had that tiny waist and shimmering blonde hair. Some of us never outgrew playing with dolls.

March 1983

Designer Genes

ATLANTA. She once was a 98-pound weakling. Now she's "Most Physical Female" of Atlanta. And the State of Georgia.

Hell, she's next to the most physical female in the nation.

Kelly Cargel struts through the parking lot of an Atlanta fitness center and causes a minor disturbance. One man grimaces and bites down on his racquetball. Another revolves slowly in place, a chicken on a rotisserie, his eyes pulled by Kelly.

They all watch silently, appreciatively, until the white sliver of Spandex and the body it doesn't cover disappear inside the house of mirrors.

It is one of those places where everybody's too busy looking at their own physique to pay attention to anybody else's. They make an exception for Kelly.

"If you're going to do something, you might as well be the best at it," says Kelly. She tosses a tangle of golden hair that matches her tanning-parlor skin tone and then checks the mirror. There's nothing there she doesn't like.

Five years ago she was just a skinny teenager in rural Douglas County. She weighed 98 pounds. Then she started working out, lifting weights two hours daily, on top of teaching four or five aerobics classes.

Now she's 21 years old, 5-foot-7 and 110 pounds. And if that doesn't sound all that remarkable, then you haven't seen The Poster.

Kelly and another woman are shown from their noses to knees in a poster promoting the latest in Atlanta's aerobics competitions. The high-stakes contests are becoming increasingly popular here and are held at stylish bars and sponsored by beer companies or fitness centers. Or both. Women in incredible physical shape do competitive routines for an audience drinking itself in the other direction.

We're not talking pony league, either. The purse in tonight's competition is $25,000. Female contestants have arrived from as far away as California to perform in a bar called "Sneakers."

And concerned men from all over Atlanta have come to see the women work on their heart rate. There's so much drooling they should rent bibs.

"I can't compete in this one since I won the last," says Kelly. "The health club thought it might look funny if I won again."

She wins a lot.

She would have won the "Miss Fitness USA" in California last year, she believes, "if I'd had a breast job." It stressed shape over stamina.

There are more health clubs in Atlanta than peach stands in Georgia. It's fitness capital of the South. Women who will never win an aerobics competition haunt the health clubs, too, sheathed in shiny tights and great expectations. They are the housewives and insurance clerks and mothers who are into aerobics to work on thighs and tummies and postnatal fat.

Once, twice, three times a week they groan in rhythm to "We Are Family" and "Boys Will Be Boys," trying to keep up with Kelly or Angie or whatever Super Body is assigned the class.

"I don't lie to my classes," says Kelly of her less-perfect clientele. "I don't tell them they'll look like me, even if they exercise as much.

"It's all up to your genetics, really. It's as simple as that."

Kelly's genes are designer.

The title Kelly won last year meant television commercials and several thousand dollars in prize money. But more importantly, it meant a psychological return on an incredible investment of time and energy. Because staying fit is all she does.

"I don't have time for anything else. I stay here 16 hours a day. If somebody special came along, I would try to fit him in."

But the young woman with the career body has at least 10 good competing years, she thinks. Her ultimate goal?

"To get married. To have kids."

The most important quality in a male? That's easy, for Kelly.

"Someone secure. He'll have to be very secure."

March 1985

Flat On Her Rear

She would have made a good Harlequin heroin. Auburn hair, blue eyes, sweet face and lots of teeth.

Andrea Shepard once was a cheerleader whose friends called her Andie. Life and love followed a pleasant, predictable rhythm.

She was pursued, pinned, engaged and then married. She eagerly climbed aboard the white horse that galloped up on schedule carrying her very own Navy ensign. Life for Andrea, however, did not end with a lingering kiss at sunset.

Ten years, three children, 14 moves and many tears into the marriage, Prince Charming took a powder. The lady of the house was left with no home.

What she did have was a dry-rotting English degree, a Pinto with a bad muffler, $400, a rented apartment in Cincinnati, Ohio, and three little girls.

Everyone has known at least one, and that's one too many. . . .

THE CHEERLEADER: Cute, Bright, Popular, Good Grades, Lots of Dates, Marries a Winner, Bears Gorgeous Children Who will all grow up to be great CHEERLEADERS!

And everyone has the desire to see her fall flat on her rear.

Well, I was
and I did,
and it hurt . . . .

Andrea fought insomnia by writing down such bittersweet thoughts, in longhand, on the back of bus schedules and plane tickets. Some of them funny. Some of them not so. Part Emily Dickinson, part Erma Bombeck.

"Honesty is their only merit," she admits. "Had I known they would be published ten years later, I might have cleaned them, and me, up a little."

And though a large Christian publishing house, Zondervan, recently compiled a book—"Sing A New Song"—from 42 of her secret, decade-old, grief-laced poems, Andrea Shepard refuses to call herself a poet.

"Most of the poetry I read I don't understand. I think poetry has been taken over by people who write things that are so ethereal that most of us can't understand."

While she is now a devout Christian, this book of verse clearly was not written by any Dale Evans. But then those struggling with divorce don't need sanctimonious philosophizing; they need hope.

I'm encouraged by this single state.
I think I might just love it.
No rhythm, no rhyme, no dinner on time.
Just handsome men to secretly covet.

Zondervan deleted the "offending" swear words that cluttered her thoughts like wadded tissues. But the obscene hurt and intense longing still come through.

"One of my daughters read the book and said, 'You sure had a lot of sexual thoughts, Mom. It's kind of embarrassing.'"

Don't look for any harsh accusations in the book. Andrea Shepard isn't the type. She sent the poems to her ex-husband before publication, inviting him to delete anything that offended him. The only thing he asked was for her not to use her old "married" name. She didn't.

"I know so many angry men and women whose whole life is a somebody-done-me-wrong song," says Andrea. "Their faces get funny wrinkles. Nobody wants to be around them. So I said to myself, 'He had my past, I'll be damned if he'll have my future.'"

Her ex-mother-in-law peddles the little book of poems to chain bookstores. She believes it should be in mainstream bookstores, not just Christian ones.

Andrea Shepard forgave. And forgot. Now she runs her own advertising agency in Cincinnati and is thinking about a second book on step-parenting. For eight years ago, Andrea Shepard remarried. Between them, she and her new husband had six teenagers.

"We had our share of problems; let me just say the kids are not all rushing off to pick up their Merit Scholarships."

But Andrea Shepard Conroy calls Andrew Conroy her "new and permanent husband." And her life is now full and happy.

Her "new" husband also read the poems before they were ever published. His only request: Don't use your "married" name.

"I was fast running out of names." So Andrea Shepard used her own.

September 1986

Poor Little Rich Single Girls

That magazine story was all about old maids. You might think, in 1986, the term "old maids" would be obsolete. But *People* magazine resurrected it.

Using statistics from a Harvard-Yale study that concludes single women over age 35 have only a five percent chance of ever marrying, *People* proceeded to reveal the chances of matrimony for a few celebrity old maids.

There's a four percent chance of marriage for both rumpled Diane Keaton and rocker Linda Ronstadt.

There's only a three percent chance for that prune Jacqueline Bisset, a 5.2 percent for Teri Garr and—get this —a mere .001 percent chance for poor old Lillian Gish.

According to the magazine, "Several well-known women have beaten the odds. Candice Bergen married Louis Malle, 47, when she was 34."

I don't know about you, but when I think of Candice Bergen—beautiful, rich, famous, talented—it is not in terms of the "odds" she had to overcome to find a man.

And, chances are, Jacqueline Bisset could march her three percent through any bar, church or boardroom in America and come out the other side with the male of her choice in tow.

All of that, of course, misses the point by an aisle. More women are choosing to remain single—longer or indefinitely.

I suppose the sociologists have to study the trends, compile the statistics and let us look long and hard at ourselves in the narcissistic way to which we have become accustomed. It's in the sociologists' contract.

And celebrity rags, of course, will use any excuse to parade out the single beauties who are infinitely more interesting than the married ones. Pretty old maids, all in a row.

But I, for one, am a little tired of a single-versus-married breakdown in everything from cookbooks to bars. The implication is this: Married people are finished and single people have yet to start.

Married people are dull and moribund and therefore do not count in the lively 1986 scheme of things. TV producers even keep their sexy starlets single so as not to lose audience interest. Yet the presumption seems to be that all single people are preoccupied with only one thing—the possibility of marriage.

Why? So they can become dull and moribund, too? We are discounting both "classes" of people for contradictory reaons. You're nobody till somebody loves you. Then you're nobody again.

What is it about human nature that makes us obsessed with organizing the world like the gangplank to Noah's Ark? And then, having accomplished it, makes us find the pairs pattern far too symmetrical and boring?

What the *People* story implies, if not the survey, is women who wait may vegetate. Those who delay may stay that way. And despite independent-sounding quotes from most of the famous old maids interviewed—"Fine with me," said Betty Thomas of her two percent options—there is a recriminatory tone that comes through.

The magazine even offered ". . . a possibly consoling reminder for women over 30 who may never toss the bouquet. If marriage is such an enviable institution, why do half of them end in divorce these days?"

Poor little rich single girls. Not married, every day their chances dwindling.

And, my, aren't they better off that way?

March 1986

Plain Pinups

COLUMBUS, OHIO. Linda Rhodes looks a little like a mermaid. Long, silver hair waiving down on her shoulders. Figure by Rubens.

She is a pink-nail-polish-and-chocolate-bonbon romantic, a woman who enjoys being a girl.

Yet there is a determined, practical side to her, too. She learned her trade by studying library books, and she stocked her shop with Salvation Army finds. She even hocked her diamonds to afford a suitable place to perform her magic. It's working.

Women come to her, from across the heartland, so she can find their beauty. Which is harder to find in some women than others but almost always is there.

And when she finds it, she documents it in glossy 8 x 10's and 16 x 20's, personalized calendars—you are the calendar girl, 12 times over—or special deal bubble bath photos.

In this Victorian house—situated cheek to jowl with a meat packing plant, formerly the home of a Christian rock group—Linda's hour-and-one-quarter photography sessions transform a teacher, an accountant, a nurse or a housewife into a suitable heroine for a perfume ad.

The women wear filmy nightgowns or underwear, wedding dresses or satin drapes, anything that makes them feel exotic. Linda shoots no nudes, much to the chagrin of the meat plant employees.

"Women have always been cheated photographically," says Linda, with feeling. "Unless they are the lover of a painter, they are never immortalized.

"Houses everywhere are full of pictures of women in navy blouses with a single strand of pearls, possibly to validate that they were ever living." No navy blouses here.

Linda's Boudoir Photography studio looks like a human-scale version of Barbie's Dream House. Pastel props are scattered everywhere—parasols so delicate they would disintegrate in a mist, ornate fans, gilded hand mirrors and more beads than Mardi Gras.

Women come here to get photographs for their husbands, their boyfriends, themselves. To look pretty for once. To prove the driver's license photo lied.

One woman, a truck driver, arrived to pick up proofs in her 18-wheeler. She had felt the strong urge to be photographed in an ultra-feminine setting.

Another woman, yet to be photographed, believes she looks like Marilyn Monroe. "Please make sure the pink ladder I have ordered is ready," she wrote Linda. "And I'll be bringing 15 yards of red satin."

"I can't quite figure the ladder," says Linda. "Should be interesting."

Linda urges her subjects to practice their "looks" and iron their clothes. She will shoot no beauty before her time. If a bruise is too prominent, if the hose has a run, Linda sends the woman home. Flaws that can't be helped, she hides.

"See this woman right here." The woman in black lingerie is beautiful.

"One of her eyes was larger than the other, and we had to work around that. Another woman was very self-conscious about her small bosom. The way the lighting worked, she looked like a C-cup in the pictures."

That in a nutshell—and a C-cup—is why Linda's business is thriving, her photography calendar full. Still, she dreams even bigger dreams. Linda Rhodes wants to shoot a Dolly Parton calendar.

May 1986

Meat Loaf On Her Diamonds

Beverly Farris likes the bars that go heavy on the stained glass and hanging plants, the ones that seed a cloud of whipped cream atop a frozen drink with a plump, red cherry.

It's the kind of place single girls in summer-white pants sit without spilling, feigning total disinterest until some young accountant calculates just the right approach. The invitations sent out are embossed and high-toned, delivered sideways over the brim of a shimmering, long-stemmed wine glass. The replies are as finely-tuned as the BMWs waiting outside. These are, after all, discriminating denizens. To a point.

Beverly just likes to watch. For the college-level English teacher, dutiful wife and mother of two, it's a vicarious refresher course in the complicated, eternal mating maneuvers that make all the rest of life's business about as exciting as folding the wash.

She sits alone, trying to look casual while picking last night's meatloaf from the crevices of her multipronged diamond ring. Sigh. It seems there's always meatloaf on her diamonds now and stretch marks striping her bikini figure.

All her friends claim Beverly is Supermom, so deft is she at juggling bottles and Beowulf, home permanents and lesson plans. She has mastered the fancy Lebanese dishes her husband favors and still finds time to read the Book of the Month. Once on her lunch hour she bought two pint-sized Easter dresses, left a watch at the repair shop, bought gas and still had time to meet her sister for a little Mexican microwave.

She's not just efficient. Within her throbs a tender heart, but one anchored with pragmatic tendencies. If personalities were equations, hers would be Heart Equals Smart, making Beverly the perfect one for friends, students and relatives to unload on.

"I need to talk to Beverly," they all say. And they do.

On her junior college office wall hang the testimonials of student converts to literacy. In glowing, competent poetry and prose her students praise her. These are the youngsters she refused to beat over the head with syntax but wooed instead with beautiful words. She gave a pilgrimage to Canterbury all the relevacy of a trip to the video arcade.

For Beverly, these students — many of whom haven't the money or grades to spend four years at a full university — keep intimate diaries, compose couplets and digest Faulkner with their Dixie beer.

After class, she's always available to listen to the serialized autobiographies of punk rock Romeos, earnest young men who conduct their romances in bars with names like "Skidmarks." She counsels a pregnant, unmarried girl, talking formulas versus breast-feeding with the same skill she gives a *Julius Caesar* lecture.

The ivory towers of this rural, catch-all college come equipped with good views of the real world.

Not long ago, Beverly decided even if she had become Everyone's Mother she needn't look the part. So she shook her permanent wave dry and snubbed the electric rollers that usually helped contain it. She put on bluejeans and a top that made her look more Jacqueline Bisset than Brownie Scout. She removed the headless doll from the back window of her Chevette.

This quiet, cosmetic rebellion didn't change much, but then she didn't really want it to. A daughter's dancing lesson still ends one hour after Literature 101 and one hour before she serves dinner. Her Calgon bathwater still keeps a rubber duck afloat.

Only occasionally does she slip into the chain bars and sip at debauchery through a rose-colored straw. She watches with a bemused, almost detached fascination while the gilded girls put themselves through the graceful motions that eventually will make them, too, somebody's mother.

How We Grow 'Em

She is a tall girl, and slim, with blonde hair and big eyes. The men are making quite a fuss over her.

One puts his fat arm around her very slender waist and calls his pal over to meet her, too.

"This is how we grow 'em in Mississippi," he chortles, and everyone around laughs heartily.

"Honey," says another man, addressing the blonde girl, "I have to shake your hand." Instead, he holds it. And holds it.

She has on the kind of dress you would not wear to work your first day on the job. It is a splashy, black and white affair, a Rorschach inkblot in which old geezers see their youth.

The dress would attract attention even without the girl's perfect figure puckering the parts that are supposed to pucker. A Mississippi State University engineering student could have earned his master's degree helping pour her in it.

It is so humid the bricks in the nearby courthouse are threatening to revert to mud. Still, the girl is smiling, not sweating. She is glowing, actually, and the sun is merely adding another layer of tan to her smooth back, already as brown as oiled pine paneling.

There is a jubilant, old-fashioned barbecue going on, in honor of a jubilant, old-fashioned politician, dean of the U.S. Senate, John C. Stennis. This is the quintessential Mississippi political gathering.

So many male dignitaries are crowding into the banquet room you can't swing a fat cat without hitting a Who's Who. The air is thick with Old Spice and bluster.

Seven U.S. senators, two former governors, an esteemed U.S. District Court judge and two current and two former congressmen all jostle for seats at the crowded, community tables. At the head table, with the honoree and his family, sits the girl.

When she stands, the men stand. When she sits, the men sit. When she walks, a hush falls over the room. Little girls and grown women rush her and ask her to put her name on a piece of napkin or notebook paper.

Seasoned, burly state troopers doff their hats and step back so as not to soil her. Then they watch her walk away from them; it is a quiet and reverent moment.

There are Phi Beta Kappas here. A Harvard man or two. A past Republican nominee for president. More lawyers than any honest citizen feels comfortable around.

There are a lot of distinguished, powerful men here today. And representing women, the girl.

Long live Miss Mississippi.

August 1985

Good Bad Books

With his mouth moving hungrily on hers and his tongue finding hers sweet and passionately willing, Nils caressed the smooth, warm skin left bare by her bikini.
— *From Carole Halston's*
A Common Heritage

Don't laugh. There's big money behind the soft-porn covers of romance novels.

"You don't have to be another William Faulkner to get published," understates Silhouette Books senior editor Mary Clare Kersten. She should know.

Mary Clare looks like a romance editor should. She has hair black as doom and fills out admirably a sweater of midnight blue. No doubt there is a brooding, bronze Nils in her life.

Right now, Mary Clare's telling a group of high school students gathered in a shopping mall how to become one of Silhouette's 250 authors who altogether grind out over 300 books a year. The more successful writers dip their pens in passion for four or more books annually, sometimes earning six-figure salaries.

And the most successful romance writers know instinctively what Ann Landers is just now finding out—women are more interested in cuddling and kissing than What Eventually Must Follow.

Women—and Silhouette knows it is mostly women who read romances—want to read exactly how the heroine and hero look, what they wear and how long they wear it before it comes off. They demand a double dose of inner-longings. Romance readers prefer a lot of adjective foreplay before verbs are injected into the relationship.

"Don't just say the heroine has lavender eyes and hair the color of moonlight," advises Dixie Browning, a North Carolina grandmother who's written 26 of the pant-filled paperbacks. "Get inside their skin and heads."

Believe it or not, these writers really worry about quality. "My first 'other woman' was about as stereotypical as you could get," laments Carole Halston, a former English teacher from Louisiana with 13 romances in print. Mrs. Halston's cliche creation was blonde, beautiful and buxom, incorporating the obvious Three B's of Other Womanhood.

Dixie Browning has her own regrets. She shakes her head, thinking of all the "really bad books, full of exclamation points" she had published early in her career. "Somebody said it's harder to write a good bad book than a bad good book," philosophizes Mrs. Browning.

Romance novels have changed since all the heroines had names like "Purity," "Chastity" and "Prudence" with morals to match. These days there are several romance categories, running the passion gamut from wholesome to sensuous.

Still, happy endings and emotional commitments must rise from the steam. And the books are never really X-rated. The hardcore porno is left at the truck stops for male readers. Women still want warmth not fire and the Good Housekeeping Seal of Approval on any groping.

The "Contemporary Romance" category, for instance, must have a virginal heroine, 19 to 29 years old, according to Silhouette guidelines. "The hero is 8 to 12 years older than the heroine. He is self assured, masterful and hot tempered, passionate and tender. He is rich and successful in the vocation of his choice . . . above all virile. He may be widowed, and even divorced, providing it is made clear that the divorce was not his fault."

Sex comes only after marriage in this category.

Silhouette's "Desire" series has heroines between 25 and 32, not necessarily virgins. The "Desires" allow premarital sex but should "concentrate on the highly erotic sensations aroused by the hero's kisses and caresses rather than the mechanics of sex." And so on.

You'd think women who write thousands of words about love and What Eventually Must Follow would lead tempestuous, exotic lives.

"I bought sleeping bags and scout uniforms with my first check," says Joyce Thies, half the romance-writing team of Janet Joyce. Janet Bieber, the other half, "bought new tires for my van."

Mrs. Thies' first manuscript was typed in all-caps "because I didn't want to be bothered with the shift key." The story inadvertently included a horse that remained pregnant over a two-year time frame.

Terry Herrington, new to the romance fold, says she won't even hold hands with her husband in public. The women are all romantics at heart, though, dreaming in pink and lavender. And they resent but ignore anyone who says they're writing trash.

She tucked the creamy pages under one slender arm, tossing hair the color of sunlit cornsilk. This book was good, and she knew it. It felt right. She wanted to see it published. The thought of the royalty checks inflamed her desire.

February 1984

Rivets and Ratchets

NEW ORLEANS. She has a body like a ship's figurehead, but don't tell Linda Pugh. She thinks her figure is average.

Men—and most of her customers are men—seem surprised, she says, when they come into the sex novelty shop and see her behind the counter. A demure business suit and conservative makeup are not what they expected.

This is nasty New Orleans, where there are blue notes, not blue laws, and perversion grows in the Garden District. Sex sells on Madison Avenue. In New Orleans it is sold.

So when Linda got tired of buying shower curtains for D.H. Holmes, she went to work for Linda's Love Lace, where an ambitious sort can make a killing if her car trunk can hold enough crotchless panties.

New Orleans always has been to sex what Wisconsin is to cheese, but the distinction is fast fading for the Crescent City. Today, Americans everywhere are bombarded with sex, which most of them believe was invented sometime around 1968. Fantasy's becoming franchised.

"Some people from my old department store were appalled that I left for this." She makes a demonstrative sweep with her hand and takes in an inventory of edible panties and fishnet briefs. Emotion Lotion in chocolate and butterscotch — rub it, it turns warm; blow it, it gets hot; pour what's left on your ice cream.

To her, they are the rivets and ratchets of a thriving business. Once it leaves the store, it's none of her business.

"As a buyer for a big department store, I got to do lots, travel places. I had dinner with Mary Martin and went to a reception for Princess Grace. I went on buying trips all the time to Dallas and New York and once made an extended buying tour of the Orient."

But there's more independence and, yes, titillation in selling the latest intimate apparel. So this college-educated woman from a small Alabama town went unabashedly into that good nightie market.

"Rule No. 1 is never assume the customer's buying for his wife," she says. Actually, she never assumes anything about her customers.

One man bought a pair of panties, garnished them with two $100 bills and had them wrapped for a "friend." Another man selected a lively assortment of ten different items, had them all gift-wrapped separately and tagged, each with a different name. One regular patron always does his shopping in a three-piece business suit and women's high heels.

But it's the home parties that really get Linda's entrepreneurial blood pumping. She packs the novelties like so many Fuller brushes and carts them to the house of a volunteer hostess. What follows is an impromptu fashion show, with the female customers becoming middle-aged and high-mileage models, giggling like Valley Girls.

"The women who are the big talkers are never the ones who buy much. It's that quiet, mousy little woman in the corner with the healthy sex life who ends up spending the money."

The lingerie party is fast becoming a suburban staple in many cities. Sexual savoir faire is a mark of municipal sophistication, like street lights once were. Unless suddenly the world gets less interested in sex, these neighborhood rituals seem to have a fate sealed tight as Tupperware.

Linda has as many bookings as she has time. Women roll the Big Wheels out of the den and plug in the percolator and it's show time.

She sometimes watches women compulsively spend money they obviously need to spend elsewhere. Women gambling on their own seductiveness is not always a pretty sight. But talk is cheap, and that's what most of the women really want. "This just opens the door."

Sometimes Linda ends up acting "almost like a sex therapist, since they assume I'm some kind of expert." She says while misconceptions remain widespread, "antiquated ideas still abound." Most of the women still only associate sexy clothes with getting pregnant.

And any fool knows, sex today is not about making babies; it's about making money.

Linda, 32, lives alone in one of those massive New Orleans apartment complexes that looks like every other brick on the block.

She likes interior decorating and doing volunteer work with the Red Cross. She collects hearts—ceramic, pewter and crystal ones. Still, there seems to be more lace than love in her life.

Have discount doses of depravation dulled her own sexual senses? Will she remain unmarried after selling truckloads of playthings to the unfaithful hordes?

Linda, gift-wrapping a black negligee a New Orleans policeman has ordered after a luncheon fashion show, takes her time with a ribbon and an answer.

"I'm not less trusting because of it, if that's what you mean. I never trusted men, and I still don't."

October 1984

7 / Clouds of Mystery

Children, Really

JACKSON, MISSISSIPPI. It is a church you might or might not notice, made with the routine complement of red brick and opaque glass. It has a modern-looking, silver steeple, a plain white cross and a new dead bolt lock on the front door.

The law calls them "juveniles."

They are children, really. One of them only seven, three of them merely twelve. Two of them brothers. How they spent their summer vacation is why the church has a new dead bolt lock.

For six days the boys sneaked into Emmanuel United Methodist Church, secluded by woods on three sides and an indifferent interstate on the fourth. For six days they worked their mischief.

They broke colored windows. They dumped white and blue paint on the carpet, the pews, the piano and organ. They wrote nasty words on the nursery walls.

They poured water on satin-like choir robes, until the red stoles bled all over the white robes. They busted the windows of the rickety blue church bus.

They tore up hymnals and shredded an American flag. They destroyed the pulpit Bible. They did an estimated $75,000 worth of meanness. Each day meant a new secret agenda of destruction.

And on the seventh day the maid saw everything they had done, and, behold, it was a wreck.

The pastor called the police. The 85-member congregation of Emmanuel Methodist may be able to use its sanctuary again by October. That is, if the pews are refinished, if the new carpet is down, if the windows are replaced and the paint job complete.

This is not an especially wealthy church. Insurance will not foot the entire bill. "I'm sick of the whole mess," says the Rev. J.A. Bridewell, cordial but tired.

Why did they do it?

"I haven't been able to figure it out," says Rev. Bridewell. "They just went in and entertained themselves for six days."

Because it was the worst case of Jackson vandalism in recent years, reporters asked the question of a variety of professionals:

Why?

"An attack by Satan," said one preacher.

"Hostility toward authority," said a doctor.

"Peer pressure," said a child psychologist.

"Just for kicks," said a cop.

Because she must work outside the home and leave them to fend for themselves, said the divorced mother of the brothers.

They "don't know," said the boys.

Let's face it. Nobody knows what makes a boy bad, or a good boy do bad, or one bad boy plus three good ones equal to four bad boys. If somebody did know, the prisons would not be flashing "No Vacancy" signs and churches would not need dead bolt locks. It happened. It happens.

August 1985

Murder Of A Town

BOYLE, MISSISSIPPI. The little house where they found Dud Collier Jr.'s body is empty now, like the rest of downtown Boyle.

You can tell it was an interesting house once. Built with lots of aged cypress and imagination.

Vickie Collier never went back there after the murder. She couldn't. After all, that was the house Collier brought her to see before they married in 1969, when he was only talking about restoring an old Mississippi Delta town.

Mrs. Collier would sit and watch him sketch his prototype town. "He had big dreams," she says. Her voice has that husky sound, just this side of raw emotion.

She is a handsome woman, probably the belle of Shelby when she graduated from high school in that small Delta town back in 1965. She lives in California now, far away on the map and in the mind from tiny Boyle.

"We used to go to artists' colonies, Gatlinburg and other places, to get ideas. Sometimes we laughed about putting a glass bubble over a perfect, controlled atmosphere."

In 1968 Collier found his dream town in unlikely, skeletal Boyle, less than ten miles from his hometown of Shaw and in the shadow — geographically, economically — of Cleveland, Mississippi. He opened a frame shop, bought other main street property and, from that modest beginning, gradually brought Boyle back from the dead.

There were some problems all along, setbacks. A fire destroyed a restaurant and smoked up some other shops. But the town slowly evolved from mostly arts and crafts shops in the 1970's to a sophisticated, stylish village, known regionally.

Maybe "evolved" is not the right word. Collier caused it to happen. He designed restoration projects with his pen; he accomplished them with his hammer.

During an occasional open house, thousands came. Some celebrities. Guest registers included European addresses. There hadn't been such crowds in Boyle since World War I, when the town was singled out for a visit of the Liberty Bell train.

In its heyday, Collier's Boyle had 17 solid, upscale businesses, mostly antique and specialty shops. Not bad for a town that had been down to two Chinese grocery stores and a post office. And not bad for a man with more intrinsic creativity than business sense.

And though Collier never built his glass bubble, the atmosphere in Boyle was special. If creative exchange had a Mississippi address, it probably was Boyle.

"He was both architect and janitor of Boyle," says a close friend of Collier's, artist Sammy Britt. "He was the heart of it."

Until July 8, 1982. When Jerry Lee Bland put a .38-caliber bullet between Dud Collier's eyebrows, he killed more than a man. He killed a town.

That is what Collier's family and friends say, at least. The empty Boyle sidewalks today back them up. There is one antique store here now. And the post office.

The rest of Boyle's smart shops have folded or relocated. The main drag today looks, once again, like a black and white scene in *The Last Picture Show*.

Sammy Britt and Collier met when they were 12 years old, sitting in opposite Little League dugouts. They competed on some playing field or other all the way through high school. Collier, Britt believes, was talented at almost too many things.

"Dud was painting more when he died. But there is no way a person who is creative can lay down the saw and hammer and pick up a paintbrush," Britt says. "Painting has to have your full attention. You can't be worrying about a broken commode across the street."

Trouble was, nothing really had Collier's full attention.

Thomas Durwood Collier, Jr. was an artist, an architect, a rock and roll drummer, a carpenter, an inventor. He carried three-by-five notecards in his shirt pocket to catalog his endless ideas.

He painted remarkable portraits, made a door for the Governor's Mansion down in Jackson, put a frame around a painting of Richard Nixon's daughters.

But more amazing, really, were the little things he did daily. He cooked for his wife and two daughters and took in stray dogs.

He was a perfectionist, a workaholic. His mother once said she knew he had been painting whenever she heard the sound of ripping canvas late at night. He refused to keep any work that wasn't his best; he didn't sign many of his paintings.

Collier also invented. Incessantly. Special hangers for his picture frames, automated easels, potty seats for his children, better windshield wipers for the car.

"He wouldn't just think of these things, he would draw them all out in elaborate sketches and even come up with the mottoes for selling them," Vickie Collier says.

He also invented jobs, whenever Boyle teenagers needed work. And in Boyle, somebody always needed work.

"He couldn't enjoy himself if anybody, anywhere was miserable," says Ann Fletcher, his friend and longtime frame shop employee. "He was a big brother type to all the poor kids in town. He gave them advice and money."

It was Ann Fletcher who found him, the morning after Collier surprised a 17-year-old Boyle youth burglarizing his home. Collier was lying on his kitchen floor, curled in a question mark position, blood puddled all around him.

"It was the way he died that made it so bad," Bolivar County Sheriff Harvey "Mack" Grimmett says. "A man is supposed to be able to walk into his home and feel safe.

"Dud knew that kid. He would have given him anything he asked for and helped load the car."

Bland had a record of penny-ante crimes. He also had a familiar *MO*: remove a pillowcase from the victim's bed, light a candle to work by and start filling the bed-linen bag with goods. He never bothered to remove the candle.

The police found that trademark candle at the Collier home; they found Bland hiding under his mother's house the next day. He pleaded guilty and got life for capital murder and ten years for burglary.

Dud Collier, Sr. is not an "If only . . ." sort of man. A veteran special deputy, he talks calmly about the horrible crime that ended his only child's brief life. Yet he cannot help but say "If only . . ." about the night of July 8, 1982.

Vickie and the children were at her mother's house, where relatives were visiting. Dud Jr. traveled from Boyle to nearby Shaw to see his father about 9 that night.

"I was cooking, and I asked him to stay and eat with me. If he had only stayed and had a bite, that boy might have done what he was going to do and gotten out of there," the father says.

Anna Collier, Dud, Jr.'s stepmother, seconds that regret. You can tell the two of them have swapped these thoughts many times before.

"It wasn't like Dud to hear food called and not stay," she says. "He was a small man, but he could eat. But he said he had some work he had to get back and finish."

The elder Collier has scrapbooks detailing his son's accomplishments. He has his son's first painting—a Mississippi magnolia, signed—hanging on a bedroom wall. And he has his son's high school ring, which he wears on his pinkie finger.

Funny thing about that ring. Dud Collier, Jr. lost it in a neighbor's garden shortly after he bought it in high school. The spring after he was buried, the neighbors dug up his ring. Unearthed it with a plow. There were 23 years of crud clinging to the gold, and the setting was gone.

But Dud Collier, Sr. had it cleaned and his son's initials etched in fancy script where the stone once was. It looks as good as new.

July 1985

The End of Hackberry Lane

JACKSON, TENNESSEE. She lived with a big family in a small house on a cul-de-sac at the end of Hackberry Lane.

The yard is about the size of a wallet photo, some of the window screens are missing and the driveway is strewn with toys. But inside, there was always love and support for Tammy Blakemore.

She was only 19, a high school senior. She had grown up quickly. Some would say too quickly; already she was a mother.

Tammy liked to sew, to cook and to watch "Star Search" on television. She made school clothes for her siblings and was a downright ace at grocery shopping.

"She was my nicest child," says Tammy's mother, Janet Holmes. She speaks softly, head bowed. Mrs. Holmes is 40, looks much younger, acts older.

"People from work try and get me to go out with them, but I always say 'No.' I'm the only one my children have since the divorce.

"I don't have a boyfriend. I work nights. Days, I stay home with my children."

There are six of them. Tammy made seven. The cramped living room is temporarily devoted to the oldest daughter. An eight-by-ten of a smiling Tammy is placed prominently on the bookshelf. The coffee table is covered with funeral leftovers—blue silk roses, potted plants and Easter lilies, their trumpets bruised and wilting.

Teenaged boys—tall and strapping, saddled with the awkwardness of that age—stroll about the small room, holding or handing off DeMarcus, Tammy's six-month-old son. The house is a bridge mix of death and life.

Members of Tammy's high school sorority, Beta Phi Zeta, have been dropping by all day, offering condolences. The phone has been ringing. The four days since the funeral have been full.

Nobody knows yet what happened to Tammy. First she was missing. Then she was found—dumped, dead and decomposing.

"God's gonna punish whoever it was," says Janet Holmes. "Tell him that. He may be hiding from the law, but you cannot hide from God.

"Whatever turmoil they put my Tammy through will be nothing to what they get in turn. And it won't be long, because He told me it wouldn't."

Tammy and her twin sisters Sherree and Sherron all were to finish high school next month. Janet Holmes had been saving money to rent a Winnebago and take the entire family — children, grandchildren, everybody—to California. A graduation trip, a family celebration.

Instead, Mrs. Holmes and the twins spent some of that money on three, identical blue and white outfits for Tammy's funeral. They were just like the outfit Tammy had picked out to wear for church Easter Sunday.

"I wanted to dress her in one, too, but her body was badly decomposed." Janet Holmes is tortured by things she does not know and things Tammy will never know.

"She will never see her baby have a birthday. She will never see him walk."

She also won't go to college and become a registered nurse. She won't write more poems, like the ones found in her diary. She won't see California or finish the softball season.

"People have offered to take care of DeMarcus, but there's no way I'll let this baby go. He's all I have left of Tammy."

Mrs. Holmes is quiet and far away for a moment, then strangely alert. She is remembering, suddenly, something else about Tammy.

Two days before she was missing, Tammy went to Furniture Annex and bought a new French provincial bed for the room she shared with her baby and two others. She slept in the new bed only one night.

The next evening she apparently headed to nearby Lane College, a peaceful-seeming campus of green lawns and black students. It is one of several colleges in Jackson, a town of 50,000 that is both pretty and proud, a town fit for its Chamber of Commerce slogan: "What America Is Meant To Be."

April 1986

Jimmy Buffett And John Doe

MEMPHIS. Jimmy Buffett was singing of sharks and ragtops and African parakeets when the man drowned.

A summer squall had cooled things off considerably on Mud Island. All around the little sand spit and its amphitheater, the Mississippi churned and the lights of Memphis burned. It was more than pleasant.

A Buffett concert is different from most rock gatherings. People know the words to the songs. The songs have words to know.

Buffett is the weekend side of us. He is the prodigal part deep within us that would just up and leave a good job one day to sail around the world. He is the Texas troubadour lurking in the soul of every staid, well-paid executive. He is a genius not wasting his mind writing corporate memos.

Buffett is the 12-year-old kid still alive in our 40-year-old bodies—mischievous but not malicious. Swearing if we ever got rich, we would pay the Mini-Mart back.

He is the Good Life.

Buffett said earlier: " . . . I think a lot of people would love to live the lifestyle I've been lucky enough to pull off . . . . There's a little bit of an admiration in the fact that somebody in this crazy world is actually getting to pull this off."

There is not a little but a lot of envy, tempered by an acknowledgment that if you ever wrote anything as fine as *A Pirate Looks At Forty* you'd probably be commuting from Aspen to Key West and living high, too.

Singing along with Buffett, then, is a way to escape, if only momentarily, the landlocked and responsible ways of adulthood.

So we all were singing our secret hearts out when new, ominous lights filled the skies above Mud Island.

A helicopter hovered close to the water east of the stage, behind Buffett and under the Mud Island monorail. Boats with blue police lights and search beams streaked across the dark waters, a grim indication something, or more likely somebody, was missing.

Buffett and band were unaware of the drama being played out behind the covered stage. The singer might have wondered why, for a moment, he seemed to lose the crowd. Binoculars that had been pointed at the stage all evening suddenly were moving to its left.

It was not long, though, before those who came to escape harsh reality lost interest in the criss-crossing search beams and distant divers and told themselves there was nothing to do about it anyway. The singing began again.

Yet, now, there was a nagging irony to all the lyrics, and it was prematurely the Morning After another illicit adult adventure.

That's the difference in being an adult and being a child. Adults pay dearly for their fun.

There is a bill, a guilt trip or sometimes a major tragedy to abate the times we dare to forget who and where in life we are.

The concert ended as concerts—and frivolous dreams—always do. the Buffett crowd filed across the walkway, dressed in their

Caribbean shirts from Wal-Mart. Some stopped to peer at the river below, where official boats cordoned the chocolate waters and continued the search.

They found him the next morning. He was still John Doe, as of this writing, to police. Approximate age, 42. He had been sitting on the river bank below the monorail. Mud Island security guards already had warned him once about swimming in the area. He did not listen.

Police said he waded into the water with a beer can in his hand. Witnesses heard him call for help three times before he went under. Nobody knew if he was there to hear Buffett from the free, riverbank seats. Nobody knew anything about him.

He was just another anonymous drowning, worth five paragraphs in the morning newspaper. Someone who couldn't quite pull it off.

July 1986

A History Of Violence

GOAT ISLAND, MISSISSIPPI. Winter has anchored just offshore and means to stay. Fingers of mud flats stretch across the slate-colored waters of Pickwick Lake, which is low and surly in time with the season.

But the pall of this big pond is temporary. A few degrees will make all the difference. The dark cabins that ring it soon will come alive with laughter and slamming screen doors and briquettes glowing in portable grills. The lake will rise and eventually spill over with bathers and skiers and boaters, bent on a big time.

Cabin windows will shed their polyethylene and children their shoes. The summer people will return. But for now, winter rules. There is the quiet and the eerie, dependable blinks of the channel lights. Nothing else.

This is the house.

It is a lovely cabin of redwood-colored siding. Split-level and tight. Set in the hillside facing the lake. Around it are the accouterments of normal living—a doghouse, a flowerbed, a utility room. The porch lights burn.

Nothing too out of the ordinary could happen here.

W.D. Crawford and his wife Elma Lee built the place as a retirement home. A place to enjoy nature and one another and family. For the past three years they had lived here, part of the small fraternity of full-timers who learn to endure, even love, the gray solitude of Pickwick winters.

Crawford's fishing boat is parked out by the road, still hitched to the car that pulled it. Ready for warmer days.

It was only four days after Christmas when Crawford was bludgeoned to death, in his kitchen, where he had been puttering about, cooking breakfast for his family.

His wife, shot in the abdomen and left for dead, wrote the words "K.D." and "Shotgun" in her own blood.

The law is still looking for the couple's grandson, K.D. Sanders. He has a history of mental illness and violence. His grandfather had been his ally, repeatedly helping him.

Crawford was buried. His wife hung on a while and then she, too, died.

And it was to K.D. that the bloody finger pointed.

People speculate. The locals believe K.D. might be hiding out in one of the area's empty cabins. Many of them are left vacant during winter months by Memphians who own them. Some have stocked deep-freezes and enough amenities to keep a fugitive for months.

Searches have yielded nothing. So for now, in these lifeless months when no-nonsense fishermen and the serious sailors have the lake to themselves, the crime goes unanswered.

It seems to me the most unnatural of all rages. If a man turned on the grandparents who took him in, as authorities believe, how doubly sad this story. What confusion, what discontent, could end like this?

February 1986

The M.O. Of Modern Tragedy

SAN YSIDRO, CALIFORNIA. Some come burdened with their alien status, others with ceramic pigs.

The stream of pedestrians filing through U.S. Customs from Tijuana to California moves slowly, as wary travelers hold high their passports or souvenir purchases for inspection. Then, they wander through the glass doors and onto an unmistakably Yankee street. The first store anyone sees on U.S. soil is a McDonald's.

No, not that McDonald's.

This one still has its golden arches ablaze and its registers ringing. The interior, done up in high-tech and mustard yellow, is as familiar to us as the den at home. We know where to order and where to sit, The menu, the prices are no surprise.

It is that very familiarity that makes a tragedy of mammoth dimensions—the massacre of 21 innocent patrons at another San Ysidro McDonald's—seem sadder, more threatening still. It's as if the brutal murders happened in our own backyards.

The site of the killings has been stripped of its corporate identity. They took the golden arches down from the San Ysidro Boulevard restaurant under cover of night, apparently wanting to dismantle as inconspicuously as possible such intimate association with disaster. They lowered the trademark of tragedy.

There are lights, though. They burn brightly, giving an eerie cast to a dark lapse in the neon necklace of commerce.

The lights are the flicker of candles, stuck inside fruit jars and glasses and religious decanters. There are dozens of them lining the brick fence that once surrounded a fast food joint, not a painful memory.

There are wreaths, too, and rosaries and pictures of Jesus. An American flag and a Mexican one as well hang motionless in the hot, still night. The handmade banners plead for contributions to build a memorial for the slain or simply ask that you "bring candles and flowers."

"Let us build a better world," one sign says. Plaster statues of Jesus and Mother Mary rise like gentle entreaties.

Beyond the crude but caring shrine looms the darkened parking lot, its entrances now police lines. One car, parked where the drive-through window once operated, sits in a shadow. Only the glow of a cigarette lets you know someone's guarding the empty store.

This is a shop-worn neighborhood. A post office borders the McDonald's shell on one side; postal patrons of Zip Code 92073 pass here daily or thereabouts. On the other side, a Yum-Yum Donuts is packing them in. Two small boys on bicycles pedal by in the darkness, shouting happily to one another as they pass the place they might have been.

The hillside lights of Tijuana twinkle beyond this street, this silent and morbid spot. Distance mutes the lumens of Old Mexico, and it seems to glow in tribute, too, its border town strewn with a million candles.

There was no preparing for James Huberty. You could spend your life avoiding danger and not anticipate the McDonald's massacre. That's what makes it so scary.

Capital punishment may or may not discourage violent crime by eliminating potential threats, one by one. But then a James Huberty, with no previous record, disaffected and unemployed and with every intention of dying himself, strolls into a fast food emporium and mows down half its customers. How do you plan for that? How do you discourage that?

While they were lighting candles on San Ysidro Boulevard, President Ronald Reagan was finishing public appearances 100 miles north in Los Angeles. At Century Plaza, where Reagan was to address the U.S. Olympic team, they had installed airport-style metal detectors and a contingent of police and Secret Service. A German Shephard police dog sat pawing the thick carpet of the posh banquet room.

At the invitation-only breakfast of champions, they had executed the most stringent of security measures. Can you, though, logically plan for the illogical, crazed act of a madman? Can you protect a President or a public from the isolated, freakish deed that is fast becoming the M.O. of modern tragedy?

The sad answer, of course, is "no." There is no recourse, no planning for human nature gone berserk, no matter how common the context.

The lights from here to Tijuana seem to dim, ever so briefly.

September 1984

"Can You Believe That?"

NEW YORK. If the kid was older than 12, I'd be surprised. We were somewhere between the Pan Am Building and Pennsylvania Station, stalled in that bump-and-grind routine called Manhattan traffic.

The youth was rapping his fists on the cab window, passenger side, looking desperate and screaming, "Hey, man. Hey, man."

The cab driver perhaps felt benevolent. Or maybe he was only curious. He leaned clear across the cab to lower the window.

At that exact instant, a second child—this one with a more acute sense of timing than a stand-up comic—took advantage of the orchestrated distraction and thrust his hand into the cabbie's window. He grabbed for a wad of bills, loosely attached by a rubber band to the sun visor. The young thief got a few dollars. The rest of the wad fell between the seat and the car door.

"Can you believe that?" the driver asked no one in particular. He nosed his cab ahead half a dozen car lengths.

Then he stuffed the salvaged bills in his shirt pocket and sighed, perhaps resigned to breaking even on this fare and having a story to tell the wife that night.

Suddenly, not two blocks away, a small hand was reaching into the driver's window once again, this time fishing for bills from the shirt pocket. The children were back.

The driver waged a quick, wrist-slapping struggle with the bandit, managing to keep all his money.

"Roll up your windows and lock your doors," the driver screamed to me.

When a New York taxi driver tells you to roll up your windows and lock your doors, you don't ask questions. You roll up your windows and lock your doors.

We rode along for a while, not speaking and looking over our shoulders like illicit lovers. Two 12-year-olds were a frightening prospect now, when only five mintues before they were only two 12-year-olds.

The thought of the skinny arms reappearing, of seeing those clutching fingers ripping at the heart-pocket of the driver, was like waiting for the monster-child to reappear in a horror movie.

"In 25 years, I've never had the same ones come back like that," said the clearly rattled driver. I commiserated with him for the remaining few blocks and then—for some reason—tipped like Onassis.

What a strange world we live in, when children are reared in the streets and act like something from the sewers, when adults four times larger cringe behind locked doors because they are afraid of the children.

After that eventful ride, I read a long *Times* piece about the welfare hotels in New York. The article told of large families crowded into small rooms, of hungry and street-wise children who begged and stole and routinely got beaten up by those larger and meaner.

Safe behind the locked doors of the Hotel Kitano (". . . the only Japanese-managed hotel in New York . . . even those in New York for the first time can feel as comfortable and safe as they would in Japan . . .") I read about the plight of the very same children who had robbed my cab.

They had, as if paid to illustrate that grim story, materialized the way statistics are wont eventually to do. And I wondered when or if it will end, the poverty and base scratching for survival that is so incomprehensible to those of us who have three bedrooms and three squares.

Something has to give, in the dark city ghettos and along the countless Sugar Ditches of rural America. Else all of us, from now until Doomsday, will be looking over our shoulders, afraid of our own children.

May 1986

The "Obviously Guilty"

DONALSONVILLE, GEORGIA. If you had a mind to murder, this would be the place. In rural Southwest Georgia—12 miles from the Seminole County seat of Donalsonville—the swamps and the farmers wage constant tug-of-war for the very ground. Cypress is staple vegetation in amphibious forests. Gray Spanish moss curls from live oak like a new perm on an old lady. Not far from here, in North Florida, is Wakulla Springs, where Hollywood filmed "Creature from the Black Lagoon."

Carl Isaacs, his half-brother, Wayne Carl Coleman, and their sidekick, George Dungee, rode these lonely Georgia backroads 12 years ago—May 17, 1973, to be exact. To the prison escapees from Maryland, this must have semed a good spot to get away with murder.

First they killed 62-year-old Ned Alday, shooting him seven times in the face. Ned was arthritic but active, the patriarch of the Alday farm, some 525 acres of land bordering the Chattahoochee River.

Ned and his sons farmed the land together, ate together, worshipped together—almost 19th Century-style. Ned was alone that day, though, the first to approach the double-wide mobile home where Dungee, Isaacs and Coleman crouched, waiting.

Isaacs took farmer Ned Alday into a bedroom. Only Isaacs returned.

"He came out laughing," Billy Isaacs said in testifying against his brother, Carl. Sixteen at the time, tag-along Billy completed the malevolent foursome.

"Carl told us, 'That bastard begged me for mercy.'"

Next to enter the afternoon ambush was Jerry Alday, Ned's oldest son. Jerry and his wife Mary owned the trailer. The intruders took Jerry, 35, to the opposite end of his own trailer and shot him in the head.

Jerry's brother Jimmy, 25, was close behind. Perhaps he wondered about the intruders' stolen car with Pennsylvania plates. He did not wonder long. Jimmy, in turn, was shot to death.

Ned's brother Aubrey Alday, 58, saw the growing collection of cars at Jerry's trailer and stopped to investigate. He was next to die.

Then Ned's middle son Chester, 30, fell. The fifth Alday to die. Officers later found him on a bed, dead, beside his father.

Mary Alday, 26, was last to die. She probably suffered the longest.

Mary returned from her job in town to the trailer. It was full of dead bodies. All of them her people.

The escaped convicts took turns raping her, then stole her car and finally shot her to death as she ran from them in a nearby field.

A larger marker says, simply, "Alday Family."

Beneath it, the six gray graves, side by side in the Spring Creek Baptist Church cemetery, testify to the enormity of the crime.

On Ned Alday's slab is etched: *Earth has no sorrow that heaven cannot heal.*

The funeral was one of the biggest ever held in this part of the state. The governor's mother and his wife— Lillian and Rosalyn Carter—both came. So did hundreds of others. Mary's mother, already ill and now heartbroken, dropped dead a few days after the funeral.

Carl Isaacs, Coleman and Dungee were convicted of the six brutal slayings in separate, back-to-back trials in January, 1974. All three were sentenced to die. All of them live today.

Since the trial Carl Isaacs has been vocal about the murders. "I'd like to get out and kill more of them," he told one reporter.

"They represent the type of society I don't like. The Aldays loved church so damn much they should have been killed and buried right at the church."

In an interview videotaped for public television in 1977, Isaacs said this: "I don't feel bad. The only thing the Aldays ever did that stood out was getting killed by me."

While acknowledging over-whelming evidence of guilt, three federal judges last month overturned the murder convictions. In ordering new trials, the judges said "inflammatory" publicity had made fair trials in Seminole County impossible. And that even an "obviously guilty defendant" has a right to a fair trial.

Now, for the stunned people of Seminole County, it is as if the murders have happened again.

I asked Curtis Strickland if he ever got himself involved in public affairs before, and he said, no, not much.

That's not surprising, because he probably wouldn't be very good at such things. He speaks in a low, earnest voice, choosing words cautiously, inexpertly, and punctuating them with phrases like "Am I right?" or "Don't you agree?" He fidgets. He fiddles with his coffee cup.

But Curtis Strickland is mad. Insulted. Appalled. Indignant. Disbelieving.

He has drafted a grammatically imperfect, legally naive petition aimed at impeaching three federal judges, and he says people all over South Georgia are beating his doors down to sign it, because they feel the same way he does. Tens of thousands of signatures will be no problem, he hopes.

Strickland is riled about the reversal of the Alday killers' 1974 murder convictions.

The three judges decided the convicts could not have gotten a fair trial in Seminole County. The people there, they said, were too upset by the crimes and the attendant publicity.

The citizens of Seminole County readily admit that it stuck in their craw when a hard-working, God-fearing farm family was viciously wiped out by low-life misfits. But the three men convicted were given a "fair trial," they will contend.

For sure, the trial was not a circus. It was conducted in a civilized manner, by the book, by educated lawyers in an atmosphere as calm as possible for a sextuple murder case. The news media, of course, were panting heavily, churning up as many details as they could for the morbidly fascinated, and there were many. But was the trial fair?

Maybe. Maybe not.

But there is one thing for certain, one thing that even the convicts don't dispute. The three are guilty. The verdict was correct.

Fingerprints, ballistics tests, a trail of stolen vehicles, the eyewitness account of a teenager traveling with the killers — all those things constituted Georgia's case. Since the trial, one of the killers has given hours of taped interviews to reporters, owning up to the murders and even bragging about them.

Although the men were sentenced to die in 1974, their cases have rattled around the legal system for more than a decade, twice reaching the Supreme Court, which refused to hear them.

Even while deciding to throw out the verdicts, the three-judge panel acknowledged overwhelming evidence of guilt.

It's a case that caused a federal judge to declare he had never seen a more clear-cut need for a change of venue. And caused a state judge sitting on the Georgia Supreme Court at the time to declare he had never seen defendants more obviously guilty.

It's really a fascinating textbook case. One that has raised a briar patch of prickly questions. What is Justice? How is it obtained?

But the disillusioned people of Seminole County don't understand it that way. They see it as them against three dangerous, unrepentant criminals, and the federal court has taken the side of the killers.

The people of South Georgia don't understand anything anymore.

January 1986

Military Honors

JACKSON, MISSISSIPPI. There are more lawyers than sewers in this town. That's why some of the lawyers live in houses.

Ed Cates was a lawyer who diversified by dabbling in local politics and selling used Cadillacs. They take a lot of the same skills.

He was an ultraconservative, church-going, paramilitary expert. Jogging and physical fitness were an obsession. He was a small, erect man who seemed always to march instead of walk.

Business was bad for Mr. Cates. People weren't buying his legal expertise. He was losing money on his Cadillac deals. He had lost a couple of political campaigns. His house had two mortgages. So, Cates dipped into a client's trust fund and made himself welcome to about $200,000.

He didn't put all the money to selfish use. He bought his daughter a car. He sent generous checks to relatives. He made a donation to an organization for the mothers of Mississippi debutantes, another to the Boy Scouts. He even gave some of it to the church.

And, he paid bills to try and continue to live in the style to which he had become accustomed.

There was the minor matter of the missing money, however. Cates had to cover his tracks. So, he dreamed up an elaborate scheme that would make it appear as if he died, trapped in a fire in his little Honda Civic. Authorities found Cates' fire-gutted car and a faceless, unrecognizable body. The smell of gas was heavy. An investigation began.

Dorothy Cates identified her husband by a shoe. That's about all that was left. Then she buried him in the military manner he would have preferred—folded flag and saluting guns. If Cates had not started sending home money orders signed by the late Army general whose identity he'd assumed, investigators might never have tracked him down. But he did. And they did. It was a big piece, but the jigsaw puzzle was incomplete.

Probably nobody but Cates knew who died in the car fire last May. Probably nobody else ever will. The courts called the dead man "John Doe."

Authorities speculated John Doe was a derelict whose trust Cates won or bought. John Doe most likely was living still when somebody—presumably Cates—poured the gasoline and struck the match and watched the Honda holocaust. A pathologist was able to determine that much from the blackened remains.

Cates was sentenced last month to 20 years in prison. That's the maximum sentence for manslaughter, the charge for which Cates' lawyers successfully plea-bargained. The district attorney gave a polite little speech about how he probably wouldn't have been able to convince a jury a murder had taken place. He had an unidentified body and a woman who had watched two cars drive by to the fire scene. She was fuzzy on details. And, of course, he had the cagey Mr. Cates, who was no help at all.

He didn't want to risk letting Cates walk, the district attorney said. So the judge asked one, weasel-worded question: "Mr. Cates, did you, on May 14, cause the death of another human being?"

"Yes, your honor, I did." There was no further accounting. Cates got the same punishment someone might get who carelessly bends over to switch a car radio from country to rock and hits a pedestrian. He will be eligible for parole in less than five years.

Once establishment, always establishment. That seems to be the unspoken reasoning behind what happened to Edward L. Cates. Here was a man who had made his fortune by propounding the law and religion and conservative ethics. He lived in a brick house and worked in a plush office. He helped govern the city where he lived. Even if Cates had gone momentarily berserk, he was one of the boys.

To convict Ed Cates of capital murder would be to dismantle a system, to deny a winning formula. Justice was not miscarried; it was aborted.

At least poor John Doe got a fancy funeral with full military honors.

February 1984

8 / Ties That Bind

Lucille

GRIMSLEYTOWN, GEORGIA—The preacher read from Proverbs, Chapter 31, about a virtuous woman. And that was nice, as far as it went.

For Lucille was a moral woman, but much more. So much more.

I sat on the Primitive Baptist pew and thought about her. It was six years to the very day after she suffered a debilitating stroke that they called the coroner to the house. But six years ago she was a strong and robust woman, one who worked hard and demanded you work hard, too.

She had a stubborn streak and a temper, and to be on her bad side was to live on the dark half of the moon. I have heard her dress down grown men until they slunk away in silence. I have returned myself in shame to the No. 2 tub to rewash my feet to suit her.

There was a sunny side. She taught me how to play "Redwing" on the old upright. She loved her music, usually hymns done with a slightly ragtime beat. Lucille didn't sing particularly well, but she sang often, and that's what counts.

Sometimes, usually at the end of the day—after cooking three monstrous meals, working the bounteous south Georgia garden and cleaning in her furious fashion—she would go into her tiny front parlor and beat the keys of the old piano until her plump arms shook.

We would curl up on the couch behind her, watching as those arms swung the length of the keyboard in a mesmerizing, graceful pattern. Lucille had the music in her.

She believed in feeding people until they hurt, in fishing from the bank, in cleanliness on a par with godliness.

She did not believe in women wearing pants, the space program, Daylight Savings Time, ponytails or saying goodbye before hanging up the telephone.

She visited the sick, rescued the perishing, cared for the dying. And she took her grandchildren along to do the same.

She loved trips to church, to town, to the cemetery, the beauty parlor and the creek bank. She loved trips, period. She wore a sun bonnet in the garden, ear bobs to town. She could be cleaning fish one hour, scrubbed and ready for church the next.

Lucille reared six children, buried two husbands and watched a parade of grandchildren come and go. She was the first truly independent woman I ever met. Nobody else ever really stood between her and hunger or poverty or disaster. She met life head-on and won.

The church was full. Jesse Mae, who nursed her during the six silent years, sat in front of me. I wished Jesse Mae had known her before.

There were lots of flowers, and Lucille would have liked that. She could grow anything, from hothouse poinsettias to peas.

"If you ever feel bad," she once said to me, "put something in the ground."

Two women sang "Amazing Grace" and "Precious Memories" a capella. Lucille loved "How Great Thou Art," too, but nobody sang that.

We walked out into the cemetery, separated only by a hogwire fence from a cornfield. The skies threatened to open up at any moment and drench the parched field.

"I hope the rain will hold off," somebody said.

The white country church that seemed so immense to me as a child looked tiny in the distance. A toy church surrounded by toy cars in a make-believe town.

The preacher said a final prayer. Then they buried my grandmother, six years after she died.

July 1986

Arrgh!!!

People always assume it must be a laugh a minute to live with a cartoonist. Ha!

Take it from me, wife of a strip artist. People paid to be funny do not give away their good sense of humor. They do not squander it at home. They cannot afford to.

There are a few advantages to being hooked up with a cartoonist. For instance, who else could list a book like Charles Schulz, *I'm Not Your Sweet Babboo* as a tax deduction?

Mostly, though, the domesticated cartoonist sits cranky and crouched, like a cat, waiting for his family or friends to do or say something ridiculous or embarrassing. Then he pounces.

"There's a gag somewhere in that stupid remark!" he'll say, bouncing off the walls. Then he'll disappear for hours to begin the delicate process of distilling family-oriented humor from reality's ribaldry.

It is a brutal business, this job of being wholesomely funny in black and white six times a week. Not to mention once a week in living color. It is a job he takes mighty seriously.

A cartoonist, after all, must be a student of the human spirit. He must be fluent in body language. He must know how to spell words like "ARRGH."

The typical house cartoonist is a medium-build, rumpled specimen who shaves half as often as Don Johnson. He is a predator, as we have shown, feeding off the silly habits and observations of others.

He can be identified easily by a single India ink spot at the tip of his index finger.

On deadline days, he makes a low, mournful sound something like this: "Ohhhhhhh. Ohhhhhhh. Noooooo."

He is on a first-name basis with every Federal Express driver in this hemisphere. His best thoughts come while soaking in tepid water, so he hogs the bathtub and stays wet or slightly pruney approximately 18 hours a day.

When two cartoonists meet, they circle one another warily like a couple of cur dogs. Then for hours and hours they discuss things like whether or not characters really need talk balloons, what strip died last and—always, always—the genius of Charles Schulz.

It is hard to tell when a cartoonist is working. One clue only evident to the most practiced observers is a glazed look that shrouds his bloodshot eyes. Do not disturb him then. Do not try to tell him anything then. He momentarily loses his hearing and at least half his other senses.

The domesticated cartoonist has irregular eating habits and sleeps only at his drawing board. He usually is nocturnal. You can lead him to water, but you can't make him drink anything but beer.

He is conveniently absent-minded, a whiz at non-consequential games such as Trivial Pursuit and always behind on his work. He wants to drive an ice cream truck when he grows up.

Sometimes the more mature of the species does mate. Occasionally, he chooses his mate from an even lower order—the newspaper columnist.

March 1986

Baby Boomerang

I have no children.

When last I gave stock answer to the question that sprouts eternally as conversational crabgrass, I was being a child myself.

The occasion was a Halloween costume party, and I had dressed as Lucy to my husband's Snoopy. Short blue dress, black and white saddle oxfords. A big bow at the end of my sash.

Lucy, my husband said, perfectly matches my personality. Better Lucy than a blockhead, was my sweet rejoinder.

I think it was the man dressed as Julius Caesar who asked the question. You stand next to a stranger eating spinach dip smeared on Nabs and you have to say something. Besides, there seemed to be dozens of little goblins and cowboys and pirates playing down around my saddle oxfords and Julius' sandals, so it was a natural and sociable thing for him to ask, "How about you? Any children?"

"Et tu?" I wanted to cry out. But instead, as usual, I turned the simple word "no" into a heartfelt apology.

I used to add, "Not yet," but with each year that seems more and more like promising something I may never deliver.

I have known women who choose children and no career. I have known women who choose a career and no children. Trouble is, I don't like either type of woman.

I have known women who choose to have both children and a job, but they usually seem too tired to view the job as a career or children a joy.

It seems to me, barren bystander that I am, like a coin toss before a football game, one doomed to end in a thankless tie: "The blue team wins the toss and elects to conceive."

Actually, the sure-fire question probably isn't pointed at me any more often now than it ever was. It's just that these days, on the cusp of Now-or-Never, it seems somehow accusing.

I do know the pictures come more frequently now. You know the ones. Beautiful, dimpled babies, in high-gloss or matte finish, with Olan Mills taking credit on the photograph's front and the parents on the back.

For a while, I framed them. But a couple of years ago they started coming in as fast and furious as Piggly Wiggly circulars, and I was forced to hang a big cork bulletin board in the kitchen just to accomodate everyone else's babies.

It is, of course, the Baby Boomer boomerang. Now, sometimes, I have trouble remembering who belongs to whom, which infant in christening gown and studio smile is cousin Valerie's and which one cousin Peggy's.

It is not that they all look alike; they certainly do not. Only men think all babies but their own look like Winston Churchill smoking a pacifier.

Maybe I intentionally am shutting them out, these good, five-by-seven babies who never cry or insist on a two a.m. feeding. Maybe I know they are too easy—always chortling, always freshly diapered, always someone else's.

For the first time, my classmates are going on without me. We all learned to tie our shoes at age five. We read at six.

We had skin trouble at 13 and parallel parked at 16. When we were 21, most of us walked the aisle in convenient pairs.

We shuddered in concert at the thought of 30 but found its reality harmless.

Now our ways have parted. I keep my babies on cork instead of in a crib.

You'll be lonely in your old age, they say.

I won't have to wait that long, you blockheads.

October 1985

Everyday Faces

I went home the other day. Unexpected. The folks were sitting down to supper, just the two of them, next to one another at a maple dinette.

Mother had been sick. Not sick exactly, but recovering from the carelessness of an unlicensed driver.

She was better. The bruises were faded, and routine and cornbread had returned to the dinner table.

What struck me, standing there unnoticed, looking in through the mesh of a screened window, was the abysmal familiarity of the scene. The same, soft, twilight shadows that have always lighted their evening meal were playing across those faces. I remembered their motions from somewhere long ago. Maybe I was born knowing them.

They were not talking, just eating, alternately anticipating one another's needs without ever saying a word.

Most of the time when I go to the farm in the Alabama piney woods, it is an occasion. It is Christmas or Thanksgiving or somebody's birthday. And even on non-holidays, I get treated like company.

I no longer know where they keep the towels or bury their trash or hide the house key. I no longer am expected to jump up at the end of the meal and wash the good dishes; now they shoo me away.

I do not even know the intimate if routine details a child would know—the postman's name, what day the paycheck comes or whose side we are on in a neighborhood feud. The postman, the paychecks, the neighbors—even home itself—have changed since I was a girl.

As an adult, I have my own household trivia to contend with. I am a picture on the wall here now, a long-distance telephone call. Perhaps this company status in my own parents' home is a shameful admission, commentary on the shuttle-style life I now lead. I don't get home much. That is the sad truth.

And because it is true, I guess it has been a while since I've seen them with everyday faces, sitting there, unceremoniously and silently passing back and forth the staples of an existence to which I am forever, inextricably linked.

It made me sad in a way I cannot explain.

All of us of normal sensibilities get a glimpse of our parents' mortality at some time or another, sooner or later. There might be a slender wrist encircled with a hospital bracelet, or a worn pair of rubber boots left on the backporch looking somehow forlorn.

It stings you like a mother's switch, the realization that parents, of all people, have human vulnerabilities and physical limits. Never a graceful melancholy, it comes along most often after you have faced your own dimensions, perhaps after a broken marriage, a professional failure. Suddenly the canyons of difference that separate you politically, religiously, philosophically, from the parents are reduced to a mere wrinkle on your brow or theirs.

You belong to one another, after all.

There are moments to remember from any close relationship. There are moments to forget.

I always will remember my father, five seats down, catching my eye at my sister's medical school graduation. The band was playing "The Tennessee Waltz." What that particular song had to do with the occasion, I don't know. But it was my father's favorite, and I sometimes played it for him. In that solemn setting, the waltz and glance seemed magnificently significant.

Mother gave me a locket one Christmas. Not a new one but an old one, a family jewel from a family without any. I was too young to take care of it; the look on her face said she knew that. I lost the locket but hang on fiercely to the memory.

Once we leave the supper table, there is no going back. Not really. We stand outside, apart, looking through the gray mesh of time and circumstance at what once seemed unalterable.

And we see something so familiar, yet so distant.

August 1985

The Rain Lamp

Mother cried on the Christmas Daddy gave her the lamp that pumped mineral oil down catgut strings to simulate raindrops. Too tacky.

Then there was the year she made him take back a string of cultured pearls. Too fancy.

Gift-giving at my house was not easy. Daddy never scored. He always spent too much on some outlandish thing in the worst color and wrong size. It always hurt to see him try.

And Mother, never any good at pretending, would proceed to turn thumbs down on a purple velvet robe or an orange soup tureen in the midst of family festivities.

"I like it, Daddy; I really do!" my sisters and I would chant, circling the disappointed Santa and his latest rejected bounty. But

Daddy would sit dismally the rest of the day in his worn recliner, planning, we figured, how to do better next year.

He was at his most vulnerable in the sweet-smelling part of a department store, slightly embarrassed among the earbobs and kid gloves and newest Vanity Fair Christmas colors. He would take us along for courage.

Some smiling saleslady with a little holiday corsage on her collar would tell Daddy that 999 out of 1,000 women would die for a coat with fur trim. He'd act like he'd found the Rosetta Stone of feminine wiles. He'd buy at least one of whatever was suggested and then trudge happily home, confident and giddy.

Until Christmas morning, when Mother would prove to be the one woman in 1,000 whom the salesgirl had predicted, the one woman who didn't like a touch of fur. Too much.

"I told you," she said for several years running, "that I need a new vacuum cleaner."

I wanted to string her up with a Hoover automatic recoiling extension cord.

The coat touched with elegance would go back to the store the day after Christmas, where some other woman would eventually find and buy it. Mother would have her sensible, all-weather coat dry-cleaned to wear another year.

The holiday he sent her roses was the worst. They were red. So was she. You can't send roses back to the store. The best you can do against their impractical impermanence is drop a couple of aspirin in the vase, which she did, fussing all the while.

I think back on the gifts I gave Mother—the modeling clay sculptures and pink ceramic ashtrays. She always went on about them and seemed immensely pleased. Why she couldn't extend that same thought-that-counts policy to my father I'll never know.

Eventually some of his gifts worked their way into her furnishing scheme, becoming fashionable after a decade like an old dress you keep long enough to recycle. There is a long-stemmed green candy dish in the living room now that once she thought abominable.

Even the rain lamp is there. None of the gifts got rave reviews on Christmas morning, though, when Daddy sat llike a boy expecting his first BB gun and waited for her to tear the expensive wrapping. There was the inevitable chorus of "Give it to me, if she doesn't like it," from the Loyal Sisters.

Then Daddy unwrapped his Old Spice, and another Christmas was history.

December 1985

A Family Day

We are, as usual, trying to arrange the holidays by telephone.

Four children and their two parents will be in four states and three time zones on Christmas. Christmas Day itself is definitely out.

Yet it seems only proper that we convene at some point during the season to exchange gifts and hugs, at least for old time's sake.

I stand armed with calendar and road map, trying to discover some empty day or common ground on which to gather.

"Can you come to my house the weekend before Christmas, maybe, and I'll get the folks here, too?"

The long distance hum seems a sneer. I do not really expect it to be this easy, do I?

My younger sister is a cashier in a Kentucky grocery store, and the Saturday before Christmas is when her work gets frantic. People shop for last-minute candied pineapple and shelled pecans, or nog to lift and toast that glorious day. She will don her bright orange uniform and work hard and late and not dare ask off, because she is, after all, just like her daddy.

My younger brother is off at college, doing his best to prove the bromide about youth being wasted on people like himself. He works 40 hours and extra hours and as an afterthought takes too many course hours.

Besides, he is in first love. And I envy but do not begrudge him that delicious dilemma of deciding between three, old-hat sisters who may or may not get together and a beautiful, eager coed named Moly. Molly should and will win.

Then there is the other sister, the doctor. Her schedule has more complications than a transplant patient. She will fly West for the holidays, because, somewhere along the way, she left her heart in San Francisco.

The folks, only at home at home, are tethered by cows and crops and cats and the hope that one of us, at least, might somehow make it to the farm during the holidays.

That leaves me. And I am busy. Busy promising more than I can deliver. I got so busy last week I completely forgot about an appointment with a man who wanted to talk to me on his birthday. It should be a felony to disappoint someone 103 by simply forgetting.

So there you have it, a family dizzy and divided, booked on early bird flights and hooked on careers.

And yet I remember when it was different. I remember three particular bedrooms and one bath and a half on Ware Hill Drive in suburbia. The sister who would become a doctor slept with me then and had incredibly cold feet.

She could, she said, "set" an infallible internal alarm by simply slapping her forehead a certain number of times. If we wanted to wake and check our Santa Claus haul at two a.m., she slapped her forehead twice. It seemed plausible to me; I thought she could do anything.

I remember setting that crazy alarm and putting our slipper-socks in take-off position next to the bed. She woke me at two a.m. I remember the Christmas my father spent half a night in the frigid utility room guarding the secret of a cocker spaniel. And the transition years when we would quickly exclaim over penny loafers and argyle sweaters and then spend the rest of the day playing with a younger sibling's toys.

Those Christmases were all, at the roots, remarkably and reassuringly similar. By mid-afternoon we always wanted to see how our friends had fared in the Santa Claus shuffle. We'd beg to travel a block or two to inventory somebody else's goods.

No, not today, my mother always said. Today belongs to the family.

December 1984

Fish Tales

My father told me lots of things time has proven true. He would sit late at night—a guru in an ageless Naugahyde recliner—smoking and philosophizing:

"When you are feeling sorry for yourself because you have no shoes, consider the man who has no feet."

"Don't judge a book by its cover."

"Don't advertise what you can't sell."

"Blood is thicker than water."

He would deliver each platitude as if he had invented it, with feeling and flourish.

My father was first a butcher, later a traveling man, always bringing us miniature bars of soap from motels in exotic ports like Dothan and Pell City. We thought he was the cats. He wore white shirts, always white shirts, and khaki pants, back when such pants had pockets big enough to hold a huge percale square of fresh handkerchief, a Buck knife and at least $52 in loose change.

He was a tall man, and big, or we thought so then, with dark brown hair and eyes the blue-green of Pensacola Sound.

Back when he was cutting meat, before OSHA and liability, he would come home now and then with a bloody and bandaged hand, the Purple Heart of a 60-hour work week. They stitched his thumb back on more times than I tied my shoes.

But finally he left the frigid confines of the meat market, began a 25-year series of "store openings," showing other, new market managers how to trim the fat from the fledgling operations. That job put him in a company car and took him away from us.

There were vacations, though. Glorious family events. Every summer he took his 14 days and rustry green tackle box and headed toward central Florida. There was a particular lake there—Lake Harris, a drop in the bucket of Florida lakes, some with wonderful names like Lake June-in-Winter—where we rented a cabin year afteer year.

Understand, this was long before Mickey Mouse and three trillion other international visitors discovered the lush middle of The

Vacation State. My father spent the entire two weeks fishing, while my mother chauffeured my sisters and me from one tourist stop to the next.

If I have ridden to the top of the Citrus Tower once, I have ridden to the top at least 32 times. I have seen the man ski barefoot at Cypress Gardens and listened to the chimes at Bok Tower until I could hear them reverberating in my sleep.

My father took each of his children fishing, one by one, on an appointed day, an outing we both dreaded and dreamed of. For fishing with my father was an adult privilege—serious business, not play. There was no laughing, singing, horseplay or other variety of fun in that little rented boat. We were not having fun, we were by-god fishing.

I remember sitting there, daybreak painting the edges of that still Florida pond, wondering just how long I could hold off asking for a Coca-Cola, a bathroom, a new worm. Wondering why I had fought with my siblings to be first to fish. Wondering if by now the rest of the tourists were milling happily about in the clouds at the tip-top of Citrus Tower.

It was always a trial, that fishing day. As much for him, I'm sure, as me. But I would go back to the cabin and brag about the fun we had had, the adventure of floating about in a boat about the size of a cereal bowl, the camaraderie of it all.

He would back up my story, forgetting the stalled outboard, my tangled line, hung hook, short attention span and general reluctance to touch anything that smelled remotely of wide-mouth bass.

We would fib together, my father and I, weaving glorious stories of lost fish that had Sam's Taxidermy written all over them. Father and daughter, we had landed one whopper of a big time.

Some day, when I'm rich and have time on my hands, I'll return to Lake Harris, if it's still there, and spend 14 days. I want to see if the days were really that long and hot, if daybreak still comes too early among the pines and palmettos. If oranges and grapefruit hang heavy from trees rooted in gray-black dust, if blood still is thicker than water.

June 1986

Pecan Money

Winter in South Georgia is a damp, flat cold that seeps in through the cracks in the wall about Thanksgiving and refuses to stir until late March. The whole world turns the gray of old wood and the spearmint green of winter rye, as if a prolonged cooling off period is necessary after the shriveling heat of a Georgia August.

My maternal grandmother made her Christmas money about this time every year, picking up pecans and selling them, a small crouched figure foraging the hard ground to buy gifts for 11 grandchildren who inevitably forgot to write thank-you notes.

I can see her now, a head-kerchief over her ears where the cold liked to settle, a mere sweater over the thin, all-season work dress. Sometimes, after a rain, she slipped my grandfather's rubber boots over her own shoes to walk through the mired barnyard and beyond, to the pasture. She had incredibly small feet, feet none of us inherited. And she had bright blue eyes, which appear in one diluted version or another throughout the faces of the entire family.

She could fill a burlap feed bag with amazing speed, perhaps thinking, with each nut deposited, "Another bolt of cloth, another spool of thread, another gift secured."

Or maybe she was thinking something else entirely.

Sometimes I think we only half knew her. After she got sick and wandered away to another time, somebody found an essay and letter she had long ago written and mailed to a radio announcer. The short essay was all about riding to town as a child beside her father in a buggy. She asked the radio man if he would, if he could, read it over the air. So far as I know, he never did.

She had stuck the essay, pencil on lined paper, in a book where she kept important newspaper clippings.

For when the One Great Scorer comes to write against your name, He marks—not that you won or lost—but how you played the game.

That was in the book. So was a torn and taped, torn and taped clipping of a Celestine Sibley column from *The Atlanta Constitution*. It was about mothers.

I wish I had a photograph of my grandmother in that pecan orchard, not an orchard really but several fruitful old trees plotted in the pasture just above the fish pond where one summer Pop found an alligator.

It is one of the ways I remember her best, stooped near to the flat ground that always had supported her and her loved ones. I wish I could bring the picture out whenever tempted to gripe about my own Christmas shopping.

The gifts she bought or made were never late, were never the wrong size, were never given in anticipation of what she might get in return. They were, in other words, true gifts. I cannot visit a shopping mall during the pre-Christmas season without thinking of the woman who never saw one. And I cannot help but think how little such a vast selection would have improved the gifts the pecans bought.

So far as I know, my grandmother wanted nothing in return but long, healthy lives for her children and grandchildren. She wanted them to get along and get together at holidays. And we did, so long as she was the glue that held the genealogical puzzle together. Now I have to stop and think hard just to place my cousins.

Cliff, who once wanted to be a disc jockey, became a preacher, they tell me.

Donna moved up to the state capital and has a new baby.

Marshall, who ran the rodeo circuit, now runs a ranch.

Pam, the pretty one, settled in her hometown.

None of us visit. Few of us ever phone or write. I'm as guilty as the next one. I might pass a cousin on the street and not realize it.

But there is a bond, I like to believe, that comes up from the south Georgia dirt and through the heart and strangles us if we move too far, too fast. It is a gift she gave us, whether we wanted it or not. It is a gift even pecan money could never buy.

November 1986

9 / Consent Of The Governed

Suicide Missions

CAMP LEJEUNE, NORTH CAROLINA. It was pay day and Friday at Camp Lejeune. Marines with weekend passes filled motels with thin walls. Young girls disguised as women came along.

There was a fight at the Thunderbird Inn and another in the parking lot of a topless dance club. Pawn shops blinked their promise, and watches and rings went for booze.

Their buddies were fighting in Grenada and digging out the dead in Beirut, but it was combat on Court Street for the leathernecks left behind.

The day before, Major General Alfred M. Gray had spoken. His plastic coffee cup matched his fatigues; both were colored in the olive and brown swirls of camouflage. The firecracker pops of small-arms practice punctuated his words.

"We are not going to forget this one. We will long remember this barbaric, terrorist attack just like we remember Guadalcanal, Tripoli, Belleau Wood, Khe Sanh. We'll remember this, too."

At Camp Lejeune, the land of the burr cut and the bereaved, Gray's word is final. He is the top Marine official on the East Coast outside of the Pentagon. His domain is 173 square miles of North Carolina shoreline—an area larger than the entire island of Grenada.

He was saying what generals say when their men are slaughtered: "We'll remember this." Reporters had been rounded up like heifers and bussed two blocks to hear him say it. The official word. For the record. Government issue.

Then he talked of young wives who now are young widows. And he called their "performance" quiet and magnificent. In knocking on doors to deliver death, he had failed to see "one instance of anger."

What did he tell them, these girl-brides with children on the way and underfoot and diapers on the spin cycle at the laundromat? Why, "You must explain that they are not alone spiritually, and they are not alone here."

That is the way generals talk. They talk of heroes and sacrifice and revenge. And the politicians award Purple Hearts to men who will never see them. And the wooden soldiers march back home, ready to go again and die for a cause as obscure as "protecting vital interests" or as obvious as re-electing a president.

The wives don't buy it, though. Nor do the mothers. And if they are quiet, it's only because they are used to being alone.

Kathleen Kirpatrick has been married three years. She is 19 years old and 7 months pregnant. She has one daughter already. Asked if she and her Marine husband Brian have lived at Camp Lejeune their entire three-year marriage, she scoffs and says, "I have. He's been gone one place or another."

Brian's coming back from Beirut, injured but alive. He's coming back to leave again.

It is a life of goodbyes, of staggeringly high divorce rates, cramped quarters and always new assignments. It is a life their men have chosen, and they accept. But you can bet your dress blues that Tripoli and Belleau Wood and Khe Sanh are not on the minds of these women whose husbands are dead or possibly dead in Beirut. They are not thinking about American honor or Lebanese peace.

They are thinking, instead, of their military men. Men still young enough to act foolish on Friday night. Boys so pumped full of high-minded words and marshalled by protocol. Boys who fight the wars of old men.

"These young wives seem to have a much deeper understanding of the 'why' of Lebanon than many of the people I've heard talk recently on television," the major general said. Maybe the general was right, on that point at least. If anyone has witnessed close-hand the unblinking devotion of a soldier to "duty," it has been his wife or mother. She has seen the exporting and exploiting of young men throughout history. She has watched him march off to places for a good reason or for no reason. And she has waited for him to come home.

Down on Court Street, a young Marine pays to have a needle shoot ink into his arm in the design of an American flag. It is that inexplicable desire to be branded as loyal and tough and true blue that makes the tatoo a part of the uniform. A salute of the skin. A bet and a dare. A better idea after beer or bourbon.

In Grenada they were fired at from resort hotels. In Lebanon unseen enemies loaded trucks with dynamite and blew them into eternity. The women absorbed the absurdity of it all with what Gray would describe as "quiet dignity."

And the boys kept carousing on Court Street and volunteering for suicide missions of their own.

November 1983

Senator Sam

MORGANTON, NORTH CAROLINA. The acre and a half he owns of this world is in the foothills of North Carolina, where the land begins a teasing rise toward the misted grandeur of the Blue Ridge Mountains. It is sturdy, unrelenting countryside, where the dirt's too rocky for farming and the people too proud not to try.

Sam J. Ervin, Jr. is home. His residential property includes the site where he was born and the adjacent lot he purchased.

Arthritis has made inflaming attacks on his hands and feet until he must walk with pain and a wooden stick. Crossing an airport corridor is almost too much for Ervin these days, so he stays here, where he was reared and where his father learned law from books, not universities.

Sam Ervin was an old man when he dropped homespun jewels from those pendulous jowls during the Watergate hearings ten years ago. Now he is ancient.

He will be 87 this month. "At least, that's what my arithmetic tells me." Illness and time have subtracted from his size—which seemed of Sydney Greenstreet proportions on a television screen—and his twisted fingers now fumble with a law book's pages. Yet his mind is as quick as a school boy's summer and his memory awesome.

On a humid day, Ervin tap-taps into his Morganton office at One Northsquare, a chrome-and-glass building that looks slightly out of kilter in a town still centered around tradition and a courthouse square. Ervin moved to the more fashionable complex in 1974 when he retired from the U.S. Senate, leaving an old office that was identified only by an Ervin bumper sticker from an ancient campaign. It seemed, somehow, to fit him better.

But it is in the new building that the old man, his face plain and rough as unbleached muslin, now holds court.

"If my lawyer friends will do the leg work, I'll sometimes prepare a brief and argue the constitutional questions of a case," he says. His expertise last year helped a team of defense lawyers save local Great Lakes Carbon from losing seven million dollars in a pollution suit.

Downstairs, his young grandson, Sam J. 'Jimmy' Ervin IV, has a law office. His son, Sam III, a judge with the U.S. Court of Appeals, also has a Morganton office. Secretaries are likely to snap at confused callers who don't know there are three Harvard-trained lawyers in tiny Morganton with the same name. "Who did you want now? The Judge, the young lawyer or Senator Sam?"

Many of them want Senator Sam, who got 1.5 million letters during the Watergate crisis. He kept records. About 65,000 of them supported President Nixon.

"You miserable wretch. You have forced the greatest president who ever lived from office." That's what one woman of thousands wrote.

"I wrote back to her. 'Apparently,' I said, 'I have higher regard for President Nixon than you do.'" Nixon's own taped voice told of his Watergate involvement, Ervin told her, "but obviously you believe he lied."

The man who introduced the Book of Galatians to Washington chic is plugging his own book these days, *Humor of a Country Lawyer.* He also wants a publisher for his autobiography. He hopes both will sell better than his Watergate account, *The Whole Truth.*

Reading from his new book of borrowed and original anecdotes, he looks a little like an itinerant preacher in a backwoods church. He licks his fingers to make the page-turning easier. He sputters and grunts and scratches at odd moments beneath his white, short-sleeved shirt. He finally warms up to his subject and then booms forth a story he made up about God wanting more power—equal status with the Supreme Court.

He scoffs a bit when asked how he feels about the troop of former White House boys who lecture and write on their past crimes for big audiences and big bucks. His white eyebrows make sharp arches in his lined and homely face.

"If people get pleasure out of hearing them, reading them, if they want to pay them money, then that's fine with me." Ervin speaks like a man who has not yet won this argument with himself.

"I think if I would suddenly go berserk, go out into the street with a gun and shoot down about five or ten people, there would be publishers down at the jailhouse by nightfall to approach me about writing a book about it."

It was ten years ago this month that Judge John Sirica ruled President Nixon must surrender subpoenaed tapes that would shed light on the darkest presidential scandal in American history.

"To say that the only thing different about Nixon from other politicians is he got caught is an absurdity. I challenge anyone to tell me anytime $100,000 of campaign money donated to elect a U.S. president ever has been used as hush money, to pay people to keep them from telling the truth about criminal offense.

"Oh, there have been isolated, individual incidents of corruption. But tell me another time the President of the United States was involved in an obstruction of justice. Even the ten Republicans who voted against the articles of impeachment felt compelled to denounce Nixon after they heard the tapes. They said the tragedy of Nixon's political death was that it was a self-inflicted wound."

Individuals have forgotten in ten years the lesson taught. But the nation as a whole, Sam Ervin believes, remembers.

He remembers. Dates, rulings, points of law. "That's on Page 195 of my book," he'll say of some obscure moment in the Watergate drama. He praises Ervin Committee members as having conducted the most nonpartisan hearings on the most political controversy aside from the Civil War in U.S. history. The only vote that broke down along party lines was one taken to decide whether to continue or disband the committee. The Democrats wanted to investigate contributions from the milk industry; Republicans wanted to stop.

He praises Republican Howard Baker for his interrogation ability and lauds the committee's chief counsel, Sam Dash. About himself? Television, he says, "can make a celebrity out of anybody real fast."

Ervin was the unlikely star of the hearings, a man 19 years into his 20-year Senate career, daring to quote such "corny" documents as the Constitution and the Bible in the direction of slick, sarcastic types like John Ehrlichman. Ervin had been known, if at all, for his fierce defense of individual liberties and constitutional arguments against civil rights legislation.

It was a burst of unsought fame good for the lecture circuit and an American Express commercial. A local Shrine Club named a unit in his honor, and the town held a "Sam Ervin Day." He was granted a dozen or more honorary degrees.

But now, mostly, Ervin is doing what he once told Mississippi oil man Fred LaRue, a repentant dirty trickster, that everyone must do. He is reaping what he sowed.

"Miss Margaret," his wife of 59 years, still is with him. She has been ill quite a bit lately. When he speaks of her it is in the soft, endearing terms of an old man for his helpmate. When Senator Sam proposed, the story goes, he was characteristically poetic and funny at the same time. He told her he would be faithful and love her if she would "strike oars across the deep" with him. She did. He has been.

They attend the First Presbyterian Church on West Union Street and enjoy their family. Here, where he once played sandlot ball and swam in North Carolina's unbelievably blue streams, he has come to rest.

There has never been, says Senator Sam, a problem with his constituency. "There's not too much difference in the fundamental principles of North Carolina people. I was born here. I lived here. We just don't disagree much about the fundamental things."

Now, with the passing of a decade, he has found time to think. He thinks right won over might. He thinks the nation survived. He thinks there are plenty of good, honest men in politics. He knows he's glad to be home.

September 1983

Food For Thought

WASHINGTON, D.C. The Escalope de Veau Sautée Francaise—veal scallops—is $7.95 here. No seconds.

For that price in the U.S. Senators' Dining Room, however, you get to watch Alan Cranston lunching with constituents two tables away and Russell Long with his grandchildren, just one table over. And if Democrats do nothing for your digestion, Paul Laxalt is over there to your far right, as is Paul Trible.

Spark Matsunaga of Hawaii keeps a standing table for any and all of the visitors from his state who want to lunch here. His is the big table in the center of the room, the only standing table and the only table with a standing bottle of soy sauce.

An old college friend of mine who now deftly defends a senator in press releases got me in, against his better judgment. "Don't wear bluejeans," he warned me. "It's formal."

And it was very nice. I had the low-cholesterol Breast of Chicken Estragon with parslied potatoes, green peas and tossed salad for $6.75. And a few, half-baked thoughts about our brand of democracy.

It's no wonder politicians turn pompous. For most of the year they rack about Washington in real style, riding up elevators marked for "Senators Only," eating in elegant surroundings where waiters refill iced tea glasses before the lemon wedges ever touch bottom.

Then, once or twice a year the politicians go "home" and stand around for inspection by the old courthouse groupies, who shake hands and act obsequious and send the leaders back to Washington with a "Give 'em hell, Senator," whether Congress is doing anything or not. It is not a routine that fosters humility. Or accountability.

But there is something fascinating about eating in the Senators' dining room, even if you prefer a hotdog at an Orioles' game to veal and anybody to a politician. I was plastering a rather tasteless pumpernickel muffin with butter when the enormity of it all hit me. It had something to do with Duckhead pants.

Russell Long—Democrat from Louisiana, a rather typical looking man, dressed like all the others in dark suit and white shirt—was talking to his grandson. Even a dessert cart away, it seemed to me the little boy was asking lots of questions, possibly about the lights underneath the clock. (The lights signal the senators as to when they need to drain their bean soup and get back to the chamber for a vote.)

The boy was wearing jogging shoes and khaki pants labeled with the mallard that is the Duckhead brand logo. He looked like a million other little boys, happy and inquisitive and as full of potential or disaster as any young child. What could be more normal, more garden-variety than Duckhead pants, for goodness sakes?

But this boy—I thought to myself while pushing around on my plate those big, round, awful green peas that need to cook at least four hours longer—is the great-grandson of Huey Long. He is related to a man who put roads through the Louisiana bayous and textbooks in the hands of sharecroppers. Who built a skyscraper for a state capitol and who inspired one of the best books ever written.

He is a direct descendant of one of the last southern politicians who was an individualist, a character, an entertainer. Someone you either loved or hated. A southern politician who stood out in a national crowd for something other than racist reasons.

The child has inherited power, I thought, and he can use it for good or evil or keep it sleeping close to his chest like his Grandfather Russell. But he will have it, as long as Longs rule Louisiana.

That's the fascination politicians hold for us, I guess. Not that Sam Nunn, over there, eats his salad any differently than we all do or dribbles any less asparagus down his tie. It's just that someday he may be vice president, which, for some reason, makes it interesting to watch him eat.

Besides, even an outsider lunching in the Senator's Dining Room will find the prices reasonable and the service excellent. Which is a lot more than we usually get from the senators.

August 1986

An Upbeat Agenda

JACKSON, MISSISSIPPI. They had the names of prep school soccer players—Trent and Webb and Thad.

They were Mississippi's top Republicans, gathered on a bunting-banked stage in the name of fund-raising and glad-handing and electing the first Mississippi governor from their party in over a century. President Reagan himself came to town.

Here, in the nation's poorest state, people paid $10 if they wanted to see their President. That price bought a yellow ticket, good for one seat rubbing the rafters of the Mississippi Coliseum. Below, partisans who forked over $25 or $200 got a much better view and a plate of catfish. Those 49 couples willing to spend $3,000 got to stand a cocktail napkin away from the President at a local restaurant.

It was a short, purposeful visit to Mississippi for Reagan. Air Force One jetted right over the recently-flooded Mississippi landscape without so much as a dip. There was no time allotted for a public appearance—save the Republican gala, which was not free. But for the precious few who paid, what a show.

Beneath an American flag big enough to cover Tunica County, Guy Hovis of Lawrence Welk fame gave his tonsils a real workout.

Tammy Wynette bussed all the boys on the stage and stood by her man of the hour, Ronald Reagan. And the President, looking fit and humble waving a miniature Mississippi flag, played his gilded audience the way Liberace plays a baby grand.

"You know, for many years, we—all of us—used the term that I think was created by some of the liberal bent: $50,000 annual income," Reagan said in that conversational, one-on- one tone of his.

"That was the dividing line between the working people and the wealthy—$50,000 a year. It's time we looked at that again and made some adjustments for inflation . . . ."

He really stood there and said that. One would think you'd have to be a numbskull to stand up in the middle of a Mississippi crowd and say, right out, that $50,000 a year no longer represents real wealth. In a state where $50,000 is eight times the average per capita income, you might get a few tomatoes thrown your way for dismissing half a hundred grand as paltry.

But Reagan's no numbskull; he was right on target in this room full of that new Southern breed, the Oxford-cloth Republican. There were many more navy blue blazers than blue collars in the Mississippi audience that cheered when Reagan redrew the prosperity line.

It's no accident that Mississippi hasn't had a Republican governor in modern history. Before the din of race, white Southern working people understood clearly the language of the Democratic Party. Workers weren't treated to political pep-talks about how they were being unfairly classified among the rich. Then as now, nobody was poorer than the South, and the Democratic Party was the poor man's party.

That is, it was until the heretofore inconsequential black man stood up and said, "Hey, ain't nobody poorer than me." Then began a mad scramble of realignment. Southern whites who had been the leading beneficiaries of federal relief programs sprouted a fiscal conscience and tumbled into the ranks of the Republicans, muttering about give-away programs and shiftless deadbeats.

Quite aware it takes more people to win an election than it does to play mixed doubles, Republicans gladly handed out the club tie to the gallused newcomers and taught them passwords like "conservative" and "creeping socialism" and "traditional values." An incongruous association was formed: the new Republicans, the silk-stockings and the rednecks, would pretend to the world and to themselves that their interest was one and the same. This entailed a rather vague manifesto that whatever is out there now is bad, and whatever they want for the future is good.

So here he was, the leader of the party of privilege, addressing the concerns of the very few Mississippi elite, propped up by the fears of those in the rafter seats, the damnable, cursed fear of the working white man of his working black brother. And white Southerners gladly followed their genteel new leaders, partners in a gentleman's agreement that the leadership may set its own agenda if it does so with utmost discrimination.

Beyond the parking lot of the Mississippi Coliseum, well after the presidential motorcade whizzed by on its way to the airport and home, a few picketers hoisted their hand-lettered signs into the muggy Jackson air.

"Segregate Forever," said one. "Ban Bussing," read another. "Integration Is Worse than the Flood," said another.

The picketers were throw-backs to another time, country cousins whose bare feet don't look right under the Republican table but who keep showing up anyway, an embarrassing reminder of the lineage of the proud, upbeat young party.

Really. Everyone knows Ronald Reagan Republicanism—like the seating arrangement in the Mississippi Coliseum—is based on economics, not race. And the rich people are all white? Well, golly gee, the Republicans are too open-minded to notice.

June 1983

Old Rivalry, New Rivals

They have nothing in common, Joe Kennedy and George Wallace Jr.

One is the product of the lush and sprawling estate called Hickory Hill in Virginia.

The other grew up roaming the capitol rotunda on Goat Hill in Montgomery.

Joe is Kennedy-handsome and Kennedy-smooth, the heir to charity tennis tournaments and Cape Cod summer homes. He heads a public service conglomerate, whatever that is, with a sales projection of $1 billion.

George, Jr., on the other hand, looks remarkably like his dark and brooding father, intense but certainly not handsome. He toured for a while on the country music circuit with Alabama's other famous junior—Hank Williams—but found the musician's life "too tentative." Now he works as "development director," whatever that is, for a state college.

No, the two have nothing much in common. Except they are the same age—33. They are Democrats. They have names bigger than themselves. They are both the sons of men shot while campaigning to become president.

And they are busy proving, lest we forget, just how strong is the lure of power and politics.

George Wallace, Jr. and Joe Kennedy both are campaigning in 1986 for their first public office. Kennedy for Tip O'Neill's congressional seat, Wallace to become Alabama state treasurer. Joe Kennedy became front-runner in his race immediately upon announcing.

Two months ago we would not have been able to pick him from a family photograph of the prolific Kennedy clan. But suddenly, after going public and political, Joe Kennedy is hot. The endless, inevitable Kennedy comparisons already have started.

He puts his left hand in and out of the side pocket of his suit jacket just like his uncle Jack, People magazine observed. And: "He walked into the bitter New England night without an overcoat."

The nation, no doubt, is ready for a fresh Kennedy face to satisfy, if nothing else, its pulp appetite. Preferably a face on a head not bloated by drugs or hung in scandal. Handsome, wholesome Joe Kennedy is a natural.

George Wallace, Jr. is not really a junior at all. He is George Wallace III. But Alabama voters would never concede that Governor George Wallace is not the original article. So the son has always been called George, Jr., or, even earlier, Little George.

Four years ago, when a weak and pain-tortured Wallace was contemplating a run for his fourth gubernatorial term, a veteran Alabama lawmaker explained why. "George Wallace is not a rich man. He wants to leave his son something. And that something will have to be the state."

Now nobody with the name "Kennedy" or "Wallace" interested in politics would be content forever with a mere congressional post or a treasurer's title would he?

If I wore a bowtie and wrote for *The Washington Post*, I might be tempted to predict something like this: Kennedy might eventually "inherit" Uncle Ted's Senate seat; Wallace the Alabama statehouse.

So, conceivably, by the year 1996 or perhaps 2000, the two young men might covet the same prize—the Democratic Party nomination for president.

And the one problem neither one will have—the son of rich Boston gentry, or the son of a welterweight boxer and a dimestore clerk—is name recognition.

January 1986

A Dead Woman Or A Live Boy

BATON ROUGE, LOUISIANA. They say the only man Edwin Edwards envies or fears has been dead now for 50 years.

Back when the Louisiana backwoods were filled with just two kinds of men—Longs and anti-Longs—Edwards' sharecropper father was anti-Long. Edwards inherited the dislike for Huey Pierce Long, or so they say.

When the light intended to shine perpetually on Long's statehouse statue was snuffed in the energy-conscious 1970's, a lot of folks thought it was then-Governor Edwards' way of dimming the megawatt memory of the Kingfish. Actually, it was just a conservation measure ordered by someone else.

The Edwin Edwards of 1984 seems cowed by no man—living or dead. He is the new Louisiana legend, a virile, outspoken populist who likes to gamble, hunt elk and flirt. This cocky Cajun, who paid for his college textbooks by picking cotton, is about to become Louisiana's governor for a third term, something nobody else has ever done—including the omnipotent Huey Long or his brother Earl.

What's more, he swamped incumbent Gov. Dave Treen, that sensible but inaccessible Republican who many found plain boring. Edwards hopped into the Beechcraft twin-engine he flew himself, kissed every Louisiana lady he could flush from the swamps and rubbed out the hapless Treen like just another mosquito.

"To lose this election, I'd have to be caught in bed with a dead woman or a live boy," bragged Edwards shortly before taking last October's election with 63 percent of the vote. That's the kind of big talk he does and then backs up with accomplishment. That's the kind of talk his admirers relish.

"Oh, sure, I said it," Edwards admits, shrugging. He holds court in a transition office on the outskirts of Baton Rouge, a temporary quarters heavy with Louisiana State Police guards. "I said it on a day I was over-exuberant about my chances, and I didn't think about being quoted."

The 56-year-old lawyer—who speaks bluntly, whether in English or French—also predicted at one point during his race that "Treen couldn't win if I died tomorrow." It was a brutal evaluation his opponent might have liked to put to the test.

This week Edwards is leading a high-stepping delegation to Paris and Monte Carlo, an organized orgy of food, fashion and fun designed to erase the last of his $13 million campaign debt. About 500 supporters are paying $10,000 a person for tickets, and legislators and reporters are bumming a ride at reduced rates. Two jets full of politicians and the oil-and-money men who keep state government lubed winged their way to Europe yesterday, to ready for a black-tie dinner at Versailles, a cocktail party at the Eiffel Tower and a special mass at Notre Dame Cathedral.

"The largest single fund-raiser before this raised $2.8 million and that was Ronald Reagan's," Edwards says. He looked as if he could hear the heralds trumpeting his arrival at Versailles already.

During the trip, Edwards plans to meet with the king of Belgium, the mayor of Paris and the head of Renault Corporation, fitting company for Louisiana's Prince of Personality. He will also give audience to the gambling tables of Monte Carlo.

To call Edwards cocky is to call rain wet. He is a manikin for Godchaux's, with alligator shoes, checked coat and open shirt. He shampoos his head with silver polish and curls his chest hair. Or so it seems.

He manages, with a paradoxical ease, to preach numerous weekends at Pentecostal church services yet keep his reputation as lady-killer intact.

"Now you know you have more money than that," he once chided a reluctant tither whose meager check he tore in half before a whole congregation.

Edwards may just be the first Louisiana politician to step beyond the long Long shadow and establish himself in the region's colorful tradition. He keeps a clean, clear desk. He's an almost compulsive handwasher. He answers reporters' phone calls himself, usually within 15 minutes after they're made. He does not smoke. He never drinks anything stronger than soft drinks, to which he's addicted.

Edwards claims he won't do anything that would harm his youthful body or hurt someone else. From all reports, that creed permits gambling, which he loves, and loving women, on which he gambles.

"When he dies, he's going to leave his body to Charlie's Angels," one Capitol wag said during an Edwards roast. "He's so slick, he could sell carbon paper to Xerox."

Edwards says he'd love to be president or vice president—"I belong in the executive, not the legislative, branch."—but "I'm not sure the country's ready for this accent." Others say his image as a womanizer and gambler is what the country's not ready for. Playboy plays better in St. John the Baptist Parish than in Peoria.

Louisiana voters don't expect entertainment from their politicians, he says, "but they sure appreciate it. Politicians tend to take themselves too seriously. I've never done that."

For high-roller Edwards, politics always has been a sure bet. He's 15 for 15 now.

His first race was won in 1954, a seat on the hometown Crowley City Council. Then he won a state Senate seat. Soon he went to the U.S. House and in 1972 became Louisiana's first Cajun governor.

That was about the time oil prices skyrocketed. At Edwards' urging, the Legislature changed the state's severance tax on oil to a percentage of the per-barrel price rather than a flat fee per barrel. Soon the state had more money than bayous and Edwards' political stock went as high as Exxon.

Not that he didn't roll the ammunition and hand it to the enemy. There were numerous near-scandals and investigations. His wife, Elaine, took $10,000 from Korean businessman Tongsun Park and neglected, he said for three years, to tell him about it.

Edwards was thick with the company head who administered a tax-sheltered investment program for state employees and then mysteriously disappeared. And the Legislature passed a bill that let Edwards collect nearly $40,000 a year in retirement pay after his first two terms. His personal worth rose by $285,000 to $750,000 during his first stint as governor.

Government was for sale under Edwards, opponents charged.

And last but certainly not least, there were those persistent rumors that he liked the ladies. One Baton Rouge radio station parodied the popular song "Bette Davis Eyes": He's got "Edwin Edward's Eyes," the new version said.

Nothing seemed to hurt him. People loved his style. While Treen served four years to make another Edwards term legal, the flamboyant ex-governor cut an album of Cajun jokes and songs.

"I was doing a survey of the favorite movies of prominent people last year," says Baton Rouge Morning Advocate film critic David Foil. He called Edwards' office and relayed his question to a press aide.

Within minutes, Edwards himself was on the phone, nominating *E.T.* as his favorite. "He said it made him cry and reminded him he was human."

On the other hand, Governor Treen sent Foil a message he hadn't had time to see any movies during the year. The press aide said she thought he'd watched part of *Kramer vs. Kramer* on television.

Edwards has appointed several women and blacks—and black women—to high-level Cabinet posts. He claims he won't accept any salary until more jobs are found for Louisiana's 200,000 unemployed.

"People joked that he found the only female black doctor in the state to head the welfare department," a Capital reporter says. That's the kind of move that got him 80 percent of the black vote last go-round.

Edwards hedges all bets. "I have many friends for the ERA," he says. "I have many other friends against the ERA. I always stand with my friends."

There is a first lady, beautifully dark Elaine. She is cool to the idea of a third term, insiders say, preferring to concentrate her time and energy on her own dressmaking business. She scoffed at the European extravaganza. What fine restaurant would serve 500? That's what she reportedly asked about the trip's announced itinerary to visit ten of Paris' finest restaurants. She may be one of the few somebodies who's anybody not to make the trip.

"My father was a strict Presbyterian, very intelligent with an absolute moral code," says Edwards. "My mother was a Catholic who loved other people and who was always sympathetic. I think I got the best traits of both parents."

He inherited his modesty from Louis the 14th.

January 1984

A Mississippi Moderate

JACKSON, MISSISSIPPI. I suppose he'd come looking for the New South. He was a young, aggressive producer for the PBS show "Wall Street Week," stopping on his way to a hiking trip in Arkansas to "experience" election night in Mississippi. It was his first trip South.

I'd seen it before. He was just another stranger with an excited, quizzical gleam in his eye, looking like a teenager about to sip a forbidden beer. He was ready to sample this sinister region where kudzu and Faulkner-freaks used to grow, the place that has emerged from the shadow of cotton rows and lynchings into a Bright New Day.

He had come, unwittingly, to the loser's camp.

He had read all about former Mississippi Governor William Winter, that unpretentious and scholarly veteran of this state's political wars. He had read how this "popular" Democratic ex-governor was challenging the Republican incumbent for a U.S. Senate seat. He knew Senator Thad Cochran was well-liked, too, the kind of guy you'd pick for your golf foursome.

But Winter had given this bottom-rung state public kindergartens and education reform. Winter had focused national attention on the fact Mississippi was finally doing something about its forgotten and uneducated sons and daughters. And surely the New Southerners, the children of sharecroppers who had beat their bare-footed pasts to reshape their region, would remember. This new breed would today reward one who had worked to give them a way to topple their own destiny. Wouldn't they?

He did not know the New South is a myth, an apparition, possibly just Ted Turner. There is no New South, just new federal laws. And time is teaching us how to get around them.

We in the South are not joining the rest of the nation; the rest of the nation is joining us, in our smallness and petty prejudice and selfish motive.

School desegregation made black Southerners rejoice; they thought they had made a sizable gain, and for the first time would attend good, well-supported schools. But then the whites deserted the public schools and interest in them waned.

Blacks thought equal housing legislation meant they now could live in decent neighborhoods, with paved streets and curbs and gutters. But white flight began, and the ghettos just got new addresses.

Blacks thought they had a political party, the Democratic one, where joining fair-minded people of all races they could achieve progress through the ballot. So whites left the Democratic Party and began voting Republican.

That's the New South and the same old pattern. And that, not Thad Cochran, is what beat William Winter.

Winter had had the audacity to point out that 59 out of 100 high school students in his state still dropped out before finishing, that some children never went to school at all and that Mississippi was the last state in the union without public kindergartens. And he had the political savvy to do something about it.

Winter had invited artists and writers to the Governor's Mansion, had—by virtue of his own, thoughtful posture—given the state a start at a new image.

He seemed genuinely dedicated to public service. He could be in a room for 30 minutes before you ever noticed him, so modest and low-key was William Winter. But he had a moderate past and a progressive record, two things white Mississippi voters evidently could not forgive. He was indicted along the backroads as an intellectual or liberal, or—depending on how far back you go on the backroads—a nigger-lover.

This state is concerned about its image. The smart young producer knew that. Why, Mississippi just spent all kind of money to buy a pavilion at a World's Fair to show the world how things have changed, didn't it?

There's less substance to that change than meat on a soup bone if William Winter is retired from Mississippi public life at age 61.

The night fell heavy. The never-close race ended in a Democratic loss. But the guest still was pleasantly surprised, marveling at all the smart, sophisticated folk he'd found in Mississippi. He noted the number of educators present. We stood there, where most gaiety was forced, waiting to hear from Winter. Waiting to hear what we already knew.

There we were, not quite a room full, losers all.

December 1984

Two Buddies

TUSCALOOSA, ALABAMA. The man looked like a cross between Father Time and a television wrestler. He had a long beard and shoulder-length hair, both the color of stained porcelain. He wore blue jeans hitched to hop puddles. His socks matched the yellow-white color of his beard.

John Verdi wanted to see John Glenn. So did all the others at the small airport.

Finally, the chartered airplane landed. It looked too rusty and primitive to be carrying a real-live astronaut, but it was. Glenn stepped off jauntily with his wife. She wore a red dress and a button that said, "Hi, I'm Annie Glenn." She looked as tired as a politician's promises, but she smiled. She looked like an Annie.

Glenn spoke to the press. He shook the hands of all the would-be delegates. Then he saw John Verdi.

There was a smile of recognition, or maybe wonder, and a handshake. Then Glenn called Annie over to speak to Verdi.

There they stood, the pug-nosed, All-American John Glenn and this Santa Claus in work clothes. Just two Marine buddies talking after all these years.

Verdi, a New York native, served with Glenn in Korea in 1953. He flew 131 missions, several of them with Glenn, before retiring to California. When the West Coast got "too expensive, too crowded," Verdi moved to Alabama. All the hair seemed natural enough response to 26 years in the Marine Corps. "Everybody just goes his own way," is how Verdi explained it.

So the man who was a cinch to win the Secret Service's vote for most suspicious-looking man in a crowd won a brief, personalized moment with the candidate instead. Glenn should have more such moments.

It added a little drama, personality to the Glenn campaign. It's hard to believe, but this side could use it. Consider, for a moment, the candidate. The Smithsonian stores the cramped, tin can that Glenn rode around the earth and into the history books. It is a tiny thing; just looking at it gives you claustrophobic tremors. A normal-sized person would spend most of his time inside just trying not to bite his knees.

Yet here is a man who allowed himself to be strapped inside and hurled through several polluted layers into the black whole of space. And here is the man who made it back from orbit and emerged with a boyish grin. He also made it back from a losing senatorial race, which requires probably as much courage.

Prize-winning author Tom Wolfe and Hollywood haven't hurt Glenn, either. They painted the man as the most conscientious and patriotic of all the Mercury astronauts. Glenn was the one who'd say, "Now, fellows, let's remember ourselves," when someone was tempted to launch a little devilment.

And he has that familiar, likeable face. An Eisenhower on an ice cream binge. And Glenn is a family man in the tradition of Ward Cleaver. His patriotic credentials are impeccable. He has been ticker-taped to Kansas and back. He's the kind of American you'd want on a postage stamp.

His ideas are well-thought-out and very mainstream. His records within the party and within the Senate are as solid as his military record.

Intelligent. Combat veteran. Venerated hero. Middle of the road. Straight as an arrow. It would be hard to create a composite president more complete that John Glenn.

Yet Glenn the candidate is sputtering like a dud bottle rocket. He lacks charisma, and he lacks a proper organization. Simply, these two things are about all that matter in the made-for-TV marathon that today's presidential election has become.

They are the right stuff. There is no other stuff. Without them, not even Hollywood can help you.

May 1984

Alabama's Absentee Landlord

Alabama without George C. Wallace? I can't imagine it.

For almost all of the 25 years I lived in Alabama, he was in the statehouse and on our minds. His likeness was posted on the rest stops, junior colleges, roads and bridges—bas-relief reminders of who was in charge.

They say in just two of his four terms as governor, taxpayers paid for $505,000 worth of photographic work of Wallace. That's a lot of thick eyebrow and jutting chin, however you slice it.

Yes, we knew him well.

We knew he played high school quarterback at Clio, using his ample brains to protect his scant 98 pounds. And that he won bantamweight boxing bouts against much larger opponents. And to earn money as a young man he inoculated dogs in his home county of Barbour.

We knew, too, even as youngsters, that our future was linked somehow with his terrific ambition.

I stood with classmates on January 14, 1963, as Wallace took the oath of office. We were out of school, because inaugurations were deemed educational.

Wallace vowed that day to do away with drinking in the governor's mansion, to create more industrial jobs, to help the struggling small farmer. Then he made his more famous promise: "I draw the line in the dust and toss the gauntlet before the feet of tyranny . . . segregation now, segregation tomorrow, segregation forever."

He became, at that very instant, more than the governor of one of the nation's poorer states. He became the embodiment of resistance and a political celebrity. He gave a prevalent attitude a proper name.

Wallace would become additional things. He would become master of parry on Sunday morning news panel shows, slugging it out verbally with Lawrence Spivak or Frank McGee. He would become Alabama's absentee landlord, dropping in ever so often at Montgomery just to tell us how well he was playing in Milwaukee.

It was not unlike being married to a traveling salesman. We assumed, I supposed, it was his job to "Stand up for Alabama" in remote and misguided Boston and Baltimore.

He would become adept at fashioning his speeches for the audience he faced when touring the nation for a vote. This one for Harvard: "Let us look at the 1954 school case, Brown vs. Topeka . . . It did not, I assure you . . . spring instantly into existence full-grown and ready for action equipped with injunctive process, preferred appeal, set bayonets and all its accouterments like Botticelli would have us believe Venus came to the shores of Greece, full-grown and full-blown on the breath of Boreas."

He became comfortable conferring with everyone from Chiang Kai-shek to Aldo Moro. We never held him to specific promises for bettering our impoverished state; we simply figured he had bigger fish to fry.

We never put him out of office. Ever. Instead, we watched and cheered as he made the governorship a launching pad for national politics or anachronistic—and, yes, cruel— causes. We watched later as he used the same high office for a kind of emotional therapy, an expensive way to heal wounds.

Wallace took himself out in the end. He tearfully dismissed himself from the lives of Alabamians, saying ill health would not allow a bid for a fifth term as governor, a bid he had considered.

He had changed on the race issue. I believe that.

Some would argue that change was politically expedient, nothing more. Others believe he saw the light while on his back in a Maryland parking lot.

I have no good reason to doubt the transformation of George Corley Wallace and no way of knowing how it came about. I am glad for him, if he now knows the truth.

There are those, though, in Alabama and across the nation who have not changed. They cling to the false notion that all men are not created equal, that a man born by chance to a certain race is inherently inferior.

Wallace was the rallying point at a time when they needed true leadership, not a refuge. The continuing harm of their hatred is a heavy mantle around George Wallace's weak shoulders. As long as they can borrow from the lively wit and authority that was George Wallace, as long as they can quote him to foster hate, the governor must be accountable as the author of a shameful chapter in American history.

Those are the wounds—not the holes from five crummy bullets—that will follow George Wallace to his grave.

April 1986

10 / My Back Pages

One Long Weekend

Aretha was on the turntable. Still, after all these years, begging for just a little respect.

A fine fire had burned down to one glowing nub. The wind was howling enough to make the inside seem real cozy. A couple of old friends from college days just happened to be in the neighborhood. Their Ethiopian residence is only halfway around the world, after all.

They may live in Addis Ababa, but those two looked quite at home sprawled out on my floor in Tennessee. There were four of us, recalling our college days in Alabama and loudly debating the merits of dry versus wet barbecue.

Two couples normally separated by 11,500 miles, picking up a decade-old friendship, as if we had last parted only last night.

How do you start? Seen any good movies lately? When the four people in question live in the Third World and Counce, Tennessee, chances are the answer to that one is a brief, resounding, unanimous, "No."

Whatever happened to . . . ? That gets us going.

Jerry Ray remains in Washington, using creative prose to make some senator look good. Lauren and Fran have a new baby girl. Jim Killian has a few more scars from close encounters with asphalt; he still won't give up that motorcycle.

David Housel surprised himself and finally got married. Paul Ellen stayed in Auburn, and weren't we all tempted?

People dropped from our lives over the years like courses from a difficult schedule are remembered, one by one. College tends to cement relationships. Not unlike war. You remember a face from a foxhole or biology class.

Not that we had it rough. Nick said it all in *The Big Chill*: "Nobody ever had a cushier birth than we did."

Amen.

We were blissfully unaware that businesses sometimes fail and marriages, too. And bliss usually is ignorance. When classes ended forever, we assumed one long weekend followed. It didn't.

Most of us cope. Some of us thrive. We work in foreign embassies or southern factories. We work at marriages and rearing children and trying to remember it is stuff we didn't invent, that all of this has gone on before.

Tonight it is good to look back, for a change, instead of forward. Old times, like a favorite sweater from the trunk, don't quite fit. But they feel warm and good.

The 1960's didn't get to Auburn until the early 1970's. We wonder if the '80's have made it there yet.

What do they play now as the last song at frat dances? Used to be Joe Cocker's "You Are So Beautiful." We probably were, beautiful that is, tanned to a turn, in finery from the Polly-Tek, with as strong a grasp on youth as we'd ever have.

It's easy to feel beautiful at such times. It's easy to believe words sung in your ear.

The fire died. Aretha took a break. It was only ten o'clock when we decided to call it a night. The travelers were tired. I had this to write.

Besides, none of us were as young as we used to be.

November 1985

Someone To Buy For

From the mouths of babes come mostly indistinguishable sounds.

Jack Branston, for instance, a 19-month-old son of a reporter and a nurse, calls his rocking horse "fotchi" for no good reason. The parents do not correct him. Instead, they now, too call all horses "fotchis."

"Daddy's a fotchi. Want to ride the fotchi?" implores the father, falling to his hands and knees. Jack ignores the poor man.

It is a strange power children hold over parents. Adults only pretend to be in control. The children hold the reins and apply the spur.

I can remember when this household had dignity. When the books were all in their place on the shelves and pillows were carefully fluffed and tossed at neat angles onto the couch. It seemed only half as alive.

Now there is a battery-operated, palomino fotchi in the dining room, which accelerates from trot to canter in six seconds and even whinnies if you ride it hard enough. There are dump trucks and rubber balls and other baby accouterments.

There are photographs of the child with his red hair and cherub cheeks, moments preserved forever by silver emulsion and Sears.

Jack himself, all 35 and one-half inches of him, is sprawled out across a tangle of blankets in the middle of the living room floor. He has slipped out of his Osh-Kosh overalls into something more comfortable—the limelight.

And we, the adults, sit impatiently waiting for a naked baby boy to do something funny, watching him as we might David Letterman on late-night TV.

Jack obliges, slapping both of his hands upside his chubby cheeks and crying, "Ohhh, noooo."

"I could have had a V-8," both parents finish, expertly taking their cue.

They have seen this routine before. Then we all laugh gleefully, the sure signal for an encore.

You've come a long way, babies, from being seen but not heard.

Today's baby-boomer babies rule their parents' world. They are the unsilent screen stars of a million VCRs, the hub of households once organized, now mesmerized.

If the boomers were pampered, now they Pamper, with every imaginable child-rearing tool Madison Avenue can give birth to. Those yuppies who love to buy now have someone to buy for.

The children of the most educated generation ever to inhabit the U.S. of A. send mere tots to school, teach them to dance before they walk and work at keeping them physically fit before they can become any other way. Babies are even ranked in size percentiles now, in case you did not know.

Physically precocious Jack—measured on the scale for two-year-olds—is in the 90th percentile for weight and is off the charts in height. According to the pediatric prognosticators, Jack's 35-plus inches should translate into a full-grown height of seven feet, six inches.

So be nice to him now.

March 1986

Kangaroo Swan Song

George Schweitzer is a young, affable CBS executive who gave me any number of reasons I should not be sad Captain Kangaroo is finished, at least on his network, after a 30-year run. He sounded just a tad defensive.

"The Captain is happy," said Schweitzer. "So why should you be sad? He asked to sell his show somewhere else, to try and find a weekday slot on the Public Broadcasting System. CBS agreed. He'll be doing another show for CBS and will remain a consultant for children's programming.

"This is not the sad story of someone walking off, used up, into a sunset," Schweitzer insisted. "If this were a thing about ratings or profit, the show would have ended in 1964. This will free Bob Keeshan (the Captain), who is a genius, to do other things."

Maybe.

It's still hard to be cheerful thinking about Mister Moose being put out to pasture, or Bunny Rabbit roaming the streets and foraging for carrots while Captain Kangaroo seeks a new home. When the Captain leaves CBS, an era that has wound down slowly, like Grandfather Clock, officially will end.

The show is not just another dinosaur, too slow-paced and awkward to race against today's sleeker models of children's programming. The Captain made it more.

He was the largely unacknowledged link between several generations of young people, who might not now peacefully coexist but for a common heritage, courtesy of the Captain. Since 1955, his quiet musings have lulled future Peaceniks, Hippies, Yuppies and Preppies. Those who dull their brains with drugs and those who build their bodies with Nautilus all at some time in their childhood indulged in Captain Kangaroo. It was a constant, a pillow to clutch in the troubled night called adolescence.

You watched Captain Kangaroo like you believed in Santa Claus—until you were far too old to admit doing so.

If my mother had seen a man on the street that looked like the Captain—his walrus mustache twitching, those thick sideburns spilling from beneath his cap—she would have clutched me into her wide skirts and picked up her pace to a trot. On the screen of our black and white RCA, however, he was a trusted friend, an early morning babysitter and teacher, as much a part of breakfast as milk.

The Captain, I'm sure, inspired the leisure suit, but we won't hold that against him.

The Captain lasted, probably because he was never pounded into our consciousness like PacMan or Victoria Principal. Every now and then he'd show up on a lunch box or pencil case, but for the most part he was a homebody content to stay in his own little hour.

His departure may have nothing to do with ratings, but Schweitzer just happens to have a few numbers handy.

CBS, according to Schweitzer, is to be commended for "supporting" Captain Kangaroo 30 years. "The show lost audience since it first went on the air in '55," he said. Early weekday television time slots became important to adults who wanted to hear, not read, their news. Reruns of the Flintstones and Scooby-Doo and all manner of stuff began beating the Captain eight to one when they competed, Schweitzer claimed. Sometimes the show wouldn't even show up in the ratings at all.

"The end of Captain Kangaroo is not something negative, necessarily," Schweitzer said. "It just means that times have changed and forms and styles have changed. The standards which that show set will stay with us."

If Keeshan finds a PBS slot, he'll be able to keep the Captain Kangaroo identity. CBS agreed to that. On the new network show, CBS Storybook, Bob Keeshan will play himself, without the uniform. There may even be a prime-time special commemorating Captain Kangaroo's 30 years, though Schweitzer said no final decision has been made about that.

The show known for its rather old-fashioned, gentle approach actually pioneered several television techniques, including use of color videotape and the slow-motion disk. While other shows were mainlining on action, the Captain forced his viewers to use their imagination through music and stories. Maybe it was too much work.

There haven't been that many inquiries about the Captain and his plans, according to Schweitzer. Everybody's too busy playing Donkey Kong and watching Scooby-Doo to ask.

May 1984

As Time Goes By

MEMPHIS. When I sit in the lobby of the Peabody Hotel, I always wish I were prettier.

Prettier and richer and all the superficial things that are not supposed to matter when you have good health and three squares daily and people who will love you even when you have grown old and are forced to wear June Allyson's adult diapers.

It's just that I want to do justice to the grand old hotel, which is one of the few places in this world that lives up to advance billing. After all, you might meet Somebody in the lobby of the Peabody. You might strike a big land deal over a black marble tabletop and lean back smugly in your plush chair to sip a brandy on it.

Or, you might feel moved to appear quite suddenly on the mezzanine, a vision in black lace, dramatic as a love triangle against the soft background of coral walls and purple piano music.

Perhaps even Philip Marlowe might happen by, a bit wrinkled by Peabody standards but devilishly handsome just the same in his dark suit and rain-splattered fedora.

Philip—that's one "L"—would sit beyond the bar, cleanly out of the way of all duck traffic, contemptuously studying the rich old men who are only a watch fob away from leaving all this grandeur. Imagine the conversation you might have with Marlowe:

"You are private detective Philip Marlowe, aren't you?"

"I was three gimlets ago. Now I'm Sir Lancelot or King Arthur, I forget which. Care for a gimlet, M'Lady?"

The people in the Peabody never seem in a typical hurry. They have no dental appointment at two o'clock, no Cub Scouts waiting curbside. They are draped in the slow graciousness of another age, another mentality. They take parsimonious sips of their drinks and fight to light one another's cigarettes as time—and more time—goes by.

Newspapers and grand old hotels are two things dying in cities all over the United States. They are both, I suppose, getting too expensive to run. Last week I stood waiting for a train—not just any train, but the City of New Orleans—in a shabby depot in Jackson, Mississippi. (Ah, depots and trains, two more bits of vanishing civilization.)

Across the street from that ramshackle depot stands the skeleton of the King Edward Hotel, once as full of life as a worm farm. Mississippi lawmakers used to get off the train, check into the King Edward and begin the session in what was affectionately and accurately called the Legislature's Third House.

Now, a gray grocery sack flops about on a gray sidewalk in front of the gray King Edward, its windows boarded up and its lights doused. Pigeons drop succinct commentary on the situation. It will be a real race to see if the wrecking ball or a tramp's fire completes the city's condemnation of the King Edward.

If I had the money, I'd buy that old hotel. I'd hire the best doormen and bellhops and masseurs. I'd find me a big Italian foutain, a la the Peabody, and staff it with the most ostentatious mallards money could buy. I'd hire old men wearing creased hats to loiter about the lobby reading newspapers with lots of inky print and few photographs.

And then, if I had any money left, I'd go sit beyond the bar, order a gimlet and wait for Marlowe.

April 1986

Mixed Marriages

They are busy in the family workshop, scheming and snipping and trying to trim this Christmas into an economical one.

She is artistic, creative, born to haunt craft shops; he has an aptitude for computer science and figures. Their hobbies share space in the workroom, which is presently strewn with paints, paper and promise for the holiday season.

Just now she is adding the meticulous details that make her ceramics special, the miniscule polka dots on a bears bowtie or the whiskers on a thumb-sized cat. It is a painstaking process.

He is fiddling with his home computer, which holds somewhere in its bytes and bowels the drawing of a snowman.

"What color should I paint the eyes?" she asks, rhetorically, holding a fragile greenwear bear closer to the light. Perhaps yellow, yes, yellow button eyes for the bear.

"Watch this," says he, not really expecting her to. He is making it snow on the visual display screen where the phantom snowman now appears. Little digital flakes are falling in a herky-jerky computer motion.

He can even flip through his computer color menu and change the blizzard to cobalt blue or electric orange. The keyboard artist is becoming power-crazy as he orders the snowman through a series of electronic paces.

So here they sit, creating, she with an acrylic brush and he with a cursor. Who says mixed marriages don't work?

Technology has gotten way ahead of her, but he can't wait to get up in the morning to see what IBM hath wrought. That's the way the world's dividing. We are either computer-friendly or computer-hateful.

Some of us not only have to ask, "May I use your telephone?" we have to ask, "How do I use your telephone?" For the first time in our lives, we find ourselves feeling like turn-of-the-century Americans must have felt when electricity lit up the parlor and the horseless carriage began transforming us into the horseless society.

Others are hooked on technology, Apple addicts who can't make a major purchase anymore without agonizing over the possibility tomorrow's car/telephone/computer model will offer options not dreamed of today.

There is a legitimate concern abroad in the land that our country is becoming bilingual, but the second language isn't Spanish. It is Fortran. The border can exist within a single household.

Take this one. She thinks a function is a church supper. He thinks his memory requires alkaline batteries.

How will they rear their children? To which school of thought should they send them?

But a snowman. To that, even she can relate. Her interest, finally, is piqued. "Can you make some copies of that little snowman picture for me?" she asks her husband.

He is happy she asked. Frantically, almost, he begins switching modes and menus, throwing switches and punching buttons, a harried, hopeful scientist prepared to deliver his creation.

The quiet tapdance of ink onto paper begins. She watches for once, expectant. He anticipates a small victory.

It is not to be. This will not be the night she converts to the Church of High Tech. The snowman in the print-out is black, and her interest is lost. It looks, she says, like a little coalman with snowball eyes.

He can reverse the print-out, of course, correcting the picture that now looks like a photographic negative of a snowman. These things take time. Besides, who cares if the snowman is black—the point is, the computer drew it.

But it's too late. She's dismissed his handiwork as just another computer fraud and gone back to painting bears. And dreaming of a white Christmas.

November 1984

Holding Pattern

The only music came from one of the stuffed animals littering the living floor. Brahms Lullaby tinkled from the fuzzy belly of the bear.

The rest of the pastel menagerie silently eavesdropped, glass eyes intent, as the two of us took turns reducing our lives into tight, hurried bits of conversation.

She is a photojournalist, a good one, employed for several years now by a major southern daily. She also is the mother of two little girls, one age two and the other two months. She is holding the infant, not her Nikon, as we talk.

At 35, Beverly Crawford is a little tired. She has ridden the crest of the baby boom, and now she'd just like to fall back, float belly-up, while somebody else tests the depths. She is sick to death of being in the first wave ashore.

When Beverly switched from reporting to photography, an editor warned her she was "flying by the seat of her pants." Newspaper photography, at least in her region, was very much a male domain. For a while she was the only female news photographer in her state.

Now, a decade later and one state over, she's still wrestling with the thorny problems peculiar to people who have the dual capacity to give life and participate in it. And she's still making her living shooting pictures.

There are several women photographers at her present newspaper, but it's Beverly who's blazed the trail through the darkroom. She was the first to work seven and eight months into pregnancy. She was the first to have a baby and return to work.

Until lately, work was what her life was about. For almost 15 years she struggled to be the best at what she does. She came damn near close. Even a serious automobile accident didn't stop her. She shot from crutches for months.

The woman is anything but a whiner. She has the stamina of a bull elephant. Yet here she sits, admitting she found with her first child that breast-feeding and shooting Atlanta Braves' baseball don't mix, beginning a self-imposed, year-long hiatus from the job she loves. She is happy with her choice to become a mother, but only resigned to the prospect of professional limitations that choice seems to entail.

Women who willingly waited late to marry, postponed families and shunned domesticity, suddenly are staring in the face of biological reality like Cinderella looked at the clock. They see pumpkins in their immediate futures.

Many of them, like Beverly, have paid their dues and then some and are just beginning to realize a little success. Now they face a lose-lose situation.

Among the many inroads women have made during the last couple of decades is the right to become a company "man." Company men come in two sexes now, with the same fierce determination to put the job before marriage, family and everything else.

Now there are company men/women, as well as company men men. They are not always the most talented, or even the hardest-working, but they look the spit-shined part. And they are, by golly, always there.

The Census Bureau tells us half of all wives now are in the labor force, up ten percentage points from 1972. Most of the wives are there, like the husbands, for economic reasons. We are no longer in the antique shop phase of wives' employment.

Beverly, like everyone else, lacks solutions. She feels solutions are likely to show themselves when the men who manage banks and brokerages and photo departments find they share not only a bed but a bank account with a pregnant wife. The workplace that was for so long, for such practical reasons, structured along military lines, may be forced to make "radical" adjustments to meet the needs of modern reality.

Meanwhile, the choice is clear-cut and at hand for a lot of women.

Beverly is convinced she'll remain in a holding pattern over the second or third tier of her profession. The photogrpahs hanging on the walls insist this shouldn't be so. Their quality reflects past sacrifice. They show the huge investment she made in her professional future.

Another of her masterpieces pads in from the rubber pool in the backyard, asking for Kool-Aid. Beverly is committed, right now, to a family portrait.

June 1984

The Worst Bogeyman

Dr. Seuss should write a companion piece to "How the Grinch Stole Christmas" and call it "Why the Grown-ups Stole Halloween."

When did adults start dressing in elaborate costumes for Halloween, anyway? I wondered about that the other day while shopping for my Smurf tail in Wal-Mart. Standing next to a man halfway into his pirate get-up and well into his forties, I took quick inventory of those frantically searching the Halloween bins for disguises. All of us were far past the respectable age for trick-or-treating.

There was a pregnant lady trying on a clown's rainbow wig. A woman with gray hair broke a seal to sample the glitter hairspray. And I was busy squeezing the extra lively racketballs to see if the malleability was correct for a blue bob tail.

When I was a child, a Halloween getup was no big deal. Each year I was either a hobo or a princess, depending on my mood. I had a green, taffeta, hand-me-down evening gown that made me a princess. A pair of pedal pushers and a kerchief on a stick made me a tramp. It took me all of 30 minutes to get ready.

Certainly my parents never, ever donned costumes. Most of my friends' parents never did either.

Cindy Austin's father once put a bedsheet over his head and hid behind the hedges to scare us. The penumbra from a yellow porch light made his ghost work and caused us to litter the lawn with caramel balls. But that one episode hardly counts as full-scale adult participation.

This year it took me a week to look adequately silly for one night. I made Sam Walton, already the richest man in America, even richer by shopping three of his Wal-Marts in three states in a hunt for standard-issue, Smurf-blue tights and a floppy white toboggan. Still, all in all, my Smurfette was not half as convincing as my haphazard hobo. Actually, I looked a little like a blue hobo with a tail.

Halloween has never been the same anyway since adults and local governments started monkeying with the calendar. They will move Halloween about at the drop of a hat—for the weather, a school carnival, a ballgame, or simply a more convenient day of the week.

Trick-or-treating, of course, has gone the guilty way of most 1950's fun. One researcher says razor blades in apples were mostly urban myths, never documented. But a stainless steel fear is lodged permanently in Halloween. We scared ourselves silly with ghost stories about modern sickos.

So parents who do not accompany their children on Halloween rounds must now deal with the worst bogeyman of them all—The Adult Conscience, a lump somewhere between the heart and the throat, shaped by parental love and Donahue.

I guess I'm down on Halloween because the holiday, more than any other, points up a loss of innocence in this, the U.S.A. What used to be a child's first ritual of independence —solo trick-or-treating—is now virtually extinct. Well-lit parties and carnivals have taken the place of running pell-mell through the dark, dressed as someone, anyone more exciting than just a fifth grade child with skinned knees trying to remember that Montpelier is the capital of Vermont.

When I scurried off in my green taffeta carrying a Winn-Dixie bag, my parents might have worried about me crossing against the light. But they didn't worry about the neighbors putting poison in the popcorn. And they didn't worry about real freaks hiding in the bushes, waiting to grab me. I suppose they did not have to.

I felt a little guilty, painting my face blue for a party. As adults, we Baby Boomers are getting to enjoy Halloween again, this time with costume parties and store-bought disguises. We should be answering the door instead.

October 1986

Relentless Understanding

I have always liked the poem Phyllis McGinley wrote about mothers:
A mother's hardest to forgive.
Life is the fruit she longs to hand you,
Ripe on a plate. And while you live,
Relentlessly she understands you.
Mothers understand us, but certainly we never understand them. It was a popular cocktail-hour sport a few years back to try. To dissect all mother-daughter relationships, to stretch the coiled umbilical cord to impossible lengths in the hopeless pursuit of "understanding" your mother, yourself.

Nobody came close.

It seemed important to tackle, though, since everyone knows daughters wear their mothers' souls just inside their own, perishable skin. We wanted to know what—or rather who— we were bound to become.

That fad has faded. Replaced, I think, by the fitness craze that reassuringly let us wear the disguise of ourselves a little longer. We did not have to look like our mothers by the time we reached 30, thus our burning desire to know her cooled. We managed, though, in the brief time mothers were being speared and dipped into the conversational fondue, to divide them into nifty subcategories— domineering, permissive, abusive, jealous or saintly.

Our mothers were at the seat of all our problems, our disappointments, the ones guilty of shielding us too much or not at all, who told us wrong about men or told us nothing at all, who smothered us with love or withheld it cruelly. We were pre-destined to failure or crime because of them; we married abusive men because of them; we were doomed to repeat mistakes because of them.

It got old fast, though, picking on mothers. Such unAmerican sport, really. And the Mother's Day messages remained basically the same, dwelling on the selfless hands and lined faces of mothers who ask no earthly rewards. "You helped me over life's highest hills, showed me the handholes and shared in my thrills." Corny but indefatigable.

Mothers, as usual, won, selfless hands down. For the relationship between a mother and her offspring goes deeper than the resentment of the 1960's or the self-help books of the 1970's. It is a mystical and unquenchable thing, this bond between the one who gives a life and the one who has to live it.

No matter how old we get, we want mother's approval. No matter how much we disdain her values, we require that she not disdain, totally, ours. No matter how much we blame her for something, we forgive her everything.

May

The Sun Also Sets

I added a screened porch to my house this summer. A house without one is a face with no nose.

Carpenters came on the hottest days of the year, in the 106-degree swelter, stacked cement blocks and pulled taut the screening and battened the boards and somehow created the porch from a gap in the trees.

I was firm. The screen door had to be the old-fashioned wooden kind with a propensity for slamming and hinges that squeak. What fool, anyway, decided doors should be screened but not heard?

Now my days are just means to an end. Day's end. I live only for sitting on my porch, enjoying the woods and the sky and wondering whatever happened to the ritual of watching twilight. Remember?

Our grandparents did it quite faithfully. They left the hot kitchen after an early supper and headed straight to the porch. It was only a small slice between full days, an intermezzo. But twilight passed on a porch must have held the therapeutic value of a half dozen trips to a psychiatrist. Certainly there were fewer psychiatrists and more porches.

Nobody necessarily talked. Sometimes a sunset over a cornfield can beg utter silence. But there was the comforting sense of having a time to talk if you needed to. It usually was wistful language, slanted to better times. In the future tense. Always the future.

"Gonna plant more corn next year."

"Reckon the children will be here this time next week."

"Gonna trade that blame truck soon."

It was a conversational waltz, smooth and rhythmic. But that was then.

My parents traded the full-blown porch for a stoop in suburbia. Nobody could sit on a stoop. Salesmen stood there, looking uncomfortable, vacuum cleaners or Fuller brushes or six months of Sports Illustrated in tow, waiting for us, the occupants, to remember where we put the living room and find the front door.

Nobody monitored twilight. On the cusp of every evening we listened to Chet Huntley and David Brinkley talk about what had happened, not what would, their gray torsos imprisoned in the mesmerizing little box that sat squarely on our den floor.

And from there we watched the Wednesday Night Fights or Wagon Train or Hit Parade, and the sun had to sink without us. If something happened in the sky, we learned about it from the tube.

We timed our talk, restricting it to commercials only. We arranged the furniture around the box, built whole rooms around it. We even bought trays to eat upon so we wouldn't miss a thing. And if company came, the rule was firm. The sound from the box must go; the picture could stay. We reluctantly obeyed.

I am grown, one of the first generation of tube babies. I can make my own decisions now: TV or not TV?

My life, until lately, has had pitifully few evenings allotted to outdoor introspection, porch philosophizing; more are spent inside, in the Red Roof Inn, en route here and yon. Twilight, for me and for most of us, is frittered away on the phone, on the couch, on the road.

You might say I have nothing much to worry about when I confess to you my fear. But suppose there was a sunset nobody watched — no sailor or painter or old man on a porch. No couple honeymooning on Pensacola Sound, no Trenton housewife on the Boardwalk. Suppose the sun set one day, completely unattended.

Would the world come to an end? And would we notice if it did?

August 1986

The Last Real Man?

A *People* magazine cover recently featured actor James Garner in four-color splendor, dubbing him "The Last Real Man in America." That revelation must have given the Russians heart.

Since John Wayne, Gable and Bogart all have gone to that great dressing room in the sky, only James Garner stands between us and Wimpdom. Or that's what the magazine decided.

It is that kind of thinking that keeps Ronald Reagan so popular. Actors playing Real Men seem to be the best America can do.

A writer followed Garner all around a golf course, watching closely his manly swing and determined stride. I'm not sure what 18 holes punched in a Bel Air pasture have to do with manhood, but the *People* person was impressed.

You must, of course, consider the source. *People* makes *Reader's Digest* look like a scholarly journal. To grace the cover you should sing in a New Wave band, have a baby out of wedlock or manage a wrestler. Or all of the above.

People never fools around with qualifying phrases. Mel Gibson is the sexiest man in the world. Garner is the only real man in America. Period.

What bothers me is that people take *People* seriously. And the line between what's real and what's make-believe becomes more and more smudged. We really care about our paper doll celebrities, whose lives are about as one-dimensional as a Hollywood set. If Brooke Shields says she's a virgin, we want to know. If Cher is sleeping with somebody new, tell us. If Miss America free-lanced, declare a crisis.

In one poll, Cyndi Lauper and Sally Field showed up among the most admired women in America. Now I like the Flying Nun, and I can even tolerate Cyndi Lauper, but neither one is an Eleanor Roosevelt or a Sacajawea, for heaven's sake.

There are no celebrated woodsmen like Daniel Boone, or scouts like Lewis and Clark. Astronauts, our modern explorers, have become so commom-place we're more interested in the esperimental rats on a shuttle flight than the pilot.

Corporate laboratories have replaced Benjamin Franklin flying his kite. Sports heroes are still around, but it is getting harder and harder to choose one who prefers playing ball to snorting coke.

Our heroes now are multimillionaire rock stars who "endure" an all-night recording session to finance food for Ethiopia, then pat themselves on the back so hard it hurts to watch.

Even our President is an actor-turned-politician whose on-camera experience and by-golly demeanor won him the most important job in the world.

We have no interest in the dull and plodding thinkers who oil the machinery and wind the reels and run the projectors that keep the show going. Our Watergate criminals and vice presidential candidates and Olympic medalists alike make television commercials and get rich because, whatever else they may be, they are celebrities.

We don't associate them with a crime or a political party or a sport. We link them with a consumer product. Celebrity is about all that counts in America these days.

James Garner is a good entertainer. I wouldn't put him in a class with Bogie, but he beats Boy George. He is, for all I know, a good man.

Surely, though, we are not reduced to one, last "real" man in Amercia, especially one who makes his living in the realm of the unreal. There have to be some real men out there who perform without makeup.

June 1985

Taken For A Ride

I remember best the ritual of her shoes. Every morning Mrs. Watkins came to school wearing stiletto high heels, black with pointed toes.

Then, right after Authority crackled its morning announcements over the intercom, she carefully took the heels off, put them in the shoe box beneath her desk and slipped into something more comfortable.

For the rest of the day she scuffed around in collapsible slippers, those cardboard-soled flats that were sold wadded up in little plastic cylinders and came in gold lamé and three sizes: small, medium and large.

She was then free to relentlessly drill us, the fourth graders, on Indian chiefs Tecumseh and Pushamataha, the river systems of South America and our multiplication tables, all without fear of varicose veins.

She was a comely woman, with or without her stilts, and great playground debate raged over who was the prettiest, Mrs. Watkins or the other young teacher, the one with black hair and azure eyes, down the hall. Somehow it was to your credit, as a pupil, if your teacher was not one of the dowdier, older models, but a student-teacher-once-removed, a sapling still willing to make field trips to Kilby Prison and the Montgomery pickle factory.

Funny the things we remember about teachers. Not their first names. We never knew them. Once we had a teacher who married midyear and changed her surname; it taxed our undimpled brains to begin calling her something different. Finally, she gave it up. At home she was the proud, new Mrs. John Smith. At school she languished in the suspended state of spinsterhood.

I had not thought of Mrs. Watkins and her shoes in a long time. We remember our teachers, but only in the most irrelevant ways.

For one year and one year only they are probably the most important adults in our lives; then we trudge off to a new grade and a new routine. And a new teacher.

They are fixtures—some of them sturdy, some of them decorative. We cannot connect them, one by one, with the bits of knowledge we manage to store away.

Who first placed China on the map of our brains? Who first put the decimal point in long division?

We remember their charactrers, really, their personal habits and attitudes, whether or not they infected the classroom with enthusiasm or terror. We remember the ritual of their shoes.

I have thought a lot more about my ex-teachers, lately, since Christa McAuliffe did not return from her field trip. I have tried to decide which of them might have signed up eager to go on a shuttle ride, which ones would have loved the idea and which ones would have seen it as so much extra playground duty.

Mrs. Gleason would have gone. She taught fifth grade at Dalraida Elementary. She had guts and a gift for science. She looked a little like Imogene Coca.

Mostly I associate her with another tragedy. She nervously walked the desk rows in her plain shirtwaist and loafers while the intercom voice told us innocence was past tense. John Kennedy had been shot.

"You might want to listen," she said in her understated way. "This is history."

Most of my teachers, like most of the rest of us laymen, have a blind faith in higher technology. Teachers, especially, not only represent but believe in authority. Stage a nationwide, president-conceived, universally endorsed contest to pick a teacher for space, and the assumption would be that the ride was round-trip.

Almost no one mentions it, but it began as a Ronald Reagan campaign stunt. I doubt if the risks were emphasized. I doubt if NASA said, as John Glenn has, that it was close to a miracle no one had died in space flight before. The shuttle ride was presented as an extended airplane ride, not a death-defying feat requiring special heroics. You would not have had 30,000-plus teachers vying for the honor of dying.

A friend put it well. If Mario Andretti died in a race-related car crash, it would be sad. But somehow not as tragic as a family doing 50, killed on the highway.

The astronauts knew well the risks. Perhaps the teacher thought the release forms she signed were mere formality.

She had chosen to go. But she had not chosen to die.

February 1986

Is This The Right Spot?

Buying a washing machine really put me through the wringer. There was something so responsible, so adult, so permanent about that pivotal purchase made 12 years ago, I counted it among the crises of my sheltered life.

Every time the blasted machine changed cycles I went into a blue funk. I sighed at Spin and cried for lost youth on Rinse.

Never again would I be able to toss everything I owned into a Volkswagen bug and move on down the road. Now I would require a U-Haul.

Never again would I, the voluntary ward of an elastic womb, tote my dirty clothes home in a soiled pillowcase to Mother. I would hereafter scrub my own collars.

My carefree days of laughter and landromats were done forever. I would never live on a communal farm and spend my days plaiting daisy wreaths. Or join the Peace Corps. Or sail around the world in a homemade yacht. I would never bike cross-country or blow from youth hostel to youth hostel in the south of France. The die was cast.

I owned a washing machine.

I was at the sober point in life where you put away childish things and commence to sorting the colors and whites. I was, irretrievably and undeniably, in the market for Major Appliances.

Now, I'm buying a house, and it's move over Randall P. McMurphy. Don't get me wrong. I want a home. Just as I really, down deep, wanted a washing machine. There is nothing romantic about dirty underwear.

I want to wrap a mortgage around me and feel bound to one spot on this lovely earth. But, is this the right spot? Is this the right earth?

This house commits me the way no $100, used washing machine ever could. Not even a U-Haul can move me now. I am attached to one place, for better or worse, for richer or (not much) poorer. There is no divorce court that can erase my wobbly signature or absolve a debt due every month till the year 2005.

All of a sudden, a "career" that's been hit-and-miss had better be a job that lasts. A soul full of wanderlust had better be satisfied with a year's subscription to National Geographic.

The free spirit who once vowed never to have a life defined by a subdivision tract suddenly is about to leap willingly into the dark abyss of ballooning Fannie Mae discount points.

I find myself doing an absurd about-face, romanticizing the very things about renting that made me want to own a home. Ah, the freedom of knowing it's somebody else's roof leaking. Oh, the joys of an "attentive" landlord.

Suddenly I have more questions than there are wallpaper patterns; they roust me in the middle of the night when I have the fewest answers.

If I have to sell, will the paper mill to the north or the nuclear power plant to the south matter to the next buyers?

What if Rupert Murdoch buys the newspaper I work for?

Suppose termites start a day camp in the walls?

I think I'll be OK if we can get to the part where you hang the brass doorknocker and paint the kitchen yellow. The fun part. My idea of home decorating is fluffing the throw pillows.

Right now, though, I'm too busy figuring out how to move the washing machine from a rented house to a mortgaged one without upsetting its fragile innards. And I'm feeling old. Very old.

Once again, I'm spooked by a change in cycles.

May 1985

11 / In God's Name

No Wasted Motions

TUSCARAWAS COUNTY, OHIO. They hauled Joe Yoder's left leg home from the hospital in a black buggy and buried it in his corn field.

Two of Joe's Amish neighbors sat in the back of the buggy and held the cloth-wrapped package length-wise, taking care not to jostle the limb and cause Joe additional pain. When they reached the white farm house and massive new barn and 100 rolling acres, the men buried the lost leg in accordance with strict custom.

With the Amish, all custom is strict. The pain, they believed, would continue until the leg was properly interred.

Just weeks after last year's mowing accident that so dearly cost him, Joe was back in the fields working, which— along with some heavy-duty worshipping—is just about all the Amish do. I met Joe not long ago at milking time.

He was playing a duet with wife Mary on a holstein's pliable teats, grinning from beneath one of those wide-brimmed, stump-topped straw hats the Amish wear. Every now and then the cow's tail would swipe his face, but Joe never missed a beat. His hands kept coaxing, and the milk kept coming.

When he and Mary would finish a cow, the wife would kick away the wooden milking stools, hand Joe his crutches, and the two would carry a bucket between them to the cooling tank. No wasted motions.

Joe is a thin man with rimless spectacles, bad teeth and a sparse beard. He wears dark, utilitarian, flyless pants, the left leg of them tied off below his thigh. His shirt is buttonless, and the black shoe on his right foot is made-to-order ugly.

When you ask a question about Amish lifestyle that Joe does not want to answer, he grins widely and says, "I don't know if I can possibly explain that to you." All those of us not Amish are English, at least to the Amish. We are the iconoclastic, the suspect, the damned.

Mary, Joe's wife by parental arrangement, is pretty, despite herself. She wears a dark kerchief to hide her hair, a stark cape and skirt with shoes ordered from the same Ugly Book as her husband's.

But she cannot subdue her Natalie Wood eyes, try as she might, and when Mary pokes her oval face around the cow's rear end, it is, for all the world, a fair dairy maid's countenance right out of a storybook.

Mary's little brother Menno, 10, stands watching, his blond curls and flat-crowned hat giving him a Little Boy Blue look. He does not speak; talk is not permitted with the English around. When Mary and Joe speak to him, they use German. Menno just stares, and now and again blinks his big, sad eyes.

"He has been working since he was little," says Mary, proudly, in her somewhat halting English. "It makes him strong."

The Yoders married at age 21—again, custom—and moved to this farmhouse a little more than a year ago. They promptly ripped the plumbing from an upstairs shower—now they carry water in buckets to use in the empty stall—and stripped the place of electricity. Later, Mary will ask her English neighbor if she knows anyone who might use an almost new, double, stainless steel kitchen sink.

"I hate for nobody not to use it," she says. "It is a very good one."

But not for her. For her, no mechanized vehicles or televisions or running water. No inside toilets or frivolous furniture or frothy curtains. Even the oilcloth on Mary's kitchen table is black. Bright, light colors are forbidden.

Mary is friendly to me, a stranger. She displays her quilt pieces and entreats me to try some root beer made at home from yeast and Petersheim Root Beer Extract. She gives her neighbor fresh asparagus, for which the Amish have no taste.

I follow her to the chicken coop, curious about every move the anachronistic lady makes. "Coop" really is not the word for it, though; its construction is too neat, too solid.

"It is dirty in here," she warns us. "City people sometimes don't like the dirt. They think the whole farm is dirty. But I like it here, you know, with the chickens and cows and the hard work. I stay real busy. And that is good."

She diligently brushes the dust from her dark blouse, which is fastened not with buttons but straight pins. She wipes her feet on a burlap rug and eventually returns to the house, where the decommissioned sink and a working pump and wood-fired stove share floorspace.

"Stay and talk," she says. "The chores are done, and we are not too busy. We enjoy talking to people."

The next day will come early for these stern and simple people, religiously bent on denying time's passage. But they offer it to me now. And I, the English, who seem never to have enough time, take it.

Not long after I leave, the house grows completely dark. Dark before the sky around it. The quiet Yoder farm is a repository for things that once were. Including work at dawn.

May 1986

Praise The Largess

FORT MILL, SOUTH CAROLINA. To borrow a line from the comic strip *Pogo,* "What hath got wrought?"

Pontius Pilate is washing his hands on one street corner, Allie Alligator frolicking on the next. You can visit Billy Graham's childhood home or drop a wad on Saks Fifth Avenue seconds at the Goodie Barn.

But never mind the incongruities at the 2,300-acre compound. Heritage USA claims more than four million pilgrims visited the park just south of Charlotte, North Carolina, last year. They are still arriving in RV's and great numbers. And this is the off-season.

They are coming in search of something the brochures describe as "the godly, noble traditions that have helped make our nation and its families great."

Exactly what those traditions are is never put into so many words. But apparently television evangelists Jim and Tammy Bakker believe they can personally imbue a glittering shopping mall, a giant water park and a grand hotel with Christian virtue.

The Bakkers—founders of the PTL Club—are to Heritage USA what Mickey and Minnie Mouse are to worlds by Disney. Their images keep cropping up—on record albums and books, post cards, T-shirts and buttons. They are the faces most prominent at Heritage USA.

You can shop Der Bakkers Bakkery, right beside The Heavenly Fudge Shoppe, with its chocolate crosses and scripture cookies. Or you can visit Tammy Bakker's Cosmetics, a logical franchise if ever there was one.

People who believe the Bakker philosophy—God meant Christians to prosper—might do better to stay away from Main Street. If Noah's Toy Shoppe doesn't get you, a real estate representative will. From PTL "partnerships" to costly crystal penguins, there are a million ways to be parted from your money.

The park mixes metaphors and monuments, making the campground mildly confusing. If you come to worship, there are a lot of distractions. If you come to play, there are better places. Disney World it is not. Too many seams show at Heritage USA to make it an extraordinary theme park. The animated angels mining jewels are bush-league and arthritic compared to, say, the Hall of Presidents.

But—and this seems to be the clue to the park's success—visitors come both to worship and play. And this may be the only place you can take a break from shopping to watch girls dancing to psalms. Or expect the "Best Sellers" in the book store all to be religious books. Or buy paintings of Jesus dressed in contemporary, Miami Vice-style pants, ministering to a wino in an alley.

The Bakkers run a taut park. No smoking. No drinking. Employees must sign a statement of faith in Jesus Christ. They ask that you "please be considerate in bathing attire" at the 52-foot water slide and the world's largest wave pool.

In fact, there is a militancy about the ministry here at Heritage USA, judging by the bumper stickers in the parking lot. "Kissing A Smoker Is Like Licking An Ashtray." Or, "God Said It. I Believe It. That Settles It."

There is the implication that Christians need an exclusive mall, an exclusive water slide and, for that matter, exclusive subdivisions. That way there'll be no accidental elbow-rubbing with the heathens.

People come here to vacation or live, depending on the level of their enthusiasm and bank account. You can buy a condominium, a house or time shares in a vacation cabin. You can dine, receive counseling (financial or spiritual) almost any time of the day or night, watch the filming of "The Jim and Tammy TV Ministry Hour" in the television studio or witness a high-tech passion play. And you can buy, buy, buy to your heart's content. All in a Christian atmosphere, far from the secular crowd.

There is planned a $1.5 billion—that is BILLION dollar—golf course and condominium project for sale by parcel. The 130 condos at each hole will be done up in different international designs. There will be a total of 15,000 housing units at this site alone.

Other scheduled construction includes a $100 million, 30,000-seat auditorium based on the design of London's 19th century Crystal Palace. Not to mention a ten-story Wendy's restaurant shaped like a sand castle.

All this free enterprise, of course, is accomplished in the name of heaven, with a special discount for all PTL members who pay $15 a month to keep the "ministry" alive. There is even a VISA card that allows a percentage of every purchase the cardholder makes anywhere to be siphoned off for the "ministry." Sort of a no-sin tax.

All ages can buy into the plan. A Thanksgiving essay contest for children under 12 costs two dollars to enter.

Nearby Fort Mill seems largely untouched by all the Christian commerce inside the gates of Heritage USA. Inside, television's *Love Boat* captain Gavin MacLeod recently led off a Christmas parade that ended with the lighting of the park with over 1.5 million bulbs.

Outside, you can buy beer or smokes at a convenience store across the street. A roadside vendor is hawking socks. Tubular socks. Secular socks. Four dollars a dozen.

November 1986

Thin Walls, Late Calls

A motel room can be a depressing place. I once overheard a marriage end through the thin walls of a cheap motel in Dothan, Alabama. It wasn't a pretty sound.

The fight, believe it or not, was over an illicit Foosball game. She had been staying out late, playing too much table soccer with someone else, he said. Her side of it was muted somewhat by weeping.

Must not have been much of a marriage to begin with.

They try to dress motel rooms up a little more these days — bonbons on the pillows, pictures on the walls. Lately, the paintings are sometimes of something other than bullfighters.

Let's face it. Motel rooms are where you stay between places, or between jobs. Sometimes between marriages. They are cubical, color-coordinated substitutes for real bedrooms, and the only warmth comes from a vent in the wall.

I was in Memphis the other night, staying so close to the interstate I could almost feel the 18-wheelers rumbling by. Next to the bed, where the Gideon Bible is supposed to be, the motel placed a card: "Chaplain on Call. The Minister whose name appears below has volunteered to assist you as personal needs arise."

The Rev. Bobby Moore and his phone number were listed. I didn't call that night. My only personal need was sleep. But the more I thought about the service, the more convinced I became it was good.

"I had no idea how much time it would take or what it might entail when I agreed to do it," Mr. Moore said when I finally called him a few days later. "But it sounded to me like a good ministry, a real opportunity."

So for the past five years, often in the wee, purple hours between days, Mr. Moore has been talking with distraught motel guests who need help making it through the night. He meets them in the motel restaurant—"I don't go to the rooms. It doesn't seem like a good idea."—and listens.

Problems usually fall into two broad categories: money or love. The number of highway pilgrims calling averages one a night.

"People who have financial needs often call. They make it this far and need money for food, lodging or gasoline. We help those we can."

And the other category?

"Marital problems. Maybe a man's left home and come this far. Maybe he lives here in Memphis and had to have someplace to stay."

The stories from the motel rooms are all different. Yet somehow all the same. Mr. Moore listens and even hears. He is, at least, a face across the table where there would not be one otherwise.

"A time or two the crisis has been severe. So severe there was a potential for suicide." A few times, someone he counseled behind the Elvis Presley post card rack has gone home for a reconciliation.

"A few write letters. Not many, but it doesn't take many to make it worthwhile."

He's the chaplain on call when strangers check in, and the safety bolt cannot lock trouble out.

August 1985

A Crock Pot In Every Corner

CHURCH HILL, MISSISSIPPI. You wouldn't notice Nico Kuyt in an airport crowd. The Hare Krishna devotee and founder of The Old South Society of Vedic Life is thin, of average height and wearing ordinary clothes. He has a full head of hair.

He also has a wife, four children, some goats and a Volvo.

Last month he bought two plantations—one of them an imposing, three-story mansion called "The Cedars" and previously owned by movie actor George Hamilton. The other house, "Lagonia," is the oldest house in this old community, circa 1790.

Some in the secluded hamlet—20 miles north of Natchez, population 100—don't trust Kuyt. Because people here have never seen anyone just like Nico Kuyt.

He doesn't believe in killing cows or watching television. He doesn't drink or do drugs. He spends at least two hours each day chanting these words: "Hare Krsna, Hare Krsna. Krsna Krsna, Hare Hare. Hare Rama, Hare Rama. Rama Rama. Hare Hare."

He wants to fill the inside of The Cedars with Hare Krishna dioramas, elaborate, three-dimensional scenes stocked with hand-crafted dolls. Where tourists normally expect antique sideboards and canopy beds, he plans to have illustrations about reincarnation and the "conscious self."

And, if all that is not confusing enough, new neighbor Nico has lawyers coming at him from all directions, some trying to collect debts from bad personal investments.

Nico Kuyt and sedate Church Hill are not a marriage made in heaven. They may not even have a honeymoon. This place puts a premium on tradition. The antebellum church on the hill—yes, the one that inspired the name—is the oldest Episcopal church in Mississippi.

Hollywood has taken advantage of the picturesque setting, for everything from Civil War epics to a Tom Sawyer film. Nearby Springfield Plantation is where Andrew Jackson got married. Church Hill is storybook South—Scarlett and Mammy and the boys. It wouldn't surprise you to see the wooden-headed Ashley Wilkes strolling down a shaded driveway.

Instead, you get Nico Kuyt, cagey about his troubled finances and with his own plan for Church Hill.

"Homes like this do have an aesthetic value," says Kuyt, indicating the empty, white, Greek Revival mansion behind him. "It's a little plain for my tastes. Personally, I like Vedic architecture better." (The Vedas are the ancient books of Hinduism, basis for his religion.)

And though Kuyt plans to keep The Cedars' exterior exactly as it is, "the interior is a different story."

Kuyt toured a Natchez antebellum home once. "You had your crock pot in every corner," he says derisively, then laughs. "There's so little culture here, because this is such a new country. You find anything 200 years old, and you've really found something. That's why these antebellum homes are such good draws."

And that's how he plans to use The Cedars—as a draw. In about a year his self-styled museum should be ready for visitors, "who will discover we are human."

His inspiration was an elaborate Krishna temple in West Virginia, which draws thousands of tourists annually. Today things around Church Hill are quiet and surprisingly normal. Children playing on the porch of Kuyt's residence, Lagonia, act like anybody else's children. Except they all are beating Hare Krishna worship drums, making quite a racket.

"Please," says the mother, who is not in the mood for music. She wears traditional Far East garb and talks about a recipe for "a really mean" vegetarian pizza.

In her house is a shrine of Krishna religious figures and art. A yak's tail is fluffed and combed and displayed on the exotic altar.

The Hare Krishnas want to change things in the West— eventually. That's the way Kuyt explains it. "We want to slip in like a needle and leave like an elephant."

His museum won't be anything that "puts people off," he insists. Nothing sectarian. People of all faiths will benefit, he says, and it will be a tourist curiosity the likes of which this area has never seen.

Some neighbors believe his religion is a front, a corporate veil for evading taxes, debts or even selling drugs. "I have made mistakes, but I've done nothing illegal."

Other neighbors have stopped by to say, "Welcome." Kuyt has had one invitation to the Baptist church, which he's thinking of accepting.

There may or may not be room in Church Hill for Kuyt's church. His 225 acres, his deed and his determination say there will be. But one thing is for sure. Kuyt is not slipping into Church Hill like a needle.

April 1985

Angry Questions

BRANDON, MISSISSIPPI. The headlights just keep coming around the curves of rural Lake Road, beaming through the black night on a modest white church. Inside Sherwood Forest Primitive Baptist Church they are talking about a book. Not the Good Book. A bad book.

Elder Walter Blair, the pastor, is holding a dog-eared copy of Stephen King's *Cujo* high above the pulpit. Its dirty words, explicit scenes have been found and underlined.

"I've got a little two-year-old daughter," says Blair. "God forbid she ever lay her hands on this."

The people filling the pews on this winter evening are angry, expectant. There have been whispers about storming a county school's library to remove books the church finds offensive.

These parents want a censorship board. They want the name of the teacher who exposed their children to books they find objectionable. They want her fired.

School board members, invited to the church for the meeting, aren't here. They sent their lawyer instead.

People from the community come, some of them straight from work. They wear the uniforms of physical labor, grease-stained jeans and work shirts. Two of the women wear bedroom slippers. They have eaten hurried suppers and are skipping *Magnum, PI* and *Dynasty.*

"I personally would be arrested and prosecuted if I went up to a child on the street and started pointing out passages like this," insists church member H.L. Howard. He is holding a copy of *Headman*, a book about youth gangs with some rough language.

Howard has joined Blair near the pulpit on a simple rise, a hump in the gold indoor-outdoor carpeting. They are an emotional see-saw, Howard rising in anger as Blair takes his seat. The preacher is dark, with black hair and a long black beard. When he sits, silent and brooding, Rasputin comes to mind.

It's attorney Fred Harrell's turn. "We operate in this country under a system of laws," he says. "I don't agree with all the laws we have. The school board did everything within its power, for instance, to uphold the right of prayer in the schools.

"It went through all the trial courts. Then the federal court decided that it should not be. But I have to say, total censorship is out of the question."

The people ask angry questions:

"Have you read the books yet?"

"Who are the teachers using them and how can we get rid of those teachers?"

"Did you know the dishwasher at McLaurin High is broke? They can afford filth like that and can't afford to fix the dishwasher that washes the food off the plates. My daughter has brought chicken home that still has feathers in it from that place. Not once. But twice."

The lawyer flushes once or twice, but his answers remain polite, noncommital. He will read the books when he gets the time. Then he will form a legal opinion about whether they should be removed from county school libraries. Then he will advise the school board. Then the school board will act.

"How long is all of this going to take?" asks a woman, pointing an index finger at the lawyer in his plaid sports coat and cream-colored trousers.

"Those old men on the Supreme Court are senile," says one man. "Anybody with any sense can read about 30 seconds worth of those books and know they are not for children."

The lawyer is asked to leave. The preacher says the lawyer "has avoided answering a lot of questions here tonight" and "couldn't understand" what the church plans to talk about next. Shrugging, the lawyer leaves. His dance card isn't full here anyway. Now the Baptists get down to business.

"That young man didn't really want to leave," says Blair, once again behind the pulpit. "Every once in a while it does a fellow good to wonder what's happening. He was just as lost as a rabbit in a thousand-acre field.

"We've got to keep it stirred so strong that they can't even get any rest at night. If we work hard enough, we might even get the whole bunch of 'em committed to Whitfield (the state mental asylum)."

One woman, who has been quiet till now, suddenly speaks. There is another book, she says, that shouldn't be on the shelves. Her child was "ordered" to report on it. "It has at least ten 'damns' in it and one 'goddamn,'" she says. "And the little boy in it is cruel. To me that book has no material value whatsoever."

The book is *The Red Pony* by John Steinbeck.

March 1984

Hymn Or Her?

"I pity you on Judgment Day," wrote one angry soul.

I don't pity the 25 members of the United Methodist Church's hymn revision committee on Judgment Day. I feel sorry for them now. What a job.

There are nine million Methodists, and hymnal editor Carlton Young and his committee seem to be hearing from them all at the rate of about 80 per day.

Committee members are charged with compiling a new hymnal that is non-sexist, non-racist and ethnically sensitive. All the while respecting the traditional language, the meter, the music and the poetry of dear old hymns. They have not opened a can of worms. They have opened a worm farm.

Some people who write categorically oppose the changes. Others think changes should have been made long ago. And a whole passel of folks can go along with almost anything except rendering God genderless.

The poor committee met last month in Nashville to try out the ground rules.

Hymns of "overwhelming familiarity" will remain the same. For instance, "Faith of Our Fathers" is living still. However, alternative words may be inserted parenthetically to give sensitive congregations a choice. "Faith of Our Fathers (Martyrs/Mothers/Ancestors) living still . . . ."

That could produce an interesting sound if a single congregation cannot decide on a single word to sing.

Another ground rule: God can remain Father, King and Lord, but the committee is substituting God or Christ or other neutral deity titles for "He" or "His" or "Him." Example: "He walks with me and He talks with me . . . . has become "God walks with me and God talks with me."

"God of our fathers" is now "God of the ages." The enjoinder "Good Christian Men, Rejoice" will be "Good Christian Friends, Rejoice."

Other hymns need surgery for other reasons. "Am I a Soldier of the Cross?" is too heavy on· battle imagery for a denomination devoted to peace. In another song, the words "failing lips grow dumb" have been changed to "failing lips are stilled" so as not to offend the physically challenged.

That old familiar song, "Have Thine Own Way" has had the line "Whiter than snow, Lord, wash me just now" changed. Now the song says, "Wash me just now, Lord, wash me just now." A little repetitive, but definitely not racist.

Even "America the Beautiful" may get a facelift. Or, rather, a footlift. A Native American minister from North Carolina, member of the Lumbee Tribe, objected to words in the second verse: "Oh, beautiful, for pilgrim feet, whose stern, impassioned stress. A thoroughfare for freedom beat, across the wilderness . . . ."

Those "pilgrim feet" trod all over Native Americans in beating that thoroughfare, the minister pointed out.

"One woman wrote and said, 'We've sung these hymns for years without thinking, without meaning anyone any harm,'" says Garlinda Burton, director of the United Methodist News Service in Nashville. "Well, maybe we should have been thinking," Ms. Burton says. Mere human words are "never going to be adequate" and definitely can use occasional revision, she contends.

And she's right, of course. The Methodist motives are indeed admirable. God is love, not John Wayne.

But I'm glad not to be on that particular committee. Semantical slights seem a little silly compared to other living examples of racism and sexism, a lot of it within the church.

Picking nit is not a pretty job, but somebody, I suppose, has got to do it.

February 1986

Roloff And His Flock

Not all of the girls were pregnant. Some had been into drugs or shoplifting or skipping school. Some simply had parents who rued the way the world was heading and felt there must be a better way.

Most of them had an ashen look, their faces washed clean of all makeup and their budding bodies hidden under long skirts and loose blouses. They wore cheap tennis shoes with white crew socks and barrettes to keep their hair out of their eyes.

Not far away, thousands of college coeds were sunning and dreaming aloud as rock music rolled through cassettes onto the sundeck. Later, they would squeeze their trim, toasted bodies into designer jeans and greet their dates. But that was a world away from the Bethesda Home for Girls in Hattiesburg, Mississippi. It was at least five miles.

At Bethesda, the young girls took turns playing volleyball in the deep shade of Brother Bob Wills' neat lawn. They weren't exactly the zombie-quiet creatures described in a federal court suit the Southern Poverty Law Center filed against the home. They were farmers' daughters, happy and fat and distrustful of anything beyond the driveway.

Hard work and a disdain for the modern world were the legacies left them by Texas evangelist Lester Roloff. He had started the school and later "swapped" it with Wills for a boys' home in Tennessee. It was still the gospel according to Roloff that was taught at Bethesda. Roloff's raspy voice on Bible study tapes was the entertainment that replaced television each night. And it was his belief that corporal punishment and hard work could save teenage souls that Wills parroted.

Wills, an earnest, middle-aged man with a large, cowboy belt buckle holding up his jeans, had been tutored by the master.

Now Roloff is dead.

His most zealous supporters claimed the crash of a Cessna 210 over Texas flatlands last week not only killed their leader but signaled Doomsday. If so, it's a Doomsday the girls at Bethesda expected. They had been told just how close to the fiery gates of hell they came. And most of them eventually believed.

There was a devil painted on one wall of a crowded classroom where partitions separated the 70 students. They stood on cue and sang *a cappella* anthems thanking God and Wills for their deliverance.

They took turns telling of horrible pasts, of knife fights and group sex. They cried a lot. They said they didn't ever want to leave. Yet even in daylight, the school's doors were locked.

In Texas, there is a mournful quiet where Roloff's noisy, pulpit-pounding radio broadcasts used to be. The preacher who grabbed national headlines with a nine-year legal battle to operate his homes without state licensing is dead. Accusations that some of the homes' occupants were beaten and underfed still live.

"My old daddy spanked me, and some of these girls have to be spanked, too," Roloff always said.

His battles against rock music and state regulation probably will continue. It would be bad business not to keep fighting. The homes, financed by donations, form the basis of Roloff Enterprises, which enjoys exemption from taxes as religious work. A few years ago, Roloff himself put the annual receipts at $2.5 million.

His "branch" offices in places like Bethesda are coming increasingly under fire. A preliminary injunction is still pending against Bethesda in Montgomery, Alabama, federal court. The homes' population has dwindled to 20 since last April. Times are hard on the Hattiesburg ranch.

Bob Wills no longer is accomodating to strangers. But once, back when the trouble first started, he happily put the girls through their paces for visitors. He even had to curb the enthusiasm of their emotional avowals when they threatened to take up too much time.

"Oh, I beat you girls all the time, don't I?" he'd ask with a laugh. The girls laughed, too. In unison.

And then, once outside, he quit laughing. His eyes filled with tears, and he told of the persecution by outsiders who didn't understand about the love that was being dispensed. He looked longingly at the groomed acreage and buses and dormitories under construction and saw heaven.

"Most of these girls had nothing when they came here. Nothing." Then he went back inside, locking the door behind him.

November 1982

Santa As Satan

About 98 percent of the phone calls and letters New Yorker Jim Luce gets are positive, supportive. But, oh, the other two percent.

"I have an unlisted telephone number at home, but people get it anyway and call with messages like 'God is going to snuff you out like a candle.'"

He is a 26-year-old Episcopalian, a mild-mannered Ohio native who studied in Japan and eventually became a portfolio manager in a Japanese bank on Wall Street. Then, last April, Luce abruptly quit banking to start a group called Fundamentalists Anonymous.

FA tries to help people who want to shake a hard-line religious habit. So far, more than 14,000 people have called the small New York office to ask for advice.

"These people are isolated and suffering in silence," says Luce. Nobody before has had the guts to take an organized stand against fundamentalists, he claims, for fear they would appear to be opposing all Christianity.

FA very loosely defines "fundamentalists" as any separatist group with a judgmental, black-white mindset that believes the rest of the world is headed straight for Hell.

FA—which, some days, is mostly just Luce answering the 100 or so daily inquiries himself—gets calls from all kinds of denominational dropouts. Calls from former Independent Baptists outnumber the rest.

The idea for FA was born when Luce and a former Wall Street lawyer, Richard Yao, started comparing notes on how fundamentalism had touched their own lives. Yao once was a fundamentalist himself. Luce had family members who were.

"My five-year-old nephew had a babysitter, a sweet little old lady, who told him that his parents, as Episcopalians, were in league with Satan," says Luce. "One Christmas I asked my nephew if he was excited about Santa, and he informed me 'Santa' was just 'Satan' spelled wrong."

Another of Luce's relatives was a Jimmy Swaggart convert who quit college and isolated himself from his "Hell-bound" family to spend most days on a street corner witnessing.

FA fields some tragic calls. Luce tells this story: One woman had complained to her pastor for four years about the molestation of her daughter by her husband. The minister said the woman's own sins were being punished. "Pray," he counseled.

The day the eight-year-old daughter was hospitalized for lack of oxygen after being orally raped by the father, the mother called FA. "It took her four years to decide, 'It's them, not me.'"

Sociologists who specialize in communications tell us fundamentalism will be one of the most pervasive influences of the next century. "Fundamentalists have the tightest grip on the communications industry," says Luce. "They are very, very good at it."

How has this happened? How have a few powerful orators with fringe beliefs managed to sway millions and call it a Christian, conservative revival? Jim Luce has a theory.

Some humans want power. More prefer to be submissive. Fundamentalism adheres to a strict power hierarchy: God over minister, minister over man, man over wife.

"There's always somebody else to tell you what to do." Even if it's wrong.

March 1986

Lord, Help Us

A reader identifying herself only as "a concerned mother" sent me two, adhesive-backed, plastic Bibles, made in Taiwan for the Reverend Ewing.

Ewing instructs his congregation of the "Church by Mail" to stick the plastic Bible to an ailing body part and pray.

"Get alone," Ewing tells his sheep. "No one but you—and I mean no one—but you in the room. Peel off the back of this Bible. Be still. Be quiet. Be reverent. Slowly and prayerfully look up, then place this God's Word gently on any part of your body which needs healing as your personal act of faith to the Lord . . . ."

The mother is worried because her son and other gullible souls are sending Ewing money. "My son is one of those who can't afford to give away what little money he makes," she wrote. "Isn't this false advertising or just a plain con game?"

Ewing's instructions also include sticking the little Bible to your personal billfold and praying: "Lord, by faith, I accept all the money you are trying to send my way. Lord, I am holding Thy Word, the Bible, to rebuke the devil of poverty out of the way . . . ."

Next, Ewing tells his correspondents they must send the busy Bible back to him, along with $18.19—for Matthew 18:19 —so he, the Reverend Ewing, can wear it while he prays for them.

"By all means try your best to get this $18.19 . . . . And if after doing everything you can do to get this $18.19, you still cannot get it, then mail $9.19 to the Lord—but only, only if you have tried and cannot get $18.19 for Matthew 18:19." He pays the postage.

Ewing includes testimonials from people who were blessed by wearing the stick-on Bibles.

"The Lord blessed me with a Chevrolet."—A.J., Brooklyn, New York.

"Through Reverend Ewing's prayers I have been blessed with a home and 40 acres of land."—H.W., Philadelphia.

"I have been a Gold Book member six years now, and since joining the Gold Book Plan, God has blessed me with $10,000." —G.A., Atlanta.

"I became ill . . . and the doctor had given me up to die.

The Lord healed me. Then I met a wonderful man whom I married. Now I don't even have to work. So much has happened since writing to Reverend Ewing."—R.A., Tampa.

So, if you need a new Chevrolet, a husband, 40 acres of land, $10,000 or anything else within reason, write Bro. Ewing. He has more surprises than Vanna White. If you don't want to be sick or don't want to work, write Brother Ewing.

You will have to write. There is no telephone listing I could find for the Church by Mail. No steet address, either, just P.O. Box 3321, Atlanta.

Reverend Ewing, by the way, is no charlatan-come-lately. He claims to have been an active minister 35 years. And he most likely is prospering. The old devil of poverty probably has not stalked the good reverend since he invented the Gold Book Plan.

As the concerned mother pointed out, "If only one person a day mailed this Reverend Ewing $18.19, he would have $233,462.25 by now. This type of mail should be against the law."

The only laws it breaks, I'm afraid, are those of intelligent thought and human decency, and nobody pays much attention to them anymore. But if I were this concerned mother, I'd write the Reverend Ewing myself. I'd ask him to stop filling my son's mailbox with trash and false hopes.

Then I'd tell him where to stick his plastic Bible.

August 1986

Houses Of Worship

WILMETTE, ILLINOIS. It took 33 years to build the quartz and cement temple that rises like a giant, lacy Easter egg from this affluent Chicago suburb. It is the biggest, the only, Baha'i temple on the block. In fact, it's the only Baha'i temple on the continent.

The shrine of mystic design and majestic proportions looks somewhat misplaced in the American Midwest. But it is here, nonetheless, a cultural curiosity that has had more than 4 million visitors since it opened in 1953.

It's some of the best proof that Americans not only have freedom of religion but freedom of religious architecture as well. Style and structure seem to matter, and those with a particular message to sell know it.

The Baha' is aren't even keen on congregating. This exotic-looking house of worship was built more to pique the interest of passersby than as a place for services. Baha'is, in fact, meet in small, community groups only once every 19 days. There is no clergy or ritual.

Only a weekly devotional is held here, with no sermons or lectures allowed. The huge temple, despite its haughty exterior, is sparsely furnished with only chairs and a plain lectern.

As religions go, this one's a baby, only 140 years old. So the Baha'is see the temple as a convenient way to break the news of their existence. Tourists who know little or nothing about the Eastern religion (born in Iran) take the bait, stopping to see the gardens or unusual architecture. Guides are available, but visitors are free to roam and read the quotations of the Baha'i prophet and founder, Baha'u'llah.

Baha'is believe he is like Moses, Christ, Muhammad, Buddha—but more. They call him the "Promised One of All Religions" and claim he fulfills the Second Coming requirement for every faith.

If you fed a computer the proper data and instructed it to create the exact religious antithesis of the new prime-time fundamentalism, it just might turn up the Baha'is. "We are not allowed to argue," says a Baha'i when asked about ecumenical jockeying in the latter-day spiritual derby. "That's the one thing we cannot do."

But the Baha'is seem to believe in most of the things the fundamentalists deplore—one world government, an all-encompassing "I'm OK; You're OK" religion and complete equality between the sexes. And Baha'is accept absolutely no outside donations.

A congregation at the opposite philosophical pole also puts great stock in a distinctive physical plant. The Crystal Cathedral in Garden Grove, California, used donations exclusively to move its church from a local drive-in theater to a structure with "16,500 pillars of steel, 11,000 cathedral stars, 2,899 concert seats and 10,000 mirrored windows."

Tourists visit here, too, some for reasons having to do with design, not divinity. The cathedral looks like nothing so much as a Manhattan bank, probably not altogether accidental or inappropriate considering the philosophy of Robert Schuller, pastor.

Schuller preaches success, success and more success since "there's no doubt we need it in the United States." The sick cannot help the fallen; the poor cannot help the poor. What Schuller wants for his flock is "greater success privately, corporately and individually."

Services at the Crystal Cathedral are as slick as its mirrored exterior and effusively patriotic. One night last summer the congregation heard former football star Rosey Grier deliver the message and then raised the "world's largest" American flag to the high-tech rafters.

American sanctuaries have always meant more than a place to get in out of the rain. Even the early Spanish missions on far frontiers spared no expense or labor in building them. What remains of an old Catholic mission at Tumacacori, Arizona, is one decaying example.

There is an eerie quiet about the place, which probably would have fallen completely to the ground by now except for the care of the National Park Service.

Even in this simple adobe-brick world, those early missionaries had strong ideas about what they wanted in a church. They insisted on emulating European architecture, strategically placing windows to highlight statuary and yet keeping an overall dim interior. You can imagine how the Pima laborers must have worked, trying to please their new spiritual leaders. With what crude tools they must have struggled to mill the entry arches and bell tower.

Now the church at Tumacacori is scarred and crumbling, just another ward of the government. Just another temporal structure reaching up until it falls.

October 1984

Shaking Hell's Gates

They used to sell waterbeds in the building where Gulfport, Mississippi, preacher Ricky Edwards sold religion. The waterbeds came with a warranty.

He called the place "The Cathedral of Hope," and some of those attending services looked as if they could use a little. They came here because they had problems—husbands who cheat, wives who drink or children who smoke dope. They came because they believed Edwards a martyr in the Biblical tradition, or maybe they came because they were one of the hundreds Preacher Edwards dipped beneath the baptismal pool in happier times, when he was pastor of the huge Pass Road Baptist Church. For two years that was the fastest-growing Southern Baptist church in the state, breeding converts and critics at about the same pace.

Maybe they had seen Edwards' billboards, plastered with his distinctive profile and claims he was "Shaking the Gates of Hell." Maybe they had picked up his cards dubbing him a man of "Velvet and Steel."

Or maybe they had seen this young, strapping man on their television screens, selling "Je-a-suzzz" like a '62 Olds and exuding the kind of confidence that surely only those very close to God can have.

Edwards was getting very close to God when he piloted a Cessna 210 high in the heavens, its belly loaded with three guns, 1,049 rounds of ammunition and $115,448 in undeclared currency. He and three other Mississippi Gulf Coast men were bound on a Holy Mission to Colombia, South America, to pick up a load of cocaine.

Edwards pleaded guilty last month to charges of conspiracy to import cocaine and taking undeclared money out of the country. As part of a plea bargaining agreement, the weapons charge was dropped. Because Edwards admitted guilt and played along with federal prosecutors, the possible prison stint he faces has shrunk from 22 to 5 years. He may never have to go to prison at all, depending on how much he helps his accuser, Uncle Sam.

Last March, however, Ricky Edwards was still maintaining his innocence. He had rounded up about 50 followers too blinded by his effervescence to believe headlines and sat them all down on folding chairs in the former waterbed showroom.

There, he gave a one-man show, embroidering "One Day At A Time" with enough bump and grind to make Tom Jones blush. He wandered as far into the shrunken congregation as the leash on his portable microphone allowed, stooping and reaching and gyrating within the bounds of Christian decency. The men as well as the women were mesmerized. His wife, looking tired and not saying much, went dutifully along with the other women after the service. They were taking the children for refreshments.

Edwards stayed to talk. Some of the men stayed to listen. He sat in a small office telling his story. Three men roosted about the tiny room, a goon squad for the gospel.

A trial, Edwards kept saying, would vindicate him. Give me a trial. He had started writing a book about his ordeal. Reporters' calls had convinced him he had a marketable story. "That's why I can't get into all of the details," he said.

He said a prayer that night, a loud, community prayer designed to move mountains. "My confidence is in Him alone." Edwards pointed to the ceiling, as everyone followed his hand, perhaps expecting the roof to begin raining tiles.

There was a Ricky Edwards Benefit Fund at a Gulfport bank. Preacher Edwards was never above soliciting money from the faithful. One supporter gave him a construction job that threatened to callous hands slick as the pages of Second Thessalonians.

"I've taken a lot of ribbing, because I believe in the man," said an obviously sincere man after Edwards himself rode away into the night. "People at work keep kidding me about buying some dope. But if I didn't believe he was innocent, I wouldn't be here."

Strong headwinds near Cuba forced his craft back to Mississippi, Edwards eventually would tell a judge. When the plane landed, authorities were waiting.

There will always be faithful parishioners for Ricky Edwards. He may lose a church or two, but there always will be those who want to believe this man means the words he sings. For him, it's as easy to shake down a new group of believers as it is to shake the very gates of Hell.

May 1985

12 / Punt And Pass

The Wonder Lugs

LOS ANGELES. There are big men. Then there are the super heavyweight Olympic weightlifters.

How big are they? These men are so big the Marlboro Man calls them "Sir." This is the three-ring circus of the five-ring Olympics. We're talking Barnum and Bailey and Big Top.

Nine men with legs like California sequoias dressed in Banlon suits took turns lifting weights roughly equivalent to five soaking-wet Mary Lou Rettons. While absolute silence prevailed, these lugs with thunder thighs and garden hose veins grimaced and groaned and tried to keep from dropping the barbells on their tootsies.

Dinko Lukim of Australia did the best. He lifted a total of 909 pounds (on two lifts) without breaking into a sweat. Lukim is a rich man who fishes for tuna when he's not working out. When asked if he literally is a millionaire or if his family has the million, the low-key-to-comatose Kukim replied, "We each have a million."

He has a reasonably attractive, even intelligent face when it's not contorted by pain. He does everything slowly, as if normal movement hurts. His giant legs must create an awful chafe from rubbing against one another.

He jumped up and down when he hoisted the winning lift and people in Anaheim reported an earthquake. As he lumbered away from the audience, you couldn't help looking for the Goodyear insignia.

If a deformed body is the price of a gold medal, Lukim paid the price. His chest was so big the medal was barely noticeable, dangling like a sweat drop from where his neck once was.

Bassey Ironbar of Nigeria wasn't so lucky. With a name like "Ironbar," you have to assume he felt doomed to take up weightlifting.

Bassey was trying to lift 396 pounds when he dropped the barbell and then fell to the platform. It then took nine attendants to move the 254-pound Ironbar by stretcher from the arena. He may require surgery for a partial quadriceps rupture. The extent of injuries to stretcher-bearers is not yet known.

Then there was Manfred Nerlinger of the Federal Republic of Germany. He was blond, had a boyish face and looked about 12 years old, but for the blubber. The Incredible Hulk is Ecuador; Nerlinger is the world.

Mighty Manfred the Wonder Lug had his routine perfected. He approached the barbell as if it might bite him, sniffing it, backing off, and then going back again. Then he began a loud, rhythmic puffing, like the little train that thought it could, finally lifting with a grunt that gave new dimension to the word "primitive."

Manfred move metal. Manfred win bronze medal.

The American, of course, had the crowd on his side. Mario Martinez had to go first. He lifted a lot (903 pounds), but then he had to sit back and watch the Australian who already was rich and famous lift more. It didn't set too well with Mario.

"I should have started with 220 kilos (equal to 484 pounds)," he bellowed afterwards. He blamed his coaches. When last seen, they were in Arizona headed east.

Since I have written this far without trashing the sport, let me make this one critical observation. The different categories of the competition are poorly named. There is the "snatch" and then the "clean and jerk." Words like "snatch" and "jerk" connote anything but reaching down and lifting 300 to 400 pounds. Maybe the "clean and jerk" should be the "strain and work."

Since the Olympics is all about setting records, it should be noted the medal ceremony for the super heavyweight weightlifters was the biggest ceremony of the games. The three men together weighed more than 885 pounds. The rainbow-colored ribbons holding the medals had to be made from elastic to fit over their heads.

After the awards ceremony, the winners made polite chit-chat with reporters, refusing by and large to address any weighty topics. What would a bruiser like Lukim, with millions of dollars and women, do with a lousy gold medal?

Atlas shrugged.

August 1984

A Good Cry

LOS ANGELES. American wrestler Jeff Blatnick sat on a shaded spot of green grass outside the Anaheim Convention Center, the receiver of a pay telephone dangling close to his right ear.

The inexhaustible California sun was shining. Disneyland was just across the street. His pretty, ponytailed girl was two feet away, looking at him like Nancy Reagan looks at Ron, as if all 248 pounds might suddenly evaporate or blow away.

Someone on the other end of the silver receiver was asking about his gold medal performance, and Blatnick was shrugging his way through the interview, crediting coaches and other wrestlers and God and everyone but himself with the win.

Not since Ed Muskie cried in the snows of New Hampshire have a man's tears mattered so much to the American public. This was not tiny Olga Korbut tearing up, either, but a big, bad, brute of a man, bawling with abandon in front of 2.5 billion viewers.

Blatnick, in showing his emotions, became more than just a one-dimensional sports figure. He became real. More importantly, he injected something into the 23rd Olympiad that definitely had been missing—humility. He seemed grateful to win. It showed.

There has been a kind of cockiness exhibited here that's not becoming to America or her athletes. With the ABC misers daily counting only gold, it must be hard for some 16-year-old whose life has been a swimming lane or a balance beam to keep things in perspective. It shouldn't be beyond the rest of us.

A television technician from Sarajevo, Yugoslavia, preparing for a long ride in the school buses shuttling journalists from one Olympic venue to the next, understated the obvious. "Americans put all the emphasis on the very top-most winners. It seems less like an international event with the coverage they are doing here."

There are foreign athletes participating in these games, regardless of what you have—or haven't—seen. Their fans are in town, too, spending their savings to watch participants who are simply glad to be here, participating.

There are Americans here, too, other than that huggable minx Mary Lou or Michael Jackson's showboat friend Carl Lewis. We just don't see them on the tube. Maybe they are a tenth of a second off the world's fastest time or a fraction of a judge's point away from a bronze. We don't hear their names, much less delve in up close and personal. We don't hear about the losers unless they were expected to be winners.

The complaints from foreign Olympic athletes and coaches about the televised cheerleading of ABC were sniffed at, mostly, by the American athletes. "Tough," one American handball team player was quoted as saying. "We're winning medals. We're winning gold medals."

Sportsmanship, much less humility, seems to be as dead to the Olympic games as croquet. An athlete with a silver medal might as well have an unmentionable social disease. American gymnast Bart Conner griped for print that his individual chances were sacrificed to help the team. Swimmer Rick Carey, who did win the gold, pouted poolside during the awards ceremony, because his time wasn't his personal best. Later he fluffed up his Vidal Sassoon haircut for viewers and hemmed and hawed and finally allowed as how he shouldn't have thrown a tantrum while they were stringing the gold around his neck, but, golly gee, he demands a lot of himself.

"The important thing in the Olympic games is not winning but taking part. The essential thing in life is not conquering but fighting well." That was the cornball philosophy of Baron de Courbertin, founder of the modern Olympics. Most of his ideas have been left so far behind, applying them to the 1984 games is like vaulting with a wooden pole.

"Faster, Higher, Stronger," seems to match the mood much better.

A foreigner in a shiny new suit shared my hotel elevator one day. He didn't speak a word of English. He was beaming, though, and holding an Olympic event ticket ready in his hand. His country's athletes may not have been winning; if they were, they probably weren't being mentioned. But he was in America and on his way to the most international of all events, the 23rd Olympiad. He was proud to be here. Just proud to be here.

August 1984

Woody Hayes

COLUMBUS, OHIO. It had not been a particularly good week for Woody Hayes.

His former assistant, Wisconsin coach Dave McClain, was dead of a heart attack at the presumably lusty, middle age of 48. The death, the funeral, the untimely circumstance, obviously had troubled the man most of Ohio simply and familiarly calls "Woody."

"Forty-eight," said Woody, shaking his head in disbelief at that low number. "But, you see, he made a mistake. There's always a mistake."

For a moment I expected the old coach to produce game films of McClain's life and then stop the action at the fatal error. "He went running and got away with that. And then he came in and took a sauna. That's when it happened."

No, it had not been a good week in the life of Woody Hayes, admirer of strength and vitality, Ralph Waldo Emerson and Richard Nixon.

"Gee, but I had good coaches," he said, and you could wrap yourself in his melancholy.

Still, Woody was more than gracious to a stranger, using a walker to hobble across the room to answer the door of the white house with green shutters on pleasantly middle-class Cardiff Road. Then, refusing to sit until I sat, the courtly and meticulously dressed man exchanged amenities.

"Auburn? You went to Auburn? Well, golly, my golly. I never knew Shug Jordan. Never did."

Hayes, now 73, did not even faintly resemble wire photographs I had seen of an angry coach slugging the Hi-Mom out of a shocked Clemson University football player almost a decade ago. He looked far too docile, too kindly, even to shove so much as a single, pesky television cameraman.

His tantrums and lectures on Salamis and Midway and the similarities of great battles and the game of football all are semi-retired now, like him, the stuff of Ohio legend. He has survived strokes and heart attacks. Now he gets standing ovations and honorary degrees from the school that dismissed him in disgrace. The past infamy, he said, never did bother him. You have to develop thick skin.

"You have to do it. You have to tell 'em to go to Hell. They used to circle with airplanes and banners that said, 'Goodbye, Woody.' I always thought they said, 'Good boy, Woody.'"

If Woody Hayes got rich coaching for 28 years at Ohio State University, he didn't spend the loot on home furnishings. Everything in the living room is worn and simple—a mismatched love seat and couch, a fold-up card table covered with publications, most featuring Woody.

He looked comfortable, despite the proper suit and tie. He seemed like a favorite uncle from the intellectual side of the family, slightly hard of hearing but with memory sharp enough to quote a Shakespeare sonnet or recall The Worst Winter. He has, he said, been working on a book for some time now: "Football, History and Woody Hayes."

It was a simple interception, don't you know, that won the Battle of Midway. And Dick Nixon and his China diplomacy set up a double-team block on Russia. Sherman's March to the Sea was the greatest end-run in all of history.

Hayes grew up in nearby Newcomerstown, son of a scholar. "My father was the best educated man I ever knew. He went to seven different colleges."

Woody himself wanted to go to law school, even showed up to enroll at Ohio State in the summer of 1936. But, as they say, fate lent a hand. The law school only took new students in the fall, and by then Woody was coaching football at New Philadelphia High. He never picked up law. But he could flat lay the law down.

As he did one Friday night before a big game on Saturday. An assistant coach was in charge of selecting an "appropriate" movie to herd the team to on the night before the game. He chose *Easy Rider*.

"I had to fire that coach (Earle Bruce) off the job of choosing movies. When the boys got off the bus, I knew something was wrong. It had 'em so shook up it took me a while to get them back to normal."

Even in the movies, drugs and anarchy had no part in his football plan that was part Lombardi, part Patton.

Woody still displays that Hall of Fame temper of his from time to time. At issue in a recent local election was the construction of a 65,000-seat stadium and civic center, which to Woody could mean only one thing: pro football. "We don't need that. Let them keep their goddamned drugs somewhere else."

Then he was a smiling gentleman again, quoting from Emerson's essay "Compensation." He was tiring, but still talking.

"You've got enough already to write a book," he would say, and then he would talk some more. He stood when I stood and insisted on walking me to the door.

Here was a man legendary for all the wrong reasons. One veteran college football referee told me Hayes should enjoy the venerable reputation of Bear Bryant, and Bryant should have Woody's rep as a small, vindictive tyrant.

One helluva football coach, known best for a couple of televised temper tantrums.

A classy, Emerson-spouting scholar, too quick with a left jab.

"Throw about half of what I told you away, and you'll have a good story," said the man of intellect and ire.

If only we could, Woody, if only we could.

May 1986

Greg Pratt Is Dead

It is all around, the Sunday morning rubble from the Saturday afternoon carnage. Pop tops and potato chip bags. Enough cans to see a roadside aluminum prospector through retirement.

Once again it has seduced me, this game of college football. It has thrown me across my own couch and had its way. Again, I have been suckered into believing the ol' alma mater, Auburn University, plays for me and me alone. Those knights carry my colors, my prestige and honor across a field mined with muscle.

That Greg Pratt fell dead as Auburn's football fortunes were rising and its season coming alive has bothered but not deterred me. My mind has been experiencing temporary technical difficulties; stay tuned and the interference will fade.

Here, beneath the empty cellophane sacks and mutilated snacks, is a reprieve. A copy of the coroner's report. The same thing could have happened to Pratt if he'd been cutting grass. That's what it says.

The official line, the final word to expunge the record of both a state institution and a national preoccupation. It's what Lee County Coroner Jon Williams discovered about the heatstroke that killed the fullback from Albany, Georgia. "That it happened during a football physical (workout) is purely coincidental," Williams wrote.

The August heat, the series of 440 sprints and Pratt's history of heat-related problems brushed neatly aside, perhaps it could have happened anytime, anywhere.

Moment of silence. Play ball.

Pratt's funeral delayed practice one day, but any fool believing his death might stop for one moment the actual game is as green as new Astroturf. After all, injuries are a part of the game. They are tallied and assessed and moaned about on the Sunday-after. And a player who "stays hurt" is about as popular as one who fumbles.

There is money in college football, and fun and prestige are mere afterthoughts. Coaches coach to make it. Players play for tuition or their own professional prospects. The Auburn Alumni Association recently purchased Pat Dye's $412,000 house from a Montgomery bank and will grant Dye the title if he stays at Auburn 14 more years. All he has to do is stay and win.

If college athletes and coaches were in it just for the fine fellowship, they'd all join the astronomy club.

A couple of lonely voices were raised in protest lately, politely suggesting that not enough questions had been asked about young Pratt's death. Two Auburn alumni, John E. Martin and John A. Fairbank, penned a letter to the college newspaper and dared to prick conscience.

"Why, we ask on the first day of practice, during one of the hottest, most humid days of the summer, was a talented young man with a clear history of exercise-related heat problems pushed beyond his physical capacity to endure? He apparently was having such difficulty completing the grueling series of sprints that two coaches had to run alongside him, according to the reports we read."

The two men also begged members of Auburn's coaching staff to say they didn't say they hoped the Pratt tragedy wouldn't affect their team's performance. "Please tell us that we are not that callous and self-serving, that this was a misquote."

Coaches who coddle are not in demand. Their contracts, not their mortgages, are bought up in short order and alumni help pack the bags. Cowering in the face of adversity is not part of The Code. You don't scratch a practice because of, for heaven's sakes, humidity.

In the best circles, and in the most awesome conferences, it simply is not done.

Memphis Showboats Coach Pepper Rodgers stayed in trouble with Georgia Tech alumni, because he made the mistake of treating college football as a game. His boys roomed where they liked, not in a single athletic dormitory, and went to the playing field to have a good time. And they had a good time but didn't win enough games. So Tech got a new coach.

There will be no good answers to the questions Martin and Fairbank raised. We don't want them. Besides, the "official" investigation is complete. Greg Pratt is dead. College football is not.

All because of fans like me.

October 1983

The Mississippi Mudcat

I first met Eldridge DaLee in a Mississippi alley. It was a well-traveled alley, between the Dollar Store and the old Knox Building, if I remember my Tupelo geography.

He was walking one way, and I was walking another. Then, somehow, we were walking together, talking about things.

Mr. DaLee knew a little about almost everything. He could quote Harry Truman, Bear Bryant or statistics from *Ripley's Believe It Or Not*. And he adored baseball.

He spent the hottest part of each summer day in the library, making endless Xerox copies of pertinent passages in books and magazines. He kept a pocket full of nickels for the copy machine and file folders full of baseball stories.

Many days Mr. DaLee would leave little care packages outside my Tupelo newspaper office. The brown sacks usually contained red-rind cheese, saltine crackers, Mounds candy bars and boiled eggs with writing on them. The writing told what time the egg had been boiled. Some days the egg said 4:30 a.m. Sometimes 5 a.m. Eldridge DaLee never boiled an egg later than 5:30 a.m., according to the shells I was privileged to crack.

It was Mr. DaLee who took me to see Guy Bush, the old Mississippi pitcher. "You've got to meet him," Mr. DaLee insisted. "He's a real hero."

Since true heroes seem to be the snail darters of modern sports, I immediately agreed. We drove to a nearby slip of a town called Shannon, where Guy Bush had lived and farmed since retiring from the majors in 1945.

The old ballplayer came ambling out to greet us. He was at least 80 years old then, but he didn't really look it. He still had wavy silver hair and a lady-killing grin. Time and the sun had creased his olive skin until it looked like the well-oiled pocket of your favorite fielder's mitt.

We sat around a dinette and drank ice water and talked. Mr. DaLee wanted to hear the Babe Ruth story, and Guy Bush didn't have to be asked twice to tell it.

Bush pitched from 1923 to 1934 with the Chicago Cubs. He compiled a 176-136 won-loss record, pitched in two World Series and hurled two one-hitters. But it wasn't his statistics people remembered. It was one pitch.

Guy Bush was the last pitcher to give up a home run to Babe Ruth. Bush threw home run ball 714, out of the park and into the record book. It was a dubious kind of honor. But if you have to pitch a home run ball, better to throw it to Babe Ruth on his very last at-bat.

"I never saw a ball hit so far," Guy Bush said. "Babe couldn't run much any more. But he just smiled nicely to me as he rounded third. I tipped my hat."

Bush was not on the mound in the 1932 World Series when the Babe supposedly called his own home run, pointing to the bleachers and then spiraling the ball in the same direction. But Bush was in the Cubs' dugout, needling Ruth as he stepped into the batter's box. Some said Ruth hadn't been pointing at the bleachers at all, but at Bush, who had made him angry.

Bush got a chance to ask the Babe later: "Did you or did you not call that home run in the '32 World Series?"

Babe only replied, "Well, Guy, it made a damn good story, didn't it?"

It was an even better story told the Guy Bush way. I remember how Eldridge DaLee acted that day in the presence of his hero, the old Mississippi Mudcat. Mr. DaLee, no spring chicken himself, listened intently, leaning forward in his seat like a kid at a cowboy matinee.

Somehow, I can't imagine anyone getting that excited about the war tales of any current baseball pitcher. If the Babe had gotten his last homer off Pascual Perez, Perez might still be missing.

The strike zone these days has become the months between April and October. The fans have become as cynical as the players. Who can blame them? The baseball stories to clip and save these days are all about legalities, not legends.

A decade or so ago, when Hank Aaron was on the verge of breaking Ruth's all-time homer record, some pitchers were saying they might be glad to ease up a bit and give Aaron THE hit. A UPI reporter asked Bush what he thought about that.

"I want him to break the record as much as anyone," said Guy Bush. "But that's sinful. It's not the way to do things."

A record, like a man, should not die before its time.

They buried Guy Bush on the Fourth of July. He was 83. He had been working in his garden when his heart stopped. I don't know, but I imagine Eldridge DaLee was graveside.

He probably clipped the newspaper, too—where the world was reminded that Guy Bush was best remembered for one bad pitch.

August 1985

Wadley Pummels Lineville

It is that imaginative time of the year again. It is the season when sportswriters pull out all vocabulary stops, renewing the eternal search for new and more colorful ways to describe how one high school football team defeats another.

"Frisco City Riddles Excel." "Wadley Pummels Lineville." "Roanoke Punishes LaFayette."

It is not an enviable job, believe me. There are only so many sadistic verbs, and by the second or third game of the high school season headline writers usually are forced to resort to the tried and trite: "downs," "pounds," "edges," "tops," "drubs," "nips," "outlasts," "rips," "bombs," "thumps," "tramples" and "trounces." You also have your past passive hackneyed verb, as in "falls to" and "downed by."

Below, for the layman, is a glossary of familiar terms in high school sports reporting, which often consists of taking the score by telephone from a coach who only remembers to call if his team wins:

REBUILDING. What a team not expected to win many games is doing. There is no such thing in high school sports as a bad or poorly-coached team. Under dire circumstances, for example following a five-season losing streak, a team may be called "hapless."

DISAPPOINTING. The kind of season a rebuilding team has.

CHARACTER. The resolve, determination and strength of personality fostered by participation in youthful athletics and useful in the Game of Life. Not to be confused with assorted coaches and adult boosters who never learn the difference between high school football and the Game of Life.

INTENSE RIVALRY. Rivalry.

PAYDIRT. The ten yards at either endzone of a 100-yard playing field. Not to be confused with the assistant coach's salary.

MOMENTUM. Imaginary prowess, sometimes referred to as the twelfth man, that follows the team thought to be winning at the time. Not to be confused with "fans."

WORKHORSE. Talented kid who earns the coach's paycheck.

TURNOVERS. Fumbles, interceptions and any of the other things not supposed to happen that make the game interesting.

INJURY-RIDDEN. Any team with a sufficient number of young men crippled so as to become a problem.

DESIRE. A vague, primal lust that is the underpinning for the entire autumn pageantry of football. Devoted followers of the game actually believe the caliber of players, degree of preparation and intelligence of game plan are unimportant to victory compared to "Desire."

INVOCATION. Ritual prayer before kickoff in which a deity (almost always Christian) is asked to protect the players, assure the best team wins and get the fans safely back to their respective homes. God's will for the game is not revealed at this point, else there would be no reason to stay and watch.

UPSET. When God's and the sportswriters' opinions differ.

September 1985

Burying Bear

ALICEVILLE, ALABAMA. These are the experts.

Not the sports writers, a brotherhood bound by trivia and free hot dogs. Not the University of Alabama students, whose mass grief had to be accommodated in a coliseum. Not the dignitaries, the 400 or so a downtown Tuscaloosa church would seat. Not the football players, who passed or blocked their way to big-time fame and pantyhose commercials or comfortable Alabama fortunes in insurance or used cars.

Here are the people who made Paul "Bear" Bryant important. They are the men who drive Mack trucks and the women who pour their coffee. They live on the outskirts of the college town and all it represents, just as they remain on the outskirts of the official mourning. If they help to comfort Mary Harmon, Bryant's widow, it will be through prayers offered simply and silently, as George Jones creaks a jukebox requiem.

They are holding a memorial service of their own, these patrons of the Bama Trof in Aliceville. They tell all they know about the Bear—and then some—revealing confidential tidbits about his health, his businesses and his past. They make statements riddled with inaccuracies and hyperbole but ringing with truth. They honor the dead.

"You sure as heck won't find anyone in these parts who don't think the world of Him," says Bill Romine Ensley. "Him" with a capital "H."

"He could have been governor of this state any day, just for the asking."

"I always said that, too," injects waitress Charlene Gunn. "I always said he wouldn't have had to even make one little speech, not one speech. He could have just gone on and been sworn in." She hands off a brimming cup of hot coffee to a tattooed driver, Richard Todd to Wilbur Jackson.

"You can tell what we think of him here," she says, pointing to the walls around her. There are the Bama banners and Bear posters so familiar in these parts they become almost invisible. As sure as a southerner fries a chicken or mounts a ten-pound bass, a North Alabamian pays tangible tribute to the Crimson Tide. The men in the truck stop wear their loyalty on their sleeves—and on their chests and their heads and their belts. Jerry Harper pushes his red chest forward and distorts the block white t-shirt letters exalting the Tide. "I have about two or three of these," he says.

"You know what killed the Bear, don't you?" Harper asks. He takes a slow sip of coffee to heighten the suspense. "He grieved himself to death over football, that's what. It wasn't anything else." He speaks with the authority of a man who expects the coroner to rule him right.

The eulogies are repeated in the joints and cafes along old U.S. 43, deserted like a dowdy, middle-aged woman by travelers preferring the speedier interstate running almost parallel into Tuscaloosa. It is a road flanked now by leafless hardwoods, their limbs hung heavy with kudzu vines.

School buses deliver children to homes designed with survival in mind, where no college diplomas hang to break the monotony of bare walls. It is a rather desolate region. Its philosophy a winless one by habit. This is a workaday world, where Bear Bryant and perhaps George Wallace are the only celebrities the people even pretend to know.

A young hunter sits in the Eutaw Hotel's restaurant, his camouflage coat and cap perversely serving to make him conspicuous, staring at a big, color newspaper photograph of the Bear.

It is early afternoon, when the glasses are all clean and the waitress' makeup fresh. Later the place will be full of Tuscaloosa spillover, coeds who have discovered the old hotel and its lounge and think it worth the 30-minute trip. The hunter will be tracking the dears, but now, in the quiet, almost empty cavern of a room, he stares at the picture of a man whose rather undistinguished profile is obscured by the blue and white trademark hat. A hat that clashes wildly with a red plaid suit. The hunter's long look is a silent tribute.

Up the road in bustling Tuscaloosa, motel marquees mark with plastic letters the passing of a hero. "Bear Bryant, 1913-1983. We love you," one says. Fraternity boys and school custodians drape black banners across the stately columns of the picturesque campus' hallowed halls. The Black Warrior River, normally a bright jade, looks gray today beneath a cloud-darkened sky. It flows twisted like a shroud draped across the landscape. The town itself is a tiny, cramped church, ready for services but ill-equipped to contain all the mourners.

Men sit in Holiday Inn lounges, the red lights of a bad band reflected in bifocals, talking about the giant who didn't mince his mumbled words. They muffle their grief with beer and loud talk. They know the same intimate details the Bama Trof patrons knew, the secrets broadcast on the Channel Six news. The world of traveling sales, leisure suits and giant television screens is in mourning, too.

The slurred tributes to the Bear, who won for a people used to losing, had the same lonesome sounds as a single horn blast from Jerry Harper's 18-wheeler. There is a sense of genuine loss.

January 1983

13 / Truth Is Stranger

The Secret Listing Of Walter Mitty

JACKSON, MISSISSIPPI. My hands shook slightly as I dialed the seven digits. "What manner of man will answer?" I wondered as I listened to the whirring circuitry: ta-pocketa-pocketa-pocketa-pocketa.

I had come across the name "Walter Mitty" while perusing the Jackson telephone directory one Saturday night. Don't tell me I've nothing to do.

No address. Just the name "Mitty, Walter." The only Mitty in the book.

"Hello," came an answer on my second ring.

"May I speak to Mr. Mitty, please?" I hoped with all my heart the call had not jolted him from some high adventure of the mind.

"Speaking."

"Walter Mitty" turned out to be a 36-year-old, imaginative but unemployed man whose name is not Walter Mitty. He wouldn't tell me his other name. "Walter" had had his curious telephone listing for about four years.

"It's just my way of recognizing the genius of James Thurber," he said. When nosy folks like me call asking for a "Mr. Mitty," he knows right away they are not friends of his. Either Olan Mills has a special on family protraits or, more rarely, curiosity has gotten the better of a stranger. He doesn't help those curious strangers much.

Walter Mitty is a guarded individual who allows little personal information. Gentle prodding, for example, revealed only that his line of work is "Computers." He apparently wants to keep the secret life of Walter Mitty secret.

"What," I asked, rather brazenly, "do you daydream about?"

"You're getting far too personal," the inscrutable Walter Mitty answered.

Mitty crossed his arms and pushed a strong chin stubbornly forward; he would just keep pleading the fifth, and this half-cocked Senate Committee could take its contempt citation and go straight to Hell. He would teach them to pry into billionaire industrialist Walter Mitty's affairs. Wear them down, he would. The committee stenographer sneaked him a sly, admiring smile as the pocketa-pocketa-pocketa of her machine recorded his defiance.

Mr. Mitty did allow as to how he'd had a picture of Don Quixote on his office wall—back when he'd had an office wall. "I've been tilting at windmills all my life."

Some sharpy at the telephone company originally questioned his listing, Mr. Mitty said, but imagination somehow prevailed, and the name was printed.

I called the telephone company, curious about how much of this stuff goes on. When asked about Walter Mitty, they laughed. "Sometimes we do query people about unusual listings," said Bill Dawson of South Central Bell.

"But as long as they want to pay for it, and it's not obscene, they can list anybody they want. They can be Joe Blow, as far as I know. I've never given it much thought, really."

You can call directory assistance if you want to satisfy yourself that Walter Mitty lives, but please don't call Mitty himself. I asked if Mr. Mitty would mind if I mentioned him in print. "Probably," he said, vague to the end. "I don't want to get a lot of phone calls."

Movie star and recluse Walter Mitty, beleaguered and weary, finally broke free of the all-too-familiar sea of adoring women, collapsing against the heavy oak door of his masculinely sparse mansion. The pounding of their sweaty little fists was a faint pocketa-pocketa through the dense timbers. "Why can't those wretched females give me a moment's peace?" he asked the empty walls. Then he slept.

I had intruded long enough. My new acquaintance Walter Mitty was eager to be rid of me.

"Why don't you look under 'Roast' in the phone book and see what you find," he said. "That's much more interesting."

Chuck was there, all right, the only "Roast" in the book. But he wasn't home.

May 1984

Whaddayamean Art?

WASHINGTON. They say a drug deal or two has gone down on this lovely spit into the Potomac called Hains Point. But things looked innocent enough late one weeknight not long ago.

The bureaucrats were nestled all snug in their beds. Visions of runarounds danced in their heads. And mostly teenagers—hanging out, as the hip say—were populating the hot nights of summer.

I was there to see *The Giant*. That is what most everyone calls J. Seward Johnson's remarkable sculpture; officially, it is *The Awakening*.

And seeing The Giant at night definitely will wake you up. The sight of a dimly-lighted, struggling, half-buried human is disturbing, to say the least. The giant appears to have been sleeping for a long, long time. He is just waking, or attempting to break through the earthen barrier covering him. He looks a lot like a haggard Gulliver weakened by the Rotation Diet, trying desperately to snap the invisible ties that bind.

Most of the giant appears to be underground. Only his head, a portion of a leg, an arm and a foot are sprouting from the earth. Or, maybe the grimacing giant is going the other way—down instead of up. Perhaps this is not a resurrection at all. Perhaps the big man is being swallowed up by an angry, mistreated environment or sucked down by something so ordinary as quicksand.

Only the name *The Awakening* points our imaginations in the other direction. People assign the sculpture hundreds of meanings.

Some view it as a religious statement. Others interpret *The Giant* as mankind buried in nuclear debris.

The kids simply regard it as a great roosting place. Five happy teenagers with three boom boxes were perched on the big guy's head, hanging onto his giant incisors and rapping, when I was there.

The artist, of course, is not saying what it all means. Probably he secretly titled the work "Hung Over." I phoned the Bureau of Sculpture Placement—your tax dollars at work— to find out more about *The Giant*.

"So many visitors to the city request to see it that the tour groups have extended their route encompassing the monuments, White House and Smithsonian Mall to include a stop at *The Awakening*," the spokesman replied, in writing.

The sculpture is five sculptures, really. Each a cast aluminum body part, appropriately positioned on the lawn. It is 17 feet at its highest point and 70 feet in breadth, she said.

It is also for sale at the giant price of $175,000. I suppose the National Park Service gets use of it until some private party pays to plant *The Giant* elsewhere. I hope he doesn't end up somewhere undignified, like Dogpatch USA. He does look a little like a hillbilly being swallowed in a vat of Kickapoo Joy Juice.

There is a memorable character in Joseph Wambaugh's classic cop story, *The Choirboys*. He could never quite follow the deep, philosophical discussions of life and death that went on among the cops after hours. Continually he was asking, "What do you mean? What do you mean?" So the cops nicknamed him "Whaddayamean Dean."

I felt for all the world like Whaddayamean Dean standing at the foot—really—of this struggling statue. I wanted to help him out, but I had no idea whether to push or pull.

Artists have no obligation, certainly, to explain their work. But it would sure make life easier for the rest of us to know what's going on. Even a hint would be nice.

And if *The Giant* stays buried on the banks of the Potomac, I think they might do well to add ribbons and ribbons of cast aluminum. Drape miles of tape over the poor soul's body.

Then they should paint the tape red and retitle the work "John Q. Citizen."

August 1986

Ghost Writer

At first there were only his words and they were good but not nearly enough for the young men who wanted more, always.

So then the young men who wanted to be like the "Old Man" began writing their own words and telling all about him or that which they knew, which sometimes was not very much. He endured.

Ernest Hemingway, dead nearly a quarter of a century, will have another new book out soon. He refuses to take retirement seriously.

Last year brought *The Dangerous Summer*, which had appeared, in part, in *Life* magazine but never a book. This year comes *The Garden of Eden*, a novel Scribner's is calling Hemingway's "last unpublished major work."

I doubt this will be the last virgin Hemingway, not so long as the demand for the author stays constant. Editors have deep drawers.

But if it is, Scribner's says goodbye to an industry. The "latest" Hemingway novel is about bisexuality, a drastic departure from words about fighting wars and bulls and big fish. In the book, a young American writer and his wife both fall in love with the same woman.

"The theme of bisexuality is not as strange today as it was 25 years ago," Charles Scribner, Jr. told a *New York Times* reporter.

I'll say. So, not only is Hemingway managing a book a year after death, he is managing to remain relevant as well. This particular book is supposed to show a tender, vulnerable side of the original Marlboro Man, your ol' buddy Ernest.

Now I have known a few Hemingway freaks. One in particular comes to mind. On the den wall he hung a 2-by-2-foot photograph of Hemingway. It was a print of the famous Karsh photo, with Hemingway in a high, wool turtleneck that made you itch just to look at it. Walking by the poster made my friend stand straighter and fell taller.

He had all the biographies, authorized and "un." Not just the definitive biography by Baker, but all of them, up to and including the two that have come out in the last six months. One of those latest also contained five new Hemingway short stories and promised not one, but two more volumes of biographical prattle.

The Hemingway buff I knew had a book by someone who worked on "Papa's" boat in Key West. And another by someone who cozied up to Hemingway in Cuba. He had books by a wife or two. And, I suspect, if one of those Hemingway house cats with an extra toe came out with a memoir, he'd buy that, too.

Hemingway was not just a good read to my friend; he was a mindset. I don't pretend to understand, but I figure the Hemingway book with the bisexuality theme will not be among his favorites.

"You pretty much can depend on the market (for any Hemingway book), except some fans will not buy any biography that dwells on the negative, the darker side of the writer," says a book store owner who loves Hemingway. And why shouldn't any book store owner love Hemingway?

Lee Howell's store carries roughly three dozen books about Hemingway and anything and everything by Hemingway. I was tempted to suggest a Hemingway Book-of-the-Month Club. Books by and about Hemingway exclusively. Next month a scathing memoir by a Hemingway child: "Papa, Dearest." It might just work.

For Hemingway is not unlike another great American writer. Reports of his death have been greatly exaggerated.

January 1986

"Kitty Litter" By Any Other Name

I got a polite, written reprimand the other day from the folks who invented the stuff you pour into your cat's litter box.

In a story, I used the words "Kitty Litter" generically, without capitalizing them or mentioning that Kitty Litter is a brand name. To tell the truth, I didn't know Kitty Litter was a brand name. Well, the people whose job it is to scour all the newspapers and periodicals in America for lower-cased Kitty Litters caught me.

"When not referring specifically to Kitty Litter brand, we suggest the generic term 'cat box filler,'" the note said.

Of course, nobody would know for sure what you meant if you used the words "cat box filler," so I'll just try to stay clear of the subject from now on. That shouldn't be too hard.

Newspaper people run into this kind of thing every now and then. For instance, you can't use "Kleenex" if you mean just any old tissue. Instead of "STYROFOAM" (captilalize the whole thing), the trademark watchdogs suggest you say "a light polystyrene plastic foam." Right.

You'd think it would be the ultimate compliment to have your brand name so well-known and associated with a particular product that folks use it synonymously for said product. "Coca-Cola" for "cola." "Kodak" for "camera."

"We could lose our trademark if we didn't routinely protest its misuse," said Deborah Kayden, when I called to ask about the fuss over "Kitty Litter." The folks at Lowe's, Inc., don't mind at all having such a household name that people all over America probably call their "cat box filler" "Kitty Litter", with definite lower-case in their voices.

But if some Johnny-Come-Lately tried to name his "cat box filler" "Kitty Litter," Lowe's has to have letters like the one mailed me to prove it earnestly and diligently defends its trademark. "It all gets pretty expensive," said Deborah.

"But not as expensive as losing our trademark.

"We have to send out quite a few letters a month. 'Kitty Litter' has a nice sound, I guess, and a lot of writers use it."

I just hope the trademark defenders don't get wind of my mother, who flagrantly violates their strict rules at least 96 times a day. To her, every camera ever made is a "Brownie. " As a young reporter, I spent a month's salary on a Nikon camera, but my mother brought me back to earth. I proudly strutted through the house, trying to look nonchalant about the gleaming black hardware dangling from my shoulder. "Go snap a picture of my Thanksgiving table with your new Brownie," she said.

Any cleanser is "Bon Ami" to Mother, no matter if the label says "Comet" or "Dutch". All luggage is "Samsonite." To a lot of folks, all refrigerators are "Frigidaires."

Which would bother me a lot more if I owned "Whirlpool" or "Norge" or "General Electric" than if I owned "Frigidaire, " but then there's no figuring corporate law.

Anyway, I stand corrected. If ever the occasion forces me to write about the little clay chunks that you put in your cat crapper to keep it from smelling, I'll get it right. Or you can wash out my mouth with Bon Ami.

May 1985

An Old Concept

Women in beauty shops talk about their children and their men and how long it has been since they spent the day at the beach. I had almost forgotten.

For several years now I've routinely ducked into one of those big, shopping mall clip joints, the unisex kind, where men cut women's hair and women cut men's hair, and both sexes sit side by side without shame to be shorn. Those places require no appointment and no huge investment of time. That is the appeal.

You are in and out of some stranger's turnstiled booth before the blow dryer can cool. Take a number and choose not a style but a concept. If you talk at all to the person styling your locks, it is glancing, elevator talk. The weather, hemlines, or the NFL.

They pipe in a little Duran Duran and you figure to end up stylish.

But not long ago, I got my hair cut at a different sort of place—a real, old-style beauty shop, where the smell of permanent wave solution cleared my sinuses, and the operator actually asked my name. Maybe I need to reread my Betty Friedan, but it seemed awfully right. Not a man in the place.

Women walked around the shop in their old clothes and evolving hairdos, flipping absent-mindedly through *The Inquirer* and *The Star*, complaining about children too soon grown and roots too soon black. They took turns sitting under the old-fashioned, hood-style dryers, as close to a crown and throne as any of them will ever know.

For a few, warm, glorious moments, these women were queens and someone else lady-in-waiting. The operators still bring their customers soft drinks and intermittently check their curls, ending that ritual with those catholic and decisive words: "You're done, honey."

Much has been written about the decline of the conventional barbershop, supposedly the last male enclave in a neutered world. Where, then, are the defenders of the opposite end of the barber pole?

Our mothers had weekly appointments; we have self-sufficient styles. The French twists and teased bouffants have fallen to simpler, do-it-yourself dos. Our jobs and lifestyles do not permit half-day sessions at the beauty mill. Still, there is something therapeutic, perhaps a tad decadent, about having somebody else actually wash your hair.

The other day I splurged. Suddenly I was at somebody else's mercy, thrown back like the weak partner in a dance dip. The warm water swirled over my head and down my neck, while the platinum-blonde-talk buffeted me from all directions with the force of a cotton ball.

The shop smelled and sounded like a Saturday from childhood, a sensual mixture, somehow, of pincurls and peanut butter crackers.

I had forgotten, even, the hairstyle books, with page after page of gorgeous models tossing their perfect or perfectly outlandish hair to taunt you. Women don't choose just a hairstyle from those books; they choose faces. And all the while the dye cooks or the curlers cast, there is absolute faith that the chosen face is included in the price of a shampoo.

These leatherette chairs, then, are not pastel shrines to vanity, but to hope. This is where we once came before the prom, hoping to look older. This is where we end up again, hoping to look younger.

Perhaps the greatest perversion of the last two decades—amid stiff competition—is coeducational cutting and curling. The gelding of the old-time barbershop, the tailoring of the beautician's smock.

From now on, when I get my hair cut, I want to hear stories of sin and seduction and gall bladder surgery. Hair-curling tales that women, excuse me, tell best.

January 1986

Ladies, Be Seated

A patent is pending, and interest is brewing. Gregory Matta of Cumberland, Rhode Island, had intended to keep his new product secret until it hits the market a few months from now. But some news just won't wait.

"I try to aim at problem areas and fill needs," he says simply. Gregory is being modest considering his plans might revolutionize the modern bathroom, drastically shrink the divorce rate and put Ann Landers, who generally rules on tricky matters of decorum, completely out of business.

Greg and his wife, Lois Kelly, are manufacturing an apparatus called "Down Boy," designed to lower automatically the seat of a toilet when it is flushed. Greg came up with the idea several years ago and Lois, who was working on a master's degree in business administration at Harvard, made the "Down Boy"—and, incidentally, the universal feud over positioning of the toilet seat—the subject of her MBA thesis.

Through surveys, she found households were most receptive to the "Down Boy" idea where members had less than a college education, $25,000 to $40,000 annual income and the males outnumbered females. Higher education households and higher income brackets were more resistant.

"My thought on that is the rich have the same problem but just don't want to admit it," says Gregory.

Females generally understood the "Down Boy" concept, while males had to study on it for a while. "Why would you want the toilet seat down?" they often asked.

So Gregory, 38, and Lois, 31, are making "Down Boy" extremely simple to install, the implication being "the little lady" might have to go it alone. Installation should take about five minutes. A mechanical engineer designed the prototype, and now Gregory is working on a warning label to protect himself if someone's timing is off. He does not want to be liable in case of a fluke injury. Of course, a warning label won't keep a clumsy, irate customer from shooting Gregory.

"At first I thought of 'Down Boy' as a novelty product, but since the survey I have begun to believe it might become standard bathroom equipment," says Gregory.

His young business, The Water Closet Company, has other interesting products to offer. The "Target Trainer" is a bull's-eye that hangs off the rim of the toilet bowl as a visual incentive for young males. It is popular—surprise, surprise—with mothers. And, planned for the future, is an alarm clock which slowly brings up the bedroom lights until they reach high beam. He plans to call that one "Dawn's Early Light."

People always snicker when they hear about Gregory and Lois' products. And being personable types, they usually laugh along, too. But to them it is like hearing the same joke again and again. They are preoccupied with injection molding and marketing and liability. They are trying to run a serious business, and people keep giggling. "We're getting used to it," says Greg.

There's been a lot of derisive comment about Harvard, celebrating its 350th anniversary this year. Outsiders sometimes perceive of the place as the ultimate bastion of scholastic snobbery, the highest ivory tower of them all.

Next time you are tempted to agree, think of Harvard-trained Lois Kelly and her husband Gregory Matta. Think of Harvard as the place where domestic harmony was perfected. Think of the founders of The Water Closet Company, flush with success and laughing all the way to the bank.

October 1986

Underwear And Socks

WOODBRIDGE, VIRGINIA. If it is not the largest shopping mall in the Free World, heaven help us.

The name is Potomac Mills, a modern mall in the outer suburbs of Washington, a place full of expensive, albeit discount, stores. A $500 coat here, for example, may cost you only $350.

Plus, you can watch large-screen television as you walk through the mall. Not even MTV seems odd when it screams from the ceiling in this bright carnival of commerce. Pre-teens spill from a store selling art-deco flamingoes, neon Empire State Buildings and sweat shirts with this motto: "When the going gets tough, the tough go shopping."

Potomac Mills is so expansive some clever mall architect decided to divide it into "neighborhoods." After walking at least a mile looking for the Elvis Presley Museum—which bills itself as the first such museum licensed by the Presley estate—I stopped at an information booth to ask for help.

"Elvis is in Neighborhood One," said the lady at the desk. "Keep walking." So I did. I walked past shoe shops the size of grocery stores and discount diamond outlets.

I walked past a Swedish furniture store where shoppers are provided with baby sitters. The children left behind are made to wear bibs printed with big numbers. Then they either cry or jump about happily in a glass-walled room filled with thousands of colored, plastic balls.

When a parent finishes his shopping, he presents a claim check for the child, the same way he would for his dry-cleaning. Store personnel return the correctly-numbered tot. No refunds, no exchanges.

The mall teems with people, but the day I visited not much was happening at the Elvis museum in Neighborhood One. No long line was forming at the gift shop outside, the one that sells stuffed hound dogs and Love Me Tender Milk Bath. A teenage girl busy applying her own nail polish and wearing a sweatshirt that said "Camp Beverly Hills" took her time taking my $2.75. She seemed unimpressed with Elvis; she seemed unimpressed with life.

The King's music was being piped in through the museum walls, and lavish, lighted exhibits held Elvis effluvia of a rather remakable variety. There actually was—and I would not joke about a thing like this—one lighted showcase of Elvis' Jockey shorts and black Banlon socks. "Underwear and Socks," the exhibit was carefully labeled.

There were "Swimming Pool Items," including a portable television, deflated rubber raft and swim trunks. After seeing the underwear, however, the swim trunks meant very little.

There were cars and jewelry and even the X-rays of Elvis' infected sinus. The blue, pin-striped hat Elvis bought in 1962 at a Memphis Sears was on exhibit, as was his last personal limousine, a white, 1973 Lincoln that he had admired in the movie *Shaft*. The King's cowboy shirt and books he read while on tour were all there, behind glass.

A sign said some of the artifacts belonged to a man from Columbus, Georgia, who "knew Elvis personally." I believed it. Usually you have to know someone pretty well before rifling their underwear drawer.

If it at first seemed odd that an Elvis museum—the first of its kind—existed in a discount shopping mall in the suburbs of our nation's capital, later it made perfect sense. What better setting could you find for the possessions of a man who so dearly loved possessions?

It is a fitting place to view a $75,000 diamond-studded, gold nugget ring and not think a thing in the world about it. And, if you don't think an exhibit of underwear is a fitting tribute to a King, you can always move to another neighborhood.

May 1986

Slug Burgers

CORINTH, MISSISSIPPI. "You can deep-fat fry cow pies, and they'll eat 'em," says my friend Dave Haffly. He should know, for he's in the food service industry. It is a truism of that trade that heavy frying will cover a multitude of culinary sins, says Dave. It may be true.

What else could explain the slug burger? You either love or hate a slug burger. There is no middle ground, no neutral turf. Slugs are like raw oysters or Richard Nixon. Nobody ever sat on a fence and thought about them. Reaction is fierce and unwavering.

They say the slug was born here in Northeast Mississippi during World War II or thereabouts, when meat was scarce and rationing resulted in some pretty weird recipes. Nobody is crystal clear on its origin. The butchers who devised the first slug paddies are mostly long gone.

What seems abundantly obvious, however, is that slugs—also appetizingly known as "gut-busters" and "grease burgers"—are extremely popular still, at least in these parts. But now eating slugs is more a matter of preference than practicality. You may save a few cents, but that is no longer why you eat a slug. You eat them becauseyou crave them.

I checked out the White Trolley Restaurant, which used to be housed in a genuine trolley but now is in an elongated, conventional building. Customers sit at a long lunch counter, close enough to the kitchen to hear the grease pop. Slugs are a specialty.

On the menu here slugs are called, simply, "hamburgers." They cost 50 cents. "Beef burgers" are listed below them, at 75 cents.

Out-of-towners, who periodically come in and order a hamburger without scrutinizing the menu or asking questions, express shock when they get slugs. "What's this?" they have been known to ask.

What it is is a burger made from generous portions of cereal, flour and lard, mixed with a small percentage of ground beef. Not a great meal for the cholesterol-conscious.

The mixture is patted into small paddies, which are fried once in hot grease, then frozen until needed; then they are fried again. There used to be a restaurant in town that would dip your slug bun in the hot grease, too, for an extra nickel.

Ronnie Dees, co-owner of the White Trolley, sells about 50 dozen slugs each day at lunch. "A lot of people just prefer them to regular hamburgers," he insists. "We get doctors and lawyers and laborers. People come in and order two or three dozen at a time."

I looked up and down the lunch counter. Sure enough, the dark reddish-brown paddies, not much bigger than an Oreo, were in front of just about each and every customer.

Contrary to popular rumor, they do contain some meat. But a quick, strictly unscientific survey of old men on the street showed me opinion varied wildly about exactly how much meat is in a slug.

"Not enough to make a gnat's eyeball," offered one man in a dusty gun shop. Another man allowed as to how they used to flavor slugs with the blood from ground beef. But modern slugs don't even have so much as beef blood, he swore.

I figured on some answers from Gray's Meat Market, slug supplier. I figured wrong.

Gray's is a charming, old-fashioned market that has display cases made of thick glass and full of appealing red meat. The place has atmosphere. An old woman even hobbled in to fetch her dog a bone.

Gray's is known for excellent steaks, fine sausage and slug burgers. C.F. Gray, proprietor, could not remember exactly when or how the slug began. "I've been in this over 40 years, and they've been around that long, at least."

He plundered through an old safe for a newspaper clipping that told about slugs, but he came up with nothing. "Maybe I'll find it someday," he said, shrugging and resuming his work. I left, because I was no paying customer; I don't like interruptions either.

In the interest of thorough reporting, I tried a slug. A bite of one, at least. It will suffice to say I liked it as well as I do raw oysters. Or Richard Nixon.

August 1986